D1498139

The World
of William Saroyan

Nona Balakian with author William Saroyan, in front of the Opéra in Paris, June 1975.

The World
of William Saroyan

Nona Balakian

Lewisburg
Bucknell University Press
London: Associated University Presses

Associated University Presses
440 Forsgate Drive
Cranbury, NJ 08512

Associated University Presses
16 Barter Street
London WC1A 2AH, England

Associated University Presses
P.O. Box 338, Port Credit
Mississauga, Ontario
Canada L5G 4L8

The paper used in this publication meets the requirements of the American National Standard for Permanence of Paper for Printed Library Materials Z39.48–1984.

Library of Congress Cataloging-in-Publication Data

Balakian, Nona.
  The world of William Saroyan / Nona
Balakian.
      p.   cm.
  Includes bibliographical references and index.
  ISBN 0-8387-5368-X (alk. paper)
  1. Saroyan, William, 1908– —Criticism and interpretation.
I. Title.
PS3537.A826Z59   1998
818'.5209—dc21   97-4379
                                                              CIP

SECOND PRINTING 1998

PRINTED IN THE UNITED STATES OF AMERICA

Contents

Foreword

Nona Balakian was engaged in a long voyage through William Saroyan's repertory when she died suddenly on 5 April 1991. It took me several years before I could approach without tears the manuscript she had lovingly nurtured for the last decade of her life. Through it I could hear two voices. First there was Saroyan's ebullient, explosive, exuberant one which Nona had felt her mission and duty to bring back to new readers. But there was also her own silken, culturally rich, piercingly analytical voice to support her belief that Saroyan deserved a major rank in the twentieth century world of letters. Her presentation had been microanalytical in order to let Saroyan speak as much as possible through the interstices of her commentary which followed step by step Saroyan's development as a man and formation as a writer into what she calls "a new version of the Classic American." Her basic premise was that the orphaned son of an Armenian immigrant followed in the footsteps of his great American mentors, Emerson, Melville, Sherwood Anderson, and Walt Whitman—and with lessons in modernism from Gertrude Stein.

The book is biographical only in the sense that it examines Saroyan's works in the context and sequence of his life experiences. His writings unfold in the pages of Nona Balakian's critical scrutiny as she traces the expansion and changes in Saroyan's work through the multiple genres he tackles. In her view, although Saroyan began as an ethnic writer publishing initially in Armenian periodicals, he soon emerged as a representative of the American scene and spirit, which were more cohesive than they are now at the end of the century. Along with his deep and sustained allegiance to his own roots, he depicted an assortment of first-generation Americans: Greeks, Assyrians, Jews, Japanese, Mexican, Irish, Filipino, even "a guy from Iowa," in the throes of a valiant life-struggle in the San Francisco/Fresno area of California, unwilling to collapse under the Great Depression and the advent of World War II. Their many shades and hues blended into a single, powerful brand of humans that are recognized with humor and empathy in the world of William Saroyan as he celebrates within the boundaries of mortality "the brotherhood of things alive."

After having shown the unique niche he had made for himself in the short story, Balakian saw him as a pioneer along with Thornton Wilder in the launching of a new theater, regional in its setting but universal in scope. Then she set out to examine the novels, plays, and the fragmentary confessional writings of the later period. In these she had detected a different tone and quality confirmed with her own observations of his later years when she had known him personally and communicated with him directly. In the last two years of her own life Nona had become engrossed with much philosophical reading relating to mid-century turmoils. She was trying to connect the existentialist sense of void and mortality with the alterations in Saroyan's spontaneous charm and humor so characteristic of his earlier years. She was searching for the direct impact on him of the dark clouds that were spreading over the zeitgeist of western civilization. But time ran out on Nona as she attempted to assess the changes in Saroyan's writings.

What Nona Balakian did not know then, but what we have since discovered as Saroyan's papers have become collected and housed at Stanford University, is the amazing magnitude of the unpublished works. His theatrical writing alone includes two hundred and thirty plays most of which remain unpublished and unperformed; all this body of work remains a challenging task for textual analysis.

Fortunately, Nona had taken very precise and detailed notes on the later works she had read. I was able to compose this material into a final chapter without changing a single word or intruding editorially or conceptually into the text. I offer it as a macrocosmic overview of the rest of the Saroyan writings she had intended to include in her study. With the rich research archives now accessible, future scholars will be able to probe further in the direction Nona Balakian opened up.

Balakian characterized herself as a literary journalist and was very proud of her profession, which she had exercized during her forty-three years on the staff of the *New York Times Book Review.* Thousands of books passed through her screening and many a writer's fate hung in the balance as Nona wrote previews and reviews of the literary output of her time. She was exposed to both creative writers and scholarly ones. Although she had done an earlier collection of her major reviews and critical essays, entitled *Critical Encounters,* it was in undertaking this larger venture that she enlarged on her own capabilities as a scholar. In fact, it was this twofold character as a journalist of wide cultural scope with an elegant style, and her qualities as a scholar that won her a Rockefeller Foundation Fellowship to take time off from *The New York Times* to get on with this book.

But I noted a strange thing as I read my sister's manuscript after her death: she had modestly relegated to footnote status some of her most luminous discoveries. I thought it only fair to her and to her readers to bring some of these insights into the major text where they would indeed enrich that text. I think she would forgive me for taking this liberty.

This is a book that brings the works and personality of Saroyan right before the eyes of the reader as if indeed he were still alive and was having his works appraised currently, for Nona Balakian treats them with the freshness of a first review. Besides bringing to new readers an invigorating writer who has been grossly excluded from anthologies, the author takes us into the active arena of the short story of the thirties and re-creates the panorama of the dynamic theater of social protest and the beginnings of the poetic theater that were part of the world that shaped Saroyan and to which he contributed his unique talents.

Anna Balakian
June 1997

Preface

WILLIAM Saroyan—the name evokes a period, a mood—nostalgia, perhaps?—the high spirits of youth, faith symbolized by a famished young man on a flying trapeze, and much hearty, healthy laughter. In the years of his leap to fame (in the mid-1930s), and even after his bright star had dimmed, we loved and coddled him like a favorite child because his heart was in the right place; we also ignored and chided him for his perpetual adolescence, his apparent indifference to literary art. He was that troublesome self-proclaimed "genius" who could not or would not live up to his initial promise.

An ingenuous self-promoter who would have liked the universe for his audience, Saroyan never fancied himself a "writer's writer." Behind that carefully built façade of bravado verging on arrogance, he remained equally aloof from popular taste and literary fashion. His first book of short stories, *The Daring Young Man on the Flying Trapeze,* had been the miraculous anodyne for the Great Depression syndrome, and like a doctor who arrives at the eleventh hour with new medication, Saroyan was duly embraced and celebrated. With his fresh, Adamic response to life, his superabundant faith in man's *humanity* to man, he fell easily into the roles of court jester and literary acrobat, playing both parts to the hilt. His seemingly improvised, often poetic fragments of everyday life (unlike the hefty "slices" of life most of his fellows writers presented) were so irresistible and easy to read that no one (critics included) felt the need to probe behind their benign surface appeal. Like a fact of nature, Saroyan eluded explanation.

A prolific writer who achieved worldwide readership in a career that spanned five decades, Saroyan was never in want of critical attention. But his voluminous fiction, drama, essays, and autobiographical writings failed to provoke original criticism, and his work as a whole has remained unassessed by the major critics. As a result, this essentially American writer is consistently denied a place in textbooks on American literature. Like most American writers of modern times, Saroyan never reclaimed the heights of his earliest success; critics in later years never matched the accolades he received initially from the likes of George Jean Nathan, Brooks Atkinson, and Edmund Wilson. But he also never suffered total eclipse. Past seventy, with still a flicker of the old bravado in him, he remained doggedly a presence on the literary scene, as confident and secure in his personal vision in the year of his death (1981) as in the year he won (and turned down) the Pulitzer Prize (1940) for his first full-length play, *The Time of Your Life*.

I must confess that as a young critic, I was among those readers and commentators of Saroyan's early work who (inadvertently) contributed to the absence of serious critical evaluation of his work. Taking a cue from the writer himself, we allowed the man to take precedence over the work. It was always Saroyan we were watching—the ebullient, irrepressible, earnest young Fresno-Armenian we perceived both within and outside the work—not the multifarious things he was creating. The very individual voice we heard in the stories, plays, novels, and essays evoked feelings and sentiments we had repressed or allowed to go undefined and now were eager to claim as our own. Armed with standard critical tools, we heard what he said without fully comprehending what he meant.

I do not mean to imply that there is a preponderance of philosophical content in Saroyan (though I have read two interesting Ph.D. dissertations that discoursed on Saroyan's "philosophy" apart from the vividness of the works themselves), but only to point out that a Saroyan story, play, or novel does not readily yield to formal criteria of literary structure and style. Like lyric poetry or music, his writing involves emotions (as distinct from sensations) too evanescent to be grasped by the rational mind alone. To respond fully to Saroyan's work one must be ever on the alert for the root impulse that invariably links subject, form, and meaning. When he seems most artless, he is most artful and in full control.

It is impossible to read William Saroyan over a period of time without noticing an inherent duality of vision. This is more than a literary device; it is Saroyan's way of seizing art and life simultaneously. We encounter it first in the early stories and in some of the novels; shuttling back and forth between the first person and the third, the writer repeatedly interjects his muse, as if resisting surrender to the figments of his imagination. In the very act of creating, Saroyan wants to sustain a direct correspondence between his own reality as a man and a mythic form of reality that can only be found through art. It is out of this tension between the actual and the potential that he creates his characteristic style—the Saroyanesque stance: that sinuous, discursive dialogue/monologue, with all its seeming irrelevances, that unfolds its meaning as inevitably and precisely as the peeling of an onion.

In an early story, "Panorama Unmerciful," he explicitly places art and life in close proximity. The narrator (himself) informs the reader that he sees more in writing than "making up things." "I don't know if it is ever possible for anyone actually to improve life, and I imagine that it isn't, but all the same it is worth while to want to, and the more I think about this, the more I am convinced that this is essentially the job of every man who writes, and that anything else any of us do is irrelevant." In *After Thirty Years,* he reiterates the same thought: "life and art are not separate. If they could be, art is a fraud, however wonderful." The possibility that life could be improved by art remained uppermost in Saroyan's consciousness. He could never be diverted from his obsession with "the human race" (a phrase he used repeatedly and lovingly), from his perception of what it was and what it might yet become.

Early in life Saroyan had discovered that the only weapon against despair and death was the work of art, which itself attests to the potential in life, erasing the rigid contours that appear to define the individual. If the argument he carries on in his work between life and art often places him at odds with his muse, it also releases and intensifies his intuition that man has the capacity for self-creation. The reality and the dream, the man and the artist—the dichotomy is common enough in literary art, and there is nothing new in its manifestation in Saroyan's work. What is unique to Saroyan is what he made of it. In a literary period when the tendency was to view man as the sum of his environment, there was a special freshness in Saroyan's aspiration to align the world of fact and the world of inner fantasy. There was foresight, too, in his recognition that chance and an infinitude of expectation were endemic to the American experience and hence would form the substance of a new American drama.

Like Whitman before him, Saroyan began the experiment with himself. He would meld himself with his art. In a post-Romantic era, the ambition was bold and untypical. After Henry James, modern writers wanted to distance themselves from their creations, and it was generally assumed that whatever the work might reveal of the influences of the life on the art, the life and the work belonged in separate compartments. Freud and the behaviorists provided the inevitable corollary to this in subsuming the work to the life. Thus, even though the artist might remain personally impervious to his material, the biographer-critic felt justified in hammering away at the transmutation of the man into the artist. It is the inverse of that proposition—the transmutation of the artist into the man—that we see demonstrated in Saroyan's career. However hypothetical a concern this may seem to the literary critic, it does suggest an alternate theory of literature from which to view a writer who has remained vastly underestimated.

"My work is writing, but my real work is being," Saroyan wrote in his last work, *Obituaries*. That statement, coming as it does at the end of his life, has a resonance that reaches beyond the duality of reality and dream. It touches and reflects on the power of art to alter human consciousness, to humanize and expand it by refraction. It is only when we read Saroyan in this light, it seems to me, that we begin to see properly the difference between his "successes" and his "failures."

Though it was my good fortune to know William Saroyan in his later years, I never deliberately sat down with him to discuss his work. What I absorbed through our desultory talks on matters involving anything and everything but his own writing was the stance and quality of the man in relation to his work. It was clear to me from our first meeting that what was essential to his writing was essential also to the *self*. It is to accommodate that human dimension, without placing specific emphasis on "the life," that I have veered away from a strictly aesthetic approach in my interpretation of Saroyan's work. I have sought, instead, to keep my eye on the various stages in Saroyan's career as he moved toward an inner enlargement that enabled him to equate his life with his work.

In Saroyan's "world" the writing came first, then its absorption into the writer's psyche, his "being," the cumulative impact of the insight giving rise to the next work, and so on. Yet there is little progression here in the sense of an expanding oeuvre. Rather, as in the manner of Picasso, there is the excitement of a continuous search, an unquenchable creativity. Therein lies the secret of Saroyan's self-delight and his undiminished enthusiasm for getting published until the end. The creative process ultimately became his religion, his raison d'être. From the youthful "court jester" to the jolly old man with mustachio and booming voice, he remained forever the *poète manqué* in pursuit of an unattainable dream. It was his unclouded vision of something beyond the borders of the finite self that drew him repeatedly to one of the most noble uses to which the imagination can be put—a vividly contagious response to our shared humanity.

The World
of William Saroyan

1

The Time, the Place, the Man

I was the art, I
was the whole business.

—Saroyan.

THE world in which William Saroyan first burst into print in the mid 1930s is so closely linked in our minds with America's worst economic depression that it has become almost impossible to view it historically as anything other than cheerless. A period of drab and desperate existence, spiritually void and mired in hopelessness, the thirties for most people evokes Erskine Caldwell's backwoods degenerates, the earnest young proletarians of Clifford Odets's plays, and the stolid and stunned faces of tenant farmers immortalized by James Agee and Walker Evans.

Erskine Caldwell's 1932 novel, *Tobacco Road,* called attention to the dire poverty and deterioration of life in backwoods Georgia. It became a popular play in 1933. Its hero, Jester Lester, was a degenerate sharecropper. The playwright Clifford Odets rose to instant fame in 1935 with *Waiting for Lefty* and *Awake and Sing.* These Marxist plays, along with others he wrote in the next decade, introduced working-class people as leading characters in American drama and placed emphasis on the proletarian idea of exploiter and exploited. James Agee, the *Time* magazine writer and later novelist, and the photographer Walker Evans set out in 1936 to investigate the daily life of three sharecropper families in the South. Their collaborative effort exposing the tragedies and degradation of impoverished Americans was first published as a series of magazine articles and eventually became a book, *Let Us Now Praise Famous Men* (1941). Agee's ironically worded opening to the book gives a sense of the intensity with which the work was undertaken:

This is a book about 'sharecroppers' and is written for all those who have a soft place in their hearts for the laughter and tears inherent in

17

poverty viewed at a distance, the hope that the reader will be edified, and made to feel kindly disposed toward any well-thought-out liberal efforts to rectify the unpleasant situation down South, and will somehow better and more guiltily appreciate the next good meal he eats.[1]

Yet, except for those numbered among the forgotten poor of the 1930s—and they *were* legion—the decade was far from cheerless. For all the dramatic reversal from the flushness of the twenties, this era of economic debacle was replete with more major political, social, and intellectual developments than the nation had ever known. In terms of human potential—of expectation and projection—the period was anything but hopeless.

From a global perspective, it was the first time that the possibility of extending human aspirations beyond the confines of national and racial boundaries was being tried—and Americans did not underestimate the experiment. It is easy from our present vantage to forget that Communism was initially envisioned as an international revolution whose goal was the amelioration of the human condition. The workers of the world were called to unite not only to ensure their rights as citizens but to improve the lot of the dispossessed the world over. Couched in humanitarian, utopian terms, the concept reverberated in the creative thought of the decade as it utilized the revolutionary slogan—"Change the World"—for artistic ends.

Under the presidency of Franklin D. Roosevelt, a heady euphoria mingled with a new national awareness: however grim the realities of the moment, it would all change with better planning. With the New Deal as a model on the economic front, no aspect of American life seemed to be without a potential for new beginnings. Home again, "the lost generation" was no longer feeling alienated in the same way. There was work to be done, lives to be rescued, and the Apollinairean creed of life as "the supreme art" was at least temporarily abandoned. (It is significant that in 1930 the Nobel Prize in Literature had gone to Sinclair Lewis, a writer who sought "the reality of America.") In the world of science, Sir James Jeans and Robert Millikan had sufficiently popularized "the new physics,"[2] which showed incontestibly that life was fluid and open to change. And educators and psychologists like John Dewey and Harry Stack Sullivan were adding the corollary that man is a social being defined by his experiences and interpersonal relationships.[3] It was a revival all around of the political philosophy of Jean-Jacques Rousseau, reconstructed to support the socioeconomic experiments that loomed ahead.

But there were roadblocks to progress not easy to surmount. Injustice was rampant in the 1930s. Civil rights and human rights in a legal light were as yet undreamed of; immigrants were still "foreigners," scarcely to be trusted in an immobilized economy; innocent men were still in danger of being sent to the electric chair, and the plight of coal miners and migrant workers was in fact "the shame of the nation." In the streets of the largest manufacturing center in the country, the refrain "Brother Can You Spare a Dime?" was a far cry from "I Love New York." Yet despite such prefigurations of doom, the century was still too young to invoke the apocalypse in a convincing way. Writers and artists in America had faith that they could change the face of the nation by exposing the truth, whether in novels like *The Grapes of Wrath* or in photographic documentaries like the Agee and Evans book, *Let Us Now Praise Famous Men*.[4] Social consciousness had not yet become systematized into a political scheme, and social welfare was still a matter of individual compassion, bolstered by one's sense of responsibility toward a fellow human being trapped by the unequal laws of an indifferent society.

As in the 1960s, violence converged with dynamism in American life, but unlike that subsequent period of protest, the militancy of the 1930s was restrained by the long arm of an American political tradition that favored reform by moral suasion. The Founding Fathers had been generous in their use of eloquence to defend individual rights; now, armed with the new instrument of radio, New Deal orators, with Roosevelt at the helm, became mesmerizing deterrents to radical change. Looked on with a certain condescension and even distrust by an all-powerful middle-class majority, the radical Left remained a minority voice, its reality amounting to little more than an editorial presence.

But if there was less violence on the national level in the 1930s than in the 1960s, there was every bit as much anguish and disenchantment as the bright bubble of the twenties burst, dispersing not only the great American Dream but the hard-won effects that were the rewards of individual dreams.

The impact of this crisis on American writing took the form of an unsparing realism—from its most painful, mordant echo in Nathanael West's *Miss Lonelyhearts* to H. L. Mencken's Nietzschean outcries against "saccharine liberals" with their "preposterous dreams."[5] Overnight, capitalist culture was pronounced decadent, oppressive, inhuman. Yet even in the interest of social truth, the literary voice was not predominantly the strident voice, the voice of doom. In the work of John Dos Passos, Ernest Hemingway and even the archetypal novelist of the Depression years, James T. Farrell, disenchantment curiously converged with a built-in catharsis inconceivable to the sixties generation to come.

It bears noting that all three writers brought a humanist vision absent from the works of their contemporary "proletarians." By juxtaposing his character's inner and outer worlds, Dos Passos in *U.S.A.* achieved a remarkably eclectic view of the nation in extremis. In the works of Hemingway, the hardened, macho exterior of his heroes inevitably betrayed stoic humanists. And by digging into the vagaries of human nature and searching for moral roots, Farrell made his hero, Studs Lonigan, a figure of greater depth than most fictional proletarian victims.

However sharply they reflected the depths of human degradation and a corrupt society, these writers (and others) still held to a view of life that shared certain accepted values. After World War II, the viability of such values would become much harder to defend. The bleak vision of Kurt Vonnegut in *Slaughterhouse Five,* which confronts the shocking possibility of a relativity in morals, would have unhinged the writer of the thirties.

And then there was humor. However cheerless a place it might seem, America in the 1930s did not disassociate itself from its native gift of humor. The country had not yet become self-conscious in this area—ethnic jokes caused no embarrassment, and the sophisticated response to lusty laughter had not yet turned humor upon itself to create a bitterness which in time would turn to black humor. In the Depression decade, release from tension was sought as readily by turning to the antics of the Marx Brothers or Laurel and Hardy as by a dose of Valium or other sensibility-deadening agents. Going to the movies was a surefire way of chasing away the "blues," and it could be done for less than a quarter. Sitting in the darkness of a movie house, alone or with someone congenial, one might watch a grim documentary film or newsreel only to have it followed by some frothy bit of entertainment that quickly restored one's sense of well-being. Moreover, the big stars were always handsome and beautiful and resilient, and both men and women snapped back with bright retorts that marked them as "winners." Though not liberated in today's terms, women protagonists were almost always shown as resourceful and worthy of the happy ending that almost always came to them.[6]

The time was ripe for the American moment in literature, for a conscious facing up to the deep-seated dichotomy of an indigenous political and social system. Alexis de Tocqueville had long ago pointed out the inherently contradictory if not irreconcilable elements in a society based on a pluralistic egalitarianism: When over-emphasized, the concept of equality, he had observed, can become a source of individual oppression. "As the condition of men becomes equal amongst a people, individuals seem of less and society of greater importance," he wrote in *Democracy in America*.[7] The economic leveling off that resulted from the Great Depression threatened to destroy the balance between what Tocqueville saw as the separate claims of social and individual roles. The economic emergency had perforce curtailed certain individual freedoms whose unremitting corollary was the pursuit of material success.

It is a curious paradox of American literary history that the majority of the 1920s expatriates who had fled the American scene in rebellion against philistinism and conformity chose to make their return home at a time when private enterprise was being compromised by an increasingly paternalistic government. Malcolm Cowley saw in the concurrence of the Wall Street crash and the suicide of Harry Crosby—writer-playboy best known as the publisher of Black Sun books—in the last days of 1929, a symbol of the collapse of the individualist's dream, "The religion of art had failed when it tried to become a system of ethics," he wrote at the end of his book *Exile's Return*. A new conception of art was replacing the idea that it was something purposeless, useless, wholly individual and forever opposed to a stupid world. The artist and his art has once more become a part of the world."[8]

Although "the secure world of their childhood" had fallen apart, as Cowley saw it, the Paris experience served to intensify a native individualist bent. Even in its revised and expanded form, Cowley's *Exile's Return* does not adequately project into the consequences of this "literary odyssey," and his brief interpretation (in his epilogue) of the returning exiles' altered relationship to the American scene is short of being categorical: Perhaps because Mr. Cowley had been so quick in aligning himself with the Communist Party in what he calls "the pentacostal years," he comes to mistake these writers' reluctance to commit themselves to anything outside their private vision of America for sheer social indifference. In view of their subsequent "engaged" work, it seems myopic to conclude that these writers were returning to "the more self-dependent, less organized America they had known in their childhoods."[9] In being unwilling "to march with others in disciplined ranks . . . writing socially conscious poems and proletarian novels," they were not necessarily looking "toward the past," unaware of their social roles.

Something else significant that Cowley fails to point out—having come to the end of his story—was the multiplicity of ideas that

characterized the early years of the decade. For all its adherence
to the status quo, the country had not slumbered in the exiles'
absence. A philosophical and literary ferment had filtered into the
culture via the many burgeoning journals of opinion and literary
magazines. These publications encouraged communication on a
higher intellectual level than had previously seemed possible. Edmund Wilson in *The New Republic,* H. L. Mencken in *The American Mercury,* Allen Tate in *The Hound and Horn,* and T. S. Eliot
in *The Bookman* were extending the boundaries of literary criticism and stimulating the analytical capacities of a reading public
now successively exposed to the theoretical writings of Spingarn
and Santayana, Irving Babbitt and Paul Elmer More, and John
Dewey and Karl Marx.

A few weeks before the market crash, a fierce controversy had
raged over humanism (or the "New Humanism," as some called
it). It was a viewpoint that began with a bland form of aversion to
romanticism, impressionism, and bohemianism, and then moved
on to advocate a return to the moral and ethical stance of puri-
tanism. Before it evolved into a formal manifesto drafted by Corliss
Lamont in 1933, humanism became infused with the political language of the day, even while it turned its back on politics. In one
corner was the powerful social commentator, H. L. Mencken, endlessly castigating the "bouboisie," whom he connected with the
humanitarian meddlers or "wowsers" (puritans) steeped in "the
genteel tradition." In another corner, far removed, was Irving Babbitt, the Harvard-based intellectual who regarded Mencken's
iconoclasms as "superior intellectual vaudeville . . . lacking in discrimination and judgment" . . . and as "shrewd observations within
narrow limits."[10]

The humanists' dependence on the individual conscience as a
motivating force ran counter to the Rousseauesque view of a benign nature, one that had nurtured past generations and was now
surfacing in the form of class consciousness. To hold that the only
way to alter society was to alter the individual seemed to the liberals to bolster capitalist evils and the status quo. In a changing
society laden with social injustice, Babbitt's reverence for reason
and self-control carried implications of elitist reactionism. Indeed,
to a committed Communist like Joseph Freeman, it presented "an
aesthetic fig-leaf for the politics of fascism."[11]

In 1933, when Granville Hicks published his influential literary
study, *The Great Tradition,* it was predictable that from his radical
perspective Hicks would mock Humanism, which he called "the
pleasant halfway house . . . for the writer who is not quite ready

for the Church."[12] Some years earlier, it had similarly been expected that T. S. Eliot would frown on Humanism's positivistic
aspect, pronouncing it "a by-product of Protestant theology in its
last agonies."[13] Eliot's foreboding that Humanism would be transformed into a common faith practically applied to daily life did in
fact materialize in a book by John Dewey titled *A Common Faith*.
But neither Eliot nor Hicks saw as clearly as Joseph Wood Krutch
in *The Modern Temper* the dilemma facing the Humanist in this
era. He wrote,

> The more completely human we are, the less our motives, our im-
> pulses, and our values are those which we have in common with the
> other animals. . . . Civilization has been called a dance, but the feet of
> the dancers do not rest on terra firma. It is danced on a tightrope that
> sways in the breeze.[14]

The humanist vision of man as Prometheus unbound with almost
infinite powers over his own fate paradoxically contained a destructive, anarchic element that could be classed as anti-
humanitarian. Indeed, by the middle of the thirties, all the virtues
of the Humanist, his breadth of vision, his tolerance, his equilibrium and sanity became fair game for political, radical editorials
in *The New Masses*. In one such editorial, Michael Gold was not
above demolishing the career of Thornton Wilder, whose plays
were held to be quintessentially "humanistic." Gold wrote that
Wilder

> wishes to restore, he says, through Beauty and Rhetoric, the Spirit of
> Religion in American Literature . . . that newly fashionable literary
> religion that centers around Jesus Christ, the First British Gentle-
> man. . . . It is Anglo-Catholicism, that last refuge of the American
> literary snob.[15]

What becomes apparent in this record of tug of war between
Humanists and the burgeoning Communists is the (hitherto unsuspected) capacity of the American writer to carry on a dialogue on
a theoretical plane. It also becomes apparent that however deep
their concern for a better life for Americans, neither the Humanists
nor the radical left was making specific prescriptions that would
fundamentally alter American society.

In his most impersonal, diagnostic tone, Edmund Wilson in a
letter to the poet John Peale Bishop wrote early in 1931, "I have
a feeling . . . that the money-making ideal is about played out and
the country is ripe for something new."[16] In another letter to the

poet Louise Bogan a few months later, Wilson became a little more specific,

> Everything is changing so fast and we are all more or less in a position of having been brought up in one kind of a world and having adjusted muscles, socially, sexually, morally, etc. to another which is in a stage of flux.[17]

And in still a third letter that year Wilson wrote to Christian Gauss that the Marxist "prophecy" was being fulfilled.

> with the people in the cities cut off from the earth and physically and spiritually enfeebled and the people in the country not able to make a living and the concentration of money and means of production in a very few hands.[18]

Though Wilson was himself rapidly moving toward involvement in the new politics, it was "the idea of Communism" rather than the Communist Party itself that was the real lure. Just as he invariably turned to foreign sources as a critic of modern literature, so now in his political views he looked to foreign roots for his growing faith in egalitarianism. Believing, as he wrote to Allen Tate, that "the end is not art or science but the survival and improvement of humanity—the "masterpiece" eventually becoming "human life itself"[19]—he brought eloquence as well as sympathy to his *New Republic* reports on Depression America. But the radical manifesto[20] he drafted with the help of Waldo Frank, Lewis Mumford, John Dos Passos, and Sherwood Anderson, "without the collaboration . . . of the Communists," was no sooner accomplished than it was dropped.

The change of heart that all too soon would afflict Wilson and other progressive American writers of the period is usually placed at the door of disillusionment in the Soviet experiment; but it also derived—and this is perhaps more significant—from the recognition of the incompatibility of a system of ideas and values that remained remote from American reality. The aspiration to "new social forms, new values and a new human order," which Wilson's manifesto announced originated in an editorial abstraction of "the people," not in *the people* themselves. The writers, editors, and critics who agitated for change had no direct and personal experience of hardship and abuse (or at most very little), and empathy and compassion alone could not disturb the Emersonian balance of "society and solitude" or individualism and social equality that still prevailed in the early thirties.

If the repatriates briefly resisted the new political awareness it was because America's image had dimmed for them and social consciousness precluded a renewal of faith in the nation. In the end, nothing helped bring that renewal of faith about so much as the advent of Franklin D. Roosevelt and the New Deal.

As the new gears of a paternalistic government were put into motion in the first 100 days of Roosevelt's presidency, the nation seemed to spin on a newfound solidarity that belied the Marxist view of the worker as an alienated human being. Roosevelt's canny crusade to base economic reconstruction on grassroots enterprises had the effect not only of keeping foreign revolutionary elements at bay but of exposing the profound differences that separated a free nation like the United States from those still groping for elemental concepts of democracy.

The magnetism of Franklin D. Roosevelt was more than a matter of surface personality. No previous president had placed so great an emphasis on "the rights of the common man" or as frequently evoked "the old frontier spirit" that was indigenous to the nation. In an era drawn to novelty in so many areas of life, his call for economic experimentation did not seen startling, especially when his compassionate words about "the forgotten man," or "one-third of a nation, ill-housed, ill-clothed, and ill-fed" fell eloquently from his lips. Americans working together across "class" lines at the height of the economic emergency inevitably altered the country's self-image and its potential for still further concerted effort to bring about change. As the plight of the country became better known through direct experience and observation (as the country went deeper into the Depression), "protest literature" took on a validity it had previously lacked.

With American society broadened at its base, a new kind of "outsider" emerged: the American writer of ethnic background who did not disguise his working-class origin or experience. Unlike its Soviet counterpart, the American "proletariat" was sufficiently literate to provide a ready audience for these "new American" writers, and they, in turn, often provided them with a "voice." Marcus Klein is the only critic I know to have acknowledged the cumulative impact of second-generation American writers in his engrossing study, *Foreigners, The Making of American Literature, 1900–1940*. But still to be written is a study showing how the "foreigners" helped unhinge American literature from its mooring in English literary tradition, setting it—curiously enough—on its more idiomatic American course. Coming from lands rich in folk or ancient culture, these new Americans were free from intimidation; their fictional worlds recognized no formal boundaries and excluded no experience for being too lowly. They wrote out of a dual expectation—to enhance their personal status and to improve life for everyone else.

Raised by their bootstraps and at great personal self-sacrifice, in environments not always tolerant of ethnic differences, the immigrants' sons and daughters brought a heightened sense of connection with everyday lived reality. The Jewish writer (Michael Gold, Clifford Odets, Anzia Yezierska), the Yugoslav (Louis Adamic), the Italian (Jerre Mangione), the Norwegian (Ole Rölvaag) saw America with the clarity of first exposure, before over-familiarity renders things invisible. Hardship and adversity did not always lead to negative feelings; disappointments and anger were often tempered with gratitude for opportunities undreamed of in their native lands. Whatever the feeling, its expression was vivid. Their innocent eyes and plain speech helped to restore America's concrete reality.

To a writer like William Saroyan (the son of an Armenian immigrant) who as a boy and young man had haunted the public libraries of Fresno and San Francisco in search of a literary heritage he could make his own, there was, in addition, an implicit invitation to juxtapose the larger truths of the American experience received through books with the dailiness of life around him. Could it matter that his people had come from an ancient civilization of Asia Minor, while Emerson, Hawthorne, Melville, and Whitman were products of an Anglo-Saxon culture—if, like them, he could look out on the world with the mind and eye of a poet? Did it matter that he had had to teach himself what the earlier Americans had simply taken for granted—if, like them, he identified with his environment and was able to reflect it in his writing? An orphanage child, separated from his roots, growing up in an America that had become conscious of its separation from a primordial dream, Saroyan might have caught the contagion of his generation's alienation. But expatriation was a luxury he could not afford, both literally and philosophically. For a new American to make the journey back was an admission of defeat, if not of disloyalty. If the dream was to be salvaged, might it not be more reasonable to return to the classic American tradition where it had its roots? In taking the longer view of an Emerson or Whitman, one might find not only an anchor but ultimately the means of obliterating that inner sense of "foreignness" that had nothing to do with the food one ate or the God one worshiped.

Contrary to the general impression, it was not ethnicity that initially motivated Saroyan as a writer. He was consciously more American than Armenian in his early youth, if only because circumstances had thus dictated it. Untutored in the Armenian language and remote from intellectual contact with Armenians, Saroyan was immune in his earliest years to the kind of nationalistic grandiloquence that sons of immigrants brought to their writing. He loved the sound and stir that his people made around him, was charmed and moved by their great zest and openhandedness, and stood somewhat in awe of that curious mixture in them of eccentric individuality and sense of community. Odd as they might seem, he saw them as part and parcel of "the human race"—a phrase straight out of Emerson and Whitman that he made his own. If at times his Armenians seem larger than life, even idealized, it is because the narrator is himself Adam in the New World with Adam's wide-eyed innocence and newfound faith. Now and then he stumbles on the moodiness and heavy-lidded melancholy of his people (to which he is himself confessedly addicted), but even in Saroyan's earliest stories, there are no deliberate references to the starving and abused Armenians of the headlines—a stereotype that would have been easy for a young Armenian-American writer to exploit.[21] Though it seemed unlikely and even inappropriate, Saroyan's essential optimism did not contradict reality on the whole. In the long range view, a positive attitude could be glimpsed in the tenacity with which the Armenians had countered political and religious oppression, and in the uncanny ability they had developed for balancing a transcendent Christianity with a sane and easy earthiness.

Saroyan's persistent good humor was equally improbable in view of his own beginnings. There was not a great deal to evoke well-being in a child whose father had died when he was only three years old, whose earliest years were spent in uncertainty of his self-identity, who at age of eight became part breadwinner, selling newspapers in the streets of Fresno. Nor did the circumstances of his life improve in the subsequent period when, in the absence of encouragement on every side, he doggedly pursued his impractical dream of becoming a writer.

It would be false to surmise, however, that Saroyan's inspired hopefulness was an inborn reflex that only needed public approbation to become full-blown. Scattered throughout his autobiographical writings—more often in later life, but also in the early years—are telling tracks of private struggle, searing hurt, and painful recrimination, revealed in spurts after long suppression. If the thrust of what he wants to say moves nonetheless toward an affirmative statement, it is not for want of a normal amount of self-doubt and deep-seated anger over the ways of the world. In the lean years before he was discovered by *Story* magazine, the future seemed to hold little certainty for a self-educated grade-school dropout, somewhat foreign-looking, living in a small, inland region in California and striving for national recognition. In addition, there was the nagging need, in Armenian family tradition, to make "something" of oneself, along with the realization that for himself the "something" was to become an *American* writer who could speak from the center of American experience.

To the naked eye there was nothing in Saroyan's background that would seem to encourage, much less support such a prospect. Where, in this corner of Fresno, would he look for the substance of such experience? And how would he, a latecomer on the scene, recognize what was specifically American? With nothing but his prophetic soul to guide him, he could only sense that there were certain currents in his favor. A good century after Emerson had proclaimed that "the individual is the world," that "nothing is at last sacred but the integrity of your own mind," America was being propelled toward its avowed image: In the era of the common man, which the Depression had brought home, all stood equal before good and bad fortune. It was no longer necessary, for instance, to be formally educated to become a writer in America, and the writer no longer needed to look for his subject outside his daily experiences.

With typical foresight, Emerson had rhetorically posed the questions: "What is a day? What is a year? What is summer? What is woman? What is a child? What is sleep?" And starting with Wordsworth, the romantic poets had given their answers in lyric terms, but little of a parallel nature, either in England or America, had been attempted in fiction to show "the miraculous in the common," to use Emerson's words again. For the American writer of the thirties this challenge inevitably posed another: From his recognition of the fact of social change, the writer would move to an awareness of his own inward progression. The so-called "protest" literature of the thirties was often an amalgam of the private rebellion of youth with social revolt.

It was within this dichotomy of the one and the many, the wondrous and the commonplace, the immovable ideal and the fluid reality that the writer of imagination could read the American experience in its essence. In this respect, the stage was set and the script all but written for William Saroyan when he emerged on the literary scene.

In the convergence of the "new democrat" of the thirties and the Emersonian ideal of individualism that filtered through his confrontation with American reality, Saroyan had all the support he needed to justify his intuition of his own uniqueness. Throughout his life, the Emersonian stance, if not the words, would reverberate in his mind, lending an elevated, holistic tone to his most commonplace subjects. "What Ralph Waldo Emerson put in place for me was first the school that bore his name, and then little by little a fictitious reality of an extraordinary kind of soul, born in Boston . . . Like the entire culture and society of his class, he tended to repudiate the relatively dominant realities of the body, in favor of the more exalted if finally impossible realties of the soul." Saroyan goes on to argue that although he was himself of the "poor working people," he learned at Emerson School that the writing of the working man has "as much soul as Emerson or anybody brought up in comfort and ease."[22] At the same time, Saroyan was enough of a child of the era, exposed to the harsh realities of the American scene, to know that he could not coddle his individualism in the style of a previous generation of American writers. His own life struggles had made him all too aware of the other side of the coin— the need to connect with humanity at large. Here, inevitably, he found his model in another representative American writer he avowedly admired.

In the dynamic poetry of Walt Whitman, Saroyan saw the reconciliation (or the possibility of reconciliation) of the dichotomy of self and society that he was himself seeking through his writing.

In the spiritual flights that transcended the American context and even time and space, Whitman had appropriated the universe to himself, proclaiming to have "*contained multitudes.*" "*It is I who am great, or to be great—it is you up there, or any one.*" In the leaf of grass was the emblem of a humble and diverse humanity. This self-declared "radical" had reversed the poet's image from ineffectual angel and *poète maudit* to that of a lusty, robust, disorderly "*lover of men and women above the whole of other objects of the universe,*" and in so doing would influence several generations of American poets. To the writers of the thirties, Whitman's impact became allied to humanitarian concerns, his compassionate, democratic voice serving, for some, as an instrument of propaganda. But perhaps even more than Whitman's unabashed declarations of love, what proved of most lasting influence on a writer like Saroyan was the radical aspect of Whitman's aesthetic, his minimally visible art.

"*Who touches this touches a man,*" had been Whitman's boast, and the avowal had led critics to see in his inability to distinguish

between the artist in himself and the person the source of his uneven art: the lack of form, of coherence, the spurts of sentimental
rhetoric and banality. Yet in the cohesion of the artist and the man
Whitman was seeking a new approach to the ancient claim that
poets are the true legislators of the world. The poet's stance was
new.

As the "bard of democracy," in love with humanity and living
the engaged life that Emerson had recommended for the writer,
Whitman ventured to bring together the heroic and the humble,
the poet and the propagandist. In *Leaves of Grass*, he absorbed
the experience and the vision, the sermon and the instant impression and, without limiting the imperative of self-expression, recorded the "agonies" of multitudes.

More than anything, perhaps, it was Whitman's personal dynamism, fortified by his total open-endedness toward experience, that
must have made the deepest impression on Saroyan at a time when
he was groping for a voice of his own. To hold "creeds and schools
in abeyance" would imply that a writer could reach his reader
without artificial literary intervention. It was tantamount to a declaration of independence for the writer, a refutation of dead artistic
rules and an expectation of new beginnings. This new breed of
writer could mold himself along lines of his native bent, outgrow
his "commonness," and ultimately fulfill his potential. Whitman
had said, "I consider 'Leaves of Grass' and its theory experimental,
as in a deeper sense I consider our American republic itself to be
with its theory."[23] One could translate that to mean that the artist
as experimenter was the artist endemic to a society that believed
in an evolving future.

To understand the true nature of Saroyan's work and grasp the
foundation on which his art is based one must bear in mind that
from the beginning of his career he held the belief (which he never
abandoned) that experiment was a necessary component of creativity, and creativity itself the greater part of "what is loosely called
art." Although he moved from one genre to another, from story to
play, to novel and autobiography, he did not actually abandon one
form for another but retained an open-ended relationship to each,
frequently moving back and forth. What is rarely observed in criticism of his work is the variety of styles he has used even within a
single genre, from the straightforward third-person narrative style
of the early stories to the autobiographical first-person and (especially in his plays) the impressionistic and surrealistic styles.[24]

Saroyan's reading had been sufficiently diversified from his early
days of immersion in the classics to have led him to avant-garde

magazines in the heyday of those publications in the 1920s. In 1937, only three years after the publication of "The Daring Young Man on the Flying Trapeze," his name appeared alongside that of Henry Miller and Lawrence Durrell on the cover of a French- and English-language little magazine published in Paris called *The Booster*. In a subsequent issue his name appeared in the listing of its literary editors as well. A magazine so small and dedicated that it boasted it could not pay its contributors, *The Booster* proclaimed to its readers that they were living in "A POET'S WORLD." It introduced Saroyan as a man of "divine thunder, light-bringer, dart-slinger, the man with the insane impulse." Before he turned it into a play, Saroyan had found a home for "My Heart's in the High-lands" in the pages of this fragile magazine.

In 1938, four years after his phenomenal success with "The Daring Young Man on the Flying Trapeze," Saroyan appeared in another avant-garde magazine, *transition*. The magazine's tenth anniversary issue published extracts from his unpublished work, "The Slot Machine." Written in an Eliotic imitation, it combined the linguistic experiments of Joyce and Gertrude Stein in a partial parody that is also a flashy, bravura attempt to capture the surface variety of American life:

> I saw red. I saw black. Caruso sang. The Boston Symphony Orchestra bellowed Bach. Bill Robinson danced up the stairs of the White House, tipping his derby to Mrs. Green. Valentino walked across the arena, greeted the bull with the cape, then fell, gored, the whole matinee audience weeping. A flock of airplanes projected through space. A submarine dived. A ship splashed into the sea. Nearer, my God, to thee. Mr. Fleming, I said.[25]

The Slot-Machine was initially a short play that Saroyan tried for nearly a year to convince his editors at Random House to include in his second book, *Inhale and Exhale*. Its omission from the book, along with many others that Saroyan wanted to include, would have brought the volume to an unwieldy nine hundred pages. The rejection agonized Saroyan, who was intent on including "experimental stuff." He had a firm idea "what [experimental writing] means, and what the idea is." He wrote to Donald Klopfer "I mean to show that it isn't enough to know technique, to use it effectively, and to fool, which is what experimental writing generally does."[26] It was apparent that he had done some close reading not only of Eliot, Joyce, and Stein, but of magazines like the Paris-based *transition*, where an international avant-garde assembled to proclaim "the universal man, the complete man." Eugene Jolas, *transi-*

tion's editor-in-chief since 1929, was a literary anarchist who directed his call for the uprooting of traditions to "the intellectual proletariat." On the eve of the market crash in America, he foresaw "the delusions of American prosperity, speed, mass action." In place of "the fraudulent ideologies of the masses," he proposed "the art of the future," which would depend on "man's inalienable right to dream and rebel and create in himself the possibilities of the organic cosmos." Underlining the high-fidelity decibels of Jolas's pronouncements was the "revolution of the word" that would plumb the subconscious mind while placing it alongside the conscious. In one editorial Jolas wrote that

> We need the word of movement. . . . We need the technological word, the word of sleep, the word of half-sleep, the word of chemistry, biology. . . . [T]he new vocabulary and the new syntax must help destroy the ideology of a rotting civilization.[27]

The reverberating sentence for Saroyan in all this must have been "man's inalienable right to dream and rebel and create in himself the possibilities of the organic cosmos." But very likely, too, he would read with some sense of affinity the phrase about "the new vocabulary and the new syntax."

As Gertrude Stein had demonstrated since the early part of the century, words and their usage reflected the quality and substance of human consciousness. Largely ignored by the critics of her day or at best regarded as an eccentric, Stein capitalized on that designation and set herself up as a mentor of the avant-garde writers and artists who formed a clique in Paris. Young Saroyan was never to be a part of that famous group whom Stein labelled "the lost generation," which included not only Hemingway, Fitzgerald, Dos Passos, but many other American writers and artists of the period.

From his base in San Francisco, the young and hopeful experimenter did not need propinquity to establish rapport with a writer like Gertrude Stein. Though herself a native American of German-Jewish extraction, Stein had the same need to invoke the American scene: her 1932 book, *The Making of Americans,* has a loving sense of people that closely matches that of Saroyan, even though she remains totally invisible in the narration. Saroyan would also respond to Stein's light-footed, irreverent manipulation of language, her teasing humor, and her inspired use of the vernacular and casual speech.

We have it from Saroyan himself that by 1934 he was well acquainted with Stein's work. At the public library in San Francisco, he had "read around in *Three Lives*"[28] and Bennett Cerf, his editor at Random House, had sent him a copy of *Ten Portraits*. Stein's visit to America in the year of his success had prompted a worshipful letter to her:

> Some critics say I have to be careful and not notice the writings of Gertrude Stein but I think they are fooling themselves when they pretend any American writing that is American and is writing is not partly the consequence of the writing of Gertrude Stein.[29]

Just what had struck Saroyan as "American" in her work he leaves unsaid, but it was surely more than the surface impression of the dadaist sophistication which Edmund Wilson had been quick to dismiss as "a sort of fatty degeneration of . . . imagination and style."[30] The American element was evinced in her mode of apprehending reality, a vital indeterminacy and indifference to causality that left the gates of possibility wide open, generating a new brand of Adamic excitement before the unknown. Gertrude Stein had been a student of William James in the years when his view of human consciousness had significantly changed. The consciousness which he has originally seen as a fixed entity, he now viewed as a stream with arteries that did not necessarily converge; not finite, always in motion, never free of distraction, it was a process leading to thought, not thought itself. What this meant for the writer was a sharpening of focus on the present and a separation of the object from a preconceived pattern or design. Unmistakably, Gertrude Stein had inclined to William rather than to Henry James.

The sense of fragmentation and multiplicity of life that the new physics engendered at the turn of the century had unhinged the artist who wanted to see life whole. Searching for unity and coherence toward the end of her life, Virginia Woolf in her most ambitious novel, *The Waves* (1931), turned her characters into disembodied consciousnesses stretched out over the totality of existence. It was a brave experiment that would never be duplicated. There was no comparable anxiety or challenge for the American writer grounded in a pragmatism that harked back to Whitman, the bare-throated participant in life, taking his soul down the open road in an ever-renewable, continuous present. For all her unintelligibility, there was nothing more buoyantly provocative than Stein's verbal improvisations, with their proliferating innuendoes, their De Chirico-like enigmas couched in ordinary words: "Pigeons on the grass, alas"; "when this you see remember me"; "rose is a rose is a rose is a rose." In that magical year of 1934, neither Pound's battle cry, "Make It New," nor Stein's wholehearted surrender to the aesthetics of *Now* caused any ripples on the American scene. The habit of engaging untried and unknown experiences, the book of life before philosophy, made Americans natural modernists in life, but not yet in art.

Saroyan's own experimental fervor would never lead him too far into Steinland, no matter how much drawn he might be to the precise rendering of the modern consciousness; a certain metaphysical awareness would guard him from captivity by the here and now. Saroyan's challenge as a young man of conscience with more than average pride in a freshly assimilated literary heritage would be, instead, to confront a grim social reality while embracing larger transcendent truths. The metaphor of "the daring young man on the flying trapeze"—the title of his first nationally acclaimed short story and subsequently the title of his first book—in itself suggested the risk involved in keeping a delicate balance between the inner and outer worlds, reality and dream, earth and eternity.

"Trapeze over the Universe"[31] had been Saroyan's original title, intended for a novel he was trying to write, a title suggesting a metaphysical thirst for comprehensiveness not unlike Virginia Woolf's in *The Waves,* but in turning the aborted novel into a short story and surrendering to a particular scene (America in the depth of the Depression), Saroyan escaped the trap of abstraction that had turned Virginia Woolf's characters into mere "voices." Saroyan's unnamed young hero is both emblematic and human, and because the reader can identify with him, he is able to evoke a universally shared emotional response.

The story's tour de force lies in its manipulation (not entirely unself-conscious) of two layers of consciousness experienced by a young writer dying of starvation. Since we are never wholly inside his head, we can observe him observing himself. He is clearly not from the lower dregs of society, but only recently indigent and in thrall of his hunger. When he sleeps, he dreams in surreal imagery that encompasses the totality of human experience, from

the plains of Jericho . . . Cadillac coupe to Kansas, the roar of Dostoyevsky . . . Finlandia, mathematics highly polished and slick as green onion to the teeth . . . Mr. Chaplin weeping, Stalin, Hitler, a multitude of Jews.

When he awakes, the fact of his hunger becomes a part of "the trivial truth of reality." For *"it is only in sleep that we may know that we live,"* is how the young man muses as he sets out looking for work that does not exist. The return to "the superficial truth of streets and structures" is gradual and painless because in sleep he has witnessed the wonder and enormity of existence—*"the far earth, God and his saints, the name of our fathers"*—and sensed in the cinematic rushes of his dream where the centuries merge in the moment, *"the tiny tangible atom of eternity."*

In "the gray, cold and cheerless morning," his mood is strangely euphoric as his mind sings a familiar refrain, *"He flies through the air with the greatest of ease: the daring young man on the flying trapeze."*

Distanced from himself, the young man picks up a 1923 penny from the gutter and fantasizes about buying a motor car and drinking and dining "in the fashion of a fop." A lofty apostrophe crosses his lips: "It is good to be poor, and the Communists—[his thought is cut short] but it was dreadful to be hungry." Viewing his situation objectively, he notes that he has eaten his last piece of bread, and a fleeting awareness of death makes him wonder if he'll be able to read *Hamlet* or *Huckleberry Finn* again. Now thoroughly awake, his consciousness luxuriates in the sensuous pleasures of life, and he imagines "all manner of beef, lamb, fish, cheese; grapes, figs, pears, apples, melons . . . great brown loaves of French bread." But to "buy life"—the desire comes over him like a great thirst— he must work: "If they would only allow him to sit at a desk all day and add trade figures, . . . then perhaps he would not die."

The young writer sees himself outside the pale, like a stranger in a mythic land, "He had ventured upon the wrong earth, or perhaps into the wrong age," he thinks, and wistfully he considers writing *An Application for Permission to Live.* But in that ironical edge is mingled a haughty stoicism and urge to extract meaning from his existence at the eleventh hour. Death itself can be faced. What fills him with revulsion is the thought of the Salvation Army, that haven of homeless men who "sing to God and Jesus (unlover of my soul), be saved, eat and sleep." His stoicism stops short of the surrender of the self: "His life was a private life. He did not wish to destroy this fact. Any other alternative would be better."

Though death now seems inevitable, the young man is only skirting its possibility by concentrating on the *manner* of his death. When the refrain hums through his mind again, he grandly envisions "a trapeze to God, or to nothing, a flying trapeze to some sort of eternity." He prays for strength "to make the flight with grace." Even though he goes through the motions of hunting for nonexistent jobs, he does not feel that he is involved "in all the foolishness." Convinced that there is no work to be had, he decides to go read Proust in the public library for an hour, but he quickly runs out, faint from hunger. In his empty room, he contemplates the loss of his books, "It made him very angry to think there was no respect for men who wrote."

The young man now takes a perverse kind of delight in examining the penny he has found, seeing it as a symbol of the worthlessness of the material world which he is about to leave. Turning it into an abstract problem, he absently wonders how many pennies he would need to go on living. But as his sense of life recedes, the shining penny becomes a mere thing, "How prettily it smiles, he said," looking on it "with the delight of a miser." He does not bother reading the words "*E Pluribus Unum, One Cent, United States of America*," but turning it over, he is struck by the beauty of Lincoln's face and the words "*In God We Trust, Liberty, 1923.*" His final thought is that he might have given the penny to some child who could buy a number of things with it.

> Then swiftly, with the grace of the young man on the trapeze, he was gone from his body.

Howard R. Floan, one of the few serious critical commentators on this first important story of Saroyan, misses an important element—the irony with which it is infused. Floan interprets the tone as one of self-pity and thus fails to recognize the true meaning of the ending—the "perfection" of nonbeing is something the young man becomes resigned to only at the very end, and Floan apparently does not see the use to which "the double vision" is put here; the "pity" coming from the narrator is for the *denial* of life. The young man is seen as the innocent stranger, the true alien, who realizes that "somehow he had ventured upon the wrong earth, or perhaps in the wrong age." The story bears an Emersonian overtone that reappears in many of the early stories. "His life was a private life," says Saroyan of his young man, echoing Emerson's insistence on "the infinitude of the private man." The setting of the Depression is useful for what Saroyan wanted to say about the man: the drama, sorrow, comedy of life and the world that will not allow him to release it. Yet evil as such is never defined, it is a condition of life itself.

Without pausing here to consider the story's achievement as literary art, we can weigh its importance by noting three aspects that were to become characteristic of Saroyan's style. First and foremost, a humanistic vision, firmly held in the real, the actual;

second, a reaching out to the ideal, the promise, the expectation; and finally, a continuous search for a reality that would absorb the dream.

It was in the short story that Saroyan would establish his distinctive voice—a mixture of high-minded earnestness, genial humor, and a rebelliousness that sought conciliation. In the novels and plays he would seek a distance necessary to expand his awareness of the polarity separating dream from reality. And in his autobiographical fragments, a veritable library of "confessions," Saroyan would venture to present the results of his quest as it unfolded through himself and his art. For he was his own best convert, and he was himself the experiment.

2

The Theory and Practice
of Being William Saroyan: Early Stories

> But the point is this: myself again. I must explain that nothing
> I ever say is purely autobiographical, and the fact is that I am
> always speaking and thinking of the place and of the time of
> the place, and that I myself am included in the thought because
> it is inevitable. It is not a question of pride, but a question of
> accuracy and truth. I do so objectively: myself, of this place,
> of this time.

THE quotation comes from one of Saroyan's earliest stories, and
at once gives the lie to the commonly held view of the writer as
pure romanticist. Whether or not he consistently achieved his early
claim to "accuracy and truth," he remained continually obsessed
by it, his strong feeling for exactitude carrying over into his everyday life: A Saroyan letter, for instance, would always be distinctly
dated and would often include the time begun and the time com-
pleted. This concern for documentation also held true for the first
drafts of many of his stories, plays, and autobiographical writings,
not only to establish, one felt, his "inevitable" presence—"Myself
Upon the Earth" is the title he gave the fourth story in *The Daring
Young Man on the Flying Trapeze and Other Stories*—but to indicate the speed with which he produced.

In the three-part story from which I have quoted above, "Three
Stories," the narrator (who is Saroyan externalized) is trying to
capture the essence of that corner of San Francisco that impinges
on his inner world. As he reads the *New York Herald Tribune
Books,* this unsuccessful, idealistic young writer speculates about
the books that are not getting published, books that speak of
America as the books in Greenland, for instance, speak of Greenland: "The greatest prose of America is the prose that is secret,"
he thinks, since for every book published as many as forty are not:

"America, as it was Greenland, the same." The "nonsense" that printed writers talk only obscures what is real, "the story of man on earth." This is what he hopes to write himself, "the earth" being specifically San Francisco, "the western part from Carl Street to the Pacific Ocean." "I am of Frisco," he writes,

> the fog, the foghorns, the ocean, the hills, the sand dunes, the melan-choly of the place, my beloved city, the place where I have moved across the earth, before daybreak and late at night, the city of my going and coming, the place where I have my room and my books and my phonograph.

Saroyan confesses he is not a writer and does not want to be one. "I say only what I cannot help saying, and I never use a dictionary, I never make up things. All the prose in the world is still outside of books and largely outside language, and all I do is walk around in my city and keep my eyes open."

Beyond the Whitmanesque effusion (in its variant it would become "Saroyanesque") and the stance of the guileless, self-taught writer living the common life and absorbing its flow, is the young writer's earnest conviction that an important dimension is missing in the literature of America. He goes on impressionistically:

> This is the first story, and if you do not like the style you can stop reading, because this is it, the whole thing, the place and the climate of the place, and what we think is less important than what we feel, and when the weather is this way we feel that we are alive, and this feeling is great prose and it is important, being first the place and then ourselves, and it is everything, Greenland, America, my city, San Francisco, yourself and myself, breathing, knowing we are alive. . . . [S]o if the style is unpleasant to you you can read the evening newspaper instead, and to hell with you.

The newness and promise of the Adamic dream is expressed with a snotty ingenuousness neither Whitman nor Wolfe would have been capable of.

Apart from the title story (which was earmarked for a classic) Saroyan's first book had the impact of a report from another planet—or, at least, "Greenland," his metaphor for a place both strange and familiar—and the people in it were projected through a voice like none other that American readers had heard. From our present vantage point of unlimited and unrestricted topics, scenes, and talents, it is easy to forget the limitations on literary form and subject matter that prevailed in the fiction of the thirties.

The experimentations of Faulkner were the exception. But, while Faulkner's voice was new, his characters were generically familiar. Similarly, what was new about James Farrell's novels of violent urban lives was not the characters themselves but the great earnestness and sympathy with which the author viewed them. Other major writers, such as Hemingway, Fitzgerald, Wolfe, Sinclair Lewis, Katherine Anne Porter, and even Steinbeck, were not introducing new characters in fiction so much as enlarging our capacity for identifying with different classes of people already familiar to us.

The freshness that emanated from Saroyan's "report" of small-town rural life in the southwest California derived only partly from its ethnic quaintness: The stories of struggling Armenian or Greek or Slovak immigrants of the San Joaquin Valley had more to recommend them than a surface local color. What was new in terms of American fiction, and of the short story in particular, was the author's random selection of characters with no urgent claim on our attention—ordinary persons who were not left "ordinary" for lack of a fixed place in society. Dreiser and Anderson had written about the "common life," but Dreiser had given it dramatic headline treatment, with himself distanced from his characters, while Anderson had rendered the simple life strange and even grotesque by placing too bright a spotlight on it. Saroyan's intent was different: By placing himself in the center of a specific setting that contained elements of shared experience, he sought to reach the "common reader" (who was far from "commonplace"), to show him to himself and to give him a platform from which to say what was in his heart and mind. (A corrupted version of this practice today is the television news program that brings "people" to our home screens to tell us what they, "the people," think is going on.)

In this fictive world of Saroyan's early stories there are no major dramatic situations. Indeed, large and small tragedies are so much a part of everyday life that to single one out is to render "the story of man" out of balance. Nor do heroic acts as such exist for Saroyan, who sees such actions as a characteristic human response and proof of man's instinctive aspiration toward his best self. The stories are told in a language that is simple but never banal, since the author's presence in the stories insures a mixture of common sense, extravagant insights and zany humor. In the absence of an exciting narrative, the author expects to hold the reader not simply with the strangeness of the commonplace (Emerson's "the miraculous of the common") but with the shock of recognition: if we do not live alike, we dream alike *as a people*. And they are all dreamers of one sort or another in Saroyan's kaleidoscope, where, along with human warmth and hope there is loneliness and loss, poverty and inner rebelliousness—the perennially struggling young writer so cold in his room that his hair freezes and he momentarily considers burning his books for warmth. They are the people forever swinging on the trapeze between the real world and the world toward which they aspire.

Readers of Saroyan who are mainly acquainted with his plays and his most famous volume of stories, *My Name is Aram,* may have no recollection of the solemnity underlying the stories in his first volume. There are echoes of Whitman and Thomas Wolfe in the cosmic consciousness and rhetoric of *The Daring Young Man on the Flying Trapeze.* In the more "composed" stories, there are reminders of the atmospheric gloom of Sherwood Anderson, as well as the tight-lipped factualness of Hemingway. An immense sense of mission keeps a rein on the characteristic Saroyan humor, which one glimpses nonetheless in unexpected places. "I am a story-teller and I have but a single story—man," he announces in "Myself Upon the Earth," a story that articulates the writer's credo. Self-awareness, a recognition of his own uniqueness, is at the center of Saroyan's humanistic thrust. But one has to go beyond Howard R. Floan's observation that in his first book of stories Saroyan's "ebullient sense of being alive [is] less awareness of self than responsiveness to life about him," to be able to define what "self-awareness" means to Saroyan.[1]

In his pioneering study of Saroyan's work, published in 1966, Floan goes on to point out that unlike Montaigne and others who have excelled in the personal essay, Saroyan is "not making an *enquiry* into himself: he was autobiographical without being especially aware of himself and his own processes of thought." But what Floan and other critics have tended to overlook, and what is in fact unique to Saroyan as a short-story writer, is that the "self" he acknowledges lacks a fixed entity, aspiring in fact to outgrow its original form, and thus remaining ever open and malleable. Thus the young man in "Myself Upon the Earth," desperately trying to convey "the truth of his being," without "trickery," knows that "every man is to create his own consciousness and his own precision, for these things do not exist of themselves. Only confusion and error and ugliness exist of themselves."

In Saroyan's work there is always the recognition of an *evolving* consciousness, which is in the artist's power to shape and direct. In this regard, he is closer to a modern poet like W. B. Yeats (whose lifetime pursuit was a self-created antiself) than to the romantic

Whitman, whom Saroyan resembles in other, more superficial respects. There are other esthetic parallels, too, with Yeats, which bear mentioning here in passing and are worth elaborating on later. Like the Irish poet, Saroyan demonstrates in one story after another that while the material world exists vividly for him, it derives its true meaning from the eternal and the ideal. In Saroyan's metaphysics, as in Yeats's, these correspondences are visible only to the poet, or as Saroyan would have it, to the exalted self. It is in this knowledge that Saroyan gains his sense of wholeness and euphoric optimism.

Critics of the early thirties were not normally exposed to fiction with a poetic thrust. They had a different guideline. "In American metaphysics," Lionel Trilling has observed, "reality is always material reality, hard, resistant, unformed, impenetrable and unpleasant."[2] This was how naturalism—the ontological system to which American writers of the thirties most often subscribed—could be defined. Not to relate to this system and its concomitant style meant that you failed as a representative American writer. But to Saroyan there seemed an alternative possibility. Having come along the route of a more native American stance—of Emerson and Whitman, Gertrude Stein and William Carlos Williams—he would venture to refuel that inspiration and become a test case for the recovery of the American psyche, so long hidden in a "secret prose." A decade earlier, Sherwood Anderson in "A Story Teller's Story," had proposed that Americans "were in the process of trying to make a race." For Saroyan, the "race" had been made; what was needed was a new voice to redefine it for a new generation of readers. It was this thought that allowed Saroyan to see himself as a new version of the classic American.

It would be unwise in writing about a spontaneous writer like Saroyan to belabor speculations of literary influence. He admired many writers, past and present, and was fond of crediting one or two (chiefly Maupassant and Shaw) for having given him the impetus to write. (And, one might add, the impetus to contradict.) But he repeatedly made the point that his best teacher was life and what he himself observed of life around him, unassisted by theories or traditions. The nondeterminism that invaded his fictive world had its roots as much in his own life as in any possible literary influence.

It was Saroyan's beginnings in insecurity and confused identity that initially provided the need to create a self-image. It was normal for "the orphan child of an orphan nation," as he has been called, to want to discover who he was and where he came from. Early in his childhood, in an Armenian milieu that encouraged self-

expression, his inquisitive nature flourished and he promptly recognized that "I was the art, I was the whole business."

A child of immigrant Armenians in the early years of the century,
Saroyan had the misfortune to lose his father when he was three
years old. The year was 1911, just four years before the Turkish
massacres in which more than a million and a half Armenians were
killed, driven from their homes in lands invaded and occupied by
the Turks since the fourteenth century. "The Starving Armenians"
was how affluent Americans of the 1920s instantly labelled this
small but sturdy remnant of the ancient world now in their midst,
and the phrase stuck with an overtone of mockery, since it was
assumed that you could not truly feel for what is foreign and unknown to you. Saroyan's father, a high-minded, missionary-
educated Presbyterian minister from the highlands of Armenia,
had escaped the massacres in Bitlis by coming to this country, but
he had not escaped the insecurity of the educated refugee who is
initially overqualified in a new land. Armenak Saroyan, as his son
never forgot to point out in his writings, was a failed poet who had
had the bad luck to die accidentally at the age of thirty-seven of a
ruptured appendix before he had been able to make a foothold in
the new world. His hopes of settling down with his wife and four
children in a community parish near San Francisco had been
dashed on arrival when he discovered that he could not communi-
cate with the Turkish-speaking Armenians there. Armenak Saroyan's subsequent brief period of farming had also turned into an
"episode of defeat," as his son put it.

In a taped interview Saroyan made a few years before his death,[3]
he recalled his family's arrival in San Francisco in an open wagon.
Although he was barely two years old at that time, he would have
us believe that the agony of his father's insecurity had been communicated to the child Saroyan from that day and that thereafter
he never forgot the heartbreak etched on his father's face. Though
on a commonsense level the report lacks credulity, it has a kind of
poetic truth Saroyan was always after. To Saroyan, his father's
failure was a lesson in both humility and independence.

As a young man trying to make his mark in letters, trembling
with "the responsibility" of being "a user of words" in the universal
language to which he aspired, Saroyan looked up to his father as
a spiritual mentor. "We are the same man," he wrote in "Myself
Upon the Earth, "one dead and one alive." In the youthful photograph of his father above his desk—that frustrated immigrant father he had barely known—he saw a mirror image of himself. "I
have come up from the earth with his face and his eyes," he writes

in a melancholy, self-searching awareness of something noble incompletely understood. Indeed, it is not hard to see the large impact that this silent, misfit dreamer, the poet the son cannot read, has had on the writer's character.[4]

Of Saroyan's years in the Henry Finch Orphanage in Oakland, California, we know very little. Since few writers have so fully mined their earliest years in their fiction, it would be hard indeed to explain the absence of stories of the orphanage experience on any ground other than their lack of interest to the author. Surely no one as opportunistic as Saroyan or as unsparing in his criticism of the educational process would have missed the chance, had there been one, to write another *Oliver Twist* (a book to which Saroyan has referred in another context). In one brief episode of his autobiographical work, *Here Comes, Here Goes, You Know Who,* Saroyan speaks of the orphanage years as having been ultimately beneficial:

> I was glad I had been there. It made me know what it is to be alone, and I decided it had been a good thing that I had found out almost at the beginning of my life, instead of later.

But one has to read between the lines to find out what has formed that attitude. Though himself "a small boy alone who couldn't say his family name," he is more stoical than the other little boys he hears crying when the lights go out at night: "figured they had nobody," he remembers "Willie" thinking—"Willie," who in contrast to them has a family. "It wasn't home. It was nothing and nowhere. But it was a little less nothing and nowhere when my brother showed up and we stood and talked." It becomes still less "nothing" when he learns his two sisters were in an adjoining dormitory. Later, there is a brief reunion with his mother, who has come with a picnic lunch. "What an unbelievable thing it is to be altogether for a moment, seeing each other, hearing talk about so many things," Saroyan remembers thinking, and the little boy, forgetting for a moment that his father is dead, wonders if all is not lost after all.

It is psychologically viable that the "unknown" is unsettling, indeed often frightening, especially for the innocent and inexperienced. But by leaving the field open to possibility, the unknown can also be a source of challenge. Not knowing what the future holds in any specific sense can accelerate an imagination already lively, unleashing its penchant for creativity. But the response will be positive only if there exists a center from which self-identity can emerge. The doom that prevails in Kafka's world is caused by a paralyzing anxiety that there can be no identity in a future from which the center has been removed and the contours blurred. In Saroyan's freewheeling *American* world of the early twentieth century, the initial center had been the nuclear family, which for Saroyan, was a special kind of family, with roots in "the family of man" that stretched back to legendary times.

Though much has been made of Saroyan's Armenian dimension, it has rarely been seen in its true light and never directly connected with his art. Because his Armenian characters were both colorful and articulate, they drew instant attention, and the background of his stories was valued chiefly for its quirky novelty. For readers and critics in America, at least, interest in Saroyan centered on little else. No group of readers, understandably, encouraged this emphasis more than Saroyan's fellow Armenians, who, in the sunburst of his sudden success, saw hope at last of being lifted out of their perpetual refugee designation. For himself, Saroyan, who had had his start as a published writer in the English-Armenian press, eagerly played up whatever favorable publicity he could create for the Armenians. Yet it became clear after a while, once the novelty wore off, that in overstressing the ethnic subject, damage to Saroyan's work as a whole was being done: Not only did it deflect attention from the variety of his work, but like a needle stuck in a groove, it left no leverage for critical exploration.

No one, for instance, considered the possibility that there might be a reason central to his art and thought behind Saroyan's attachment to his Armenians. Certainly not Hemingway, who equated Saroyan's repeated use of the Armenians as subject matter with attention-getting "trickery."[5] What had gone unobserved, though it had filtered exhaustively through his stories, was a certain quality of mind and being Saroyan associated with the Armenians, and it was this intangible characteristic that would give direction to his writing.

By the 1920s, certain character attributes like "industrious," "loyal," and "enterprising" had come to replace the proverbial tag "starving" when reference was made to the Armenians. Such sober traits had helped to make them generally acceptable in American society. But it was something more striking in their total behavior—something at the same time more pivotal to American life, as it surfaced in Saroyan's work—that would open up doors to them in American fiction. What Saroyan had seen in his compatriots, what was invariably to become part and parcel of his stories, and later of his plays, was an unabashed, easy, seesawing relationship between dream and reality. His characters could run the gamut of fantasy, but reality never remained far behind. If, on occasion, the absurd seemed to prevail, the hidden voice of logic, of "accuracy and truth," never entirely left the field, lending the action an indirect, double-edged irony.

The Armenians, it needs to be said in this context, are natural utopians: ultimately speaking, they had a dream instead of a country, and because territorial possession has often eluded them, they felt free to magnify the past while anticipating endless possibilities. The Armenian Soviet Socialist Republic was only one of many previous incarnations of Armenian statehood and represented but a small part of a once-extensive ancient kingdom in Southwest Asia Minor. Since the Armenians make no clear-cut division between their existence in the ancient world and their subsequent national identity, they have been able to stake a claim to one of the longest stretches of ethnic existence in that part of the world, and psychologically, at least, this has partly compensated for the consistent shrinkage of Armenia's geographical boundaries in the modern era. Where the Greeks, more practically, deposited their ancient past in a universal epic literature and went on to carve a new national identity, the Armenians, smaller and less secure, held fast to their antiquity, legends and all, lest their grandiose self-image vanish in the quicksands of time.

Saroyan had no knowledge of the Armenian written language, but as a child wise beyond his years, he could not have failed to eavesdrop on his elders—particularly those loquacious, gregarious Saroyans—as they indiscriminately bandied about the facts and legends of Armenia's past. And though he could not have had direct knowledge of the fifth-century chronicle called *History of the Armenians* by Agathangelos ("bearer of good news"), he would have heard variant accounts of stories from that book about the beginnings of the Armenian nation. As "historian" of an unrecorded time, Agathangelos based this "enigmatic" work on "received" tradition that freely intruded legend into the factually meager story of Armenia's conversion to Christianity at the dawn of the fourth century.[6] And in another much-revered work, *The History of Armenia* by Moses of Khoren (who is believed to have lived at the end of the fourth century), the creation of the land of Hayk (Armenia) itself was told through tales in which spirits, gods, and superhuman heroes confounded the separation of fact from fiction.[7] In the mists of legend, where there exists no sequence of development, events appear self-generated and hence miraculous. Yet one hard fact remains indisputable: An Armenian culture of some sophistication existed before the fourth century. If for no other reason, this is attested by the unique and pervasive Armenian Church architecture from that period and by the flow of literary production (beginning with copious translation of the Bible) that came soon after the invention of an original Armenian alphabet in 414.[8]

In the simple agrarian community where he grew up, Saroyan could not have missed observing a seeming incongruity in the Armenian character. If the Armenians he knew were any gauge, those solemn early Christians who had laid down their lives to save their immortal souls had never fully severed their pagan links with the earth, living to this day an exuberant life of here and now. Later, Saroyan's contacts with another type of Armenian would enable him to view his compatriots in a somewhat different, if analogous, light.

The Armenian journalist/patriots with whom Saroyan was to maintain a cordial relationship throughout his adult life were zealous utopians, who sought to perpetuate an Armenian consciousness in America in the hope of keeping alive the ideal of an independent Armenian nation. Remaining outside the pale of partisan politics, Saroyan wholeheartedly supported their idealism in the abstract. Early in his career, he became an assiduous contributor of fiction to their publications, and to the end of his life consistently encouraged his fellow Armenian writers.

The Armenian Revolutionary Federation, which had been publishing *Hairenik Daily* and *Hairenik Weekly* since the beginning of the century in Boston, inaugurated an English-language section in the paper in spring 1932, and in the following year published successively three stories by an unknown writer on the West Coast by the name of Sirak Goryan (a pseudonym for William Saroyan): The three stories, "A Fist Fight for Armenians," "The Broken Wheel," and "The Barber's Apprentice" brought honor to Goryan/Saroyan when Edward O'Brien singled out all three stories for his honor roll in *Best American Stories of 1934*. From then on, long after his meteoric rise to fame, Saroyan remained a regular contributor to the paper.

James H. Tashjian, in his introduction to *My Name is Saroyan*, has written a detailed account of Saroyan's lifelong faithfulness to the Hairenik publications, giving many examples of his supportiveness of the paper's endeavor to promote Armenian literary culture. Tashjian documents both Saroyan's close feelings for his people and his eagerness to identify with the Armenian heritage. But his claim that "the key to understanding what William Saroyan is all about is found in the *Hairenik* phase of his career" becomes meaningful only when we stop to examine the source and nature of Saroyan's need to relate to his roots. It is glimpsed (though not analyzed by Tashjian) in an exchange of letters between Saroyan and the editor of *Hairenik* which Tashjian provides in another publication, "The Saroyan Memorial Issue of The Armenian Review."

In a letter to the founding editor of *Hairenik,* Dr. Reuben Darbinian, on 25 April 1936, Saroyan pledges his commitment to "the Armenian spirit—a spirit of almost mad determination." Two years earlier, he had written to the same editor, "I've got what I have from my inheritance, without doubt. . . . I am proud to be an Armenian." But when the editors inadvertently put him on the spot and elicited a political stand, Saroyan unabashedly announced,

> I am interested in the great Armenia, not the petty Armenia. I am interested in the magnificence of my race which blossoms in the heart and mind of the man who finds himself and thereby finds his race.

He repeatedly made the point that if there was to be "a native Armenian consciousness," he would prefer that it be "unspoiled by politics."[9]

Clearly, there is more than simple patriotism involved here. To Saroyan, the need to know his ethnic identity is not only to be able to reach a deeper layer of himself but to find a connection, still vaguely understood, between his background and his unfolding art. What is revealed in his letters to the Armenian editors is his consistent identification of race with character rather than place—Armenia as a state of mind, a cultural entity, an immutable carrier of ancient experiences distilled by time and memory.

Looking closely at Saroyan's earliest stories, written under the name of Sirak Goryan especially for the Armenian publication between 1933 and 1934, one notes that what interests the writer, even when he is writing for an Armenian audience, is not the visible shell of ethnicity but the more elusive qualities of character and attitude. Three years of struggling to get published in San Francisco had not dulled his literary ambition, and, given a chance to write for a "ready" audience of his compatriots, Saroyan released a floodgate of stories, which *Hairenik* gratefully published.

The opportunity had come inadvertently and providentially through Saroyan's Uncle Aram, a successful lawyer and practical human being. "The crazy son of the Saroyans" was how the twenty-four-year-old William had been introduced to Armen Bardizian, an editor of *Hairenik,* who was visiting Fresno in 1932. "Only crazy boys try to be writers," the uncle had added, apologetically. But before the meeting was over, William had been invited to write "the news of Fresno" for the paper. "I write literature, not news. I write great stuff," William had demurred. "In that case, send your stuff to Reuben Darbinian [the editor in chief] and I'll talk to him about it," Mr. Bardizian had replied.[10]

Saroyan's self-confidence and determination at this point had the most fragile basis in encouragement: He had published three minor pieces in a San Francisco journal, *Overland Monthly,* and a few short stories in *The Boulevardeer,* a Detroit publication. But his attempts to get published in big magazines like *American Mercury, Scribner's,* and *The New Yorker* had met no success. Barely turned twenty-one, he had written to a San Francisco newspaperman, Charles Caldwell Dobie, "A good many years ago, I definitely decided to pursue literature as a profession." Asking Mr. Dobie for advice and help, he reinforced his determination: "I am already twenty-one and not at all displeased with the present state of society. My failure in my chosen line of work has not at all made either a socialist or an anarchist of me. I am merely insisting that I ought to be where I belong."[11] There is no evidence that Mr. Dobie ever answered the aspiring writer, and one presumes that Saroyan gave up hope of breaking into journalism, though apparently remaining unwavering in his decision to "pursue literature."

A far cry from "News of Fresno," Saroyan's earliest submissions to *Hairenik* were three poems, overtly "patriotic" in feeling and subject matter and not particularly distinguished. The first, an evocative two-part poem titled "To the Voice of Shah-Mouradian," celebrates the noted Armenian tenor whom Saroyan has acknowledged as having been "profoundly important" in his life, having heard him for the first time on a record when he was seventeen years old. His thoughts on hearing him had been, "So that's what it means to be an Armenian. That open voice, field voice, wind-voice, voice of the plains."[12] The poem emphasizes the singer's connection with the Armenian past: "Yours is the flowing of the ancient soul, While mine is but the lisping of the mind." Singing of the River, Mother Araksie, Shah-Mouradian evokes "the glory of his race," which he expects his son will seek "(Wherever he may go, to what strange place)." And if his son marries "[A] daughter of our ancient family," he muses, *his* son, listening to the singer "Of our old legend and our deathless myth" will know "how once in strength we stood, / And stand forever in her motherhood."

In two subsequent sonnets, "To the River Euphrates" and "To Lake Van," Saroyan seeks a link between that geographical locale

and the source of his spiritual strength. "In me, Euphrates is."
"Euphrates flows, however it may be / That but in dreams these
eyes its grace may see." "Lake Van, O inland sea my father saw"
is identified with his "homeland." "His blood to mine restores that
fearful awe / He felt as he from homeland's shore turned west."
He envisions the young ghost of his father there in his "spirit's
soil" long after he has left it and died. The beauty and glory of the
ancient past are eternally linked with the Armenian experience,
Saroyan suggests in his verse.

When he turns next to the story form, the abstract flights of
lyricism are held in check by a straightforward narrative style that
nonetheless conveys undercurrents of personal feeling. The first,
"Fist Fight for Armenia,"[13] published in three parts, is a story
about prejudice, something that has deeply touched him as an immigrant boy growing up in Fresno in the early part of the century.
That it is based on fact is undisputable on the recent evidence
supplied by Robert Mirak's book, *Torn Between Two Worlds*.[14] But
there is a new twist to Saroyan's story of protest, which characteristically looks for the *source* of this error.

A group of "howling schoolboys" is fighting and wrestling with
fierce animal strength. Caspar, who is caught in their midst though
obviously not one of them, feels distanced from them by their
native urge "to do. To perform. Outwardly. With the body." Re-
pelled by their sheer physicality, knowing "nothing he might do in
that way could possibly have meaning for him," he withdraws from
their "animal fun" and becomes the object of their taunts. Rejected
by all the ball-game teams, Caspar is bewildered, gauche; "too
solemn, too earnest," even his clumsiness cannot evoke the kind
of laughter that cements. What appears to be fear and timidity is
rather the effect of an inner superiority before their mindless
pugnacity:

> He was ashamed because of the direction they were taking, because
> they were not aware of the year in which they lived, not aware that all
> the history of life was accumulated in them. For their use. So that they
> could be men.

Caspar eventually decides that he must prove himself and takes
up wrestling as a sport. At first he is reluctant to strike his opponent in the face, but he soon gains an insight that justifies the
action: "The idea was to keep moving, and it didn't matter to what
end. Always. In every moment and without pause. No summary.
No documentation." What seems at first an attitude of righteous-

ness is revealed as something more far-reaching: an awareness that individual acts are immutably linked in a chain of human purpose and meaning. It is what leads Caspar to a sense of mission. In learning to wrestle, he will not only be able to defend himself but by freeing himself from his fated alienation, will be able to resist violence done to others. The only boys he will teach to wrestle are those who can handle wrestling objectively as a sport:

> He believed if he could teach the boys to box without becoming bitter, they could find it easier living. He was convinced that it was an individual's viewpoint that got him into an abnormal series of events that culminated in a violence of some sort or another.

Soon enough Caspar is put to the test. Discrimination comes out into the open when a group of younger boys is slandered as "dirty Armenians." Now Caspar's back is up against the wall as he sees little Ara George weeping "with ancient grief, wailing at the outrage of a vulgar hatred." But Caspar's strength has limits; the multiform "enemy" falls on him and the bloody fracas ends with threats of "massacre." The present moment is suddenly permeated with the past: "It seemed . . . that he had begun the fight a long time ago and that it was a thing that would never end." As he tries rising once more, he groans "O Armenia, Armenia," looking for a source from which to draw a trifle more strength.

Though they have lost the battle, Caspar's head is not bowed, nor are the heads of the boys he has tried to defend. Gathered around him, they are "silent with grief but proud somehow of their humiliation." It is Reuben, the boy who had earlier spoken with bravado—"We know we're hated, but what of it?"—who now articulates their knowledge that triumph lies elsewhere. Reuben had seen the fight as "the negation of civilization, the denial of human history, the repudiation of life itself," and the anger he now feels is for himself for having wanted "to swing a club, lowering himself to the level of a furious and unreasonable beast."

Saroyan's second "Sirak Goryan" story for *Hairenik*, "The Broken Wheel," printed in three installments,[15] reestablishes—this time in a nostalgic mood—the inner security of the child brought up in the shade of an ethos strong in its scale of values. Foremost among the supportive elements is the family, its self-contained world englobed in love and trust. Whatever deprivation, material or spiritual, the individual experiences, within the family circle laughter and hope commingle with tears and despair to restore and maintain the sense of proportion which makes renewal possible.

"Everything was solid and permanent at our house," the sensitive
eight-year-old narrator observes, "and we didn't notice the time
that was passing." The story is not a romanticization of a time
past, but rather an attempt to distill from the past an elixir for the
present. Created out of childhood recollections that retain their
freshness by being evoked through a child's eye, "The Broken
Wheel" contains many of the elements that will come to earmark
the Saroyan story, most especially the commingling of humor and
sentiment with a youthful energy that transforms the commonplace
into something unique and memorable. The feeling it projects of
family relationships will surface again most prominently in *The
Human Comedy* a decade later.

The small house on Santa Clara Avenue (in the foreign district
of Fresno) with its "clean, wholesome smell," is here introduced
for the first time as the locale of the numerous Aram Garoghlanian
stories that will eventually become *My Name is Aram*. Earthy in
essence, it abounds in the beauty of flourishing trees, among them
the English walnut, the olive, the honeysuckle plant, the peach,
the castor, and the cactus. The peach tree, which has "happened
accidentally," growing outside their yard proper, is appropriated as
their own, not for the fruit it yields (which could be had cheaper
from the store) but for the esthetic pleasure this family of meager
means derives from it. Every spring, his sister Naomi cuts a bunch
of blossoms from it and places it in a black vase: "we used to see
the blossoms in the black vase," the boy recalls, "and suddenly we
used to feel it was all splendid. It seemed to mean that we were
alive and we used to laugh about it."

> In the winter [he remembers] we laughed a great deal. We would be
> sullen and sorrowful for weeks at a time and then suddenly all of us
> would begin to laugh. We would laugh fifteen or twenty minutes and
> then we would be sullen and sorrowful again.

He suspects that "it was in us to feel bewildered and futile."

Yet the story is not about that; or about that only incidentally.
The atmosphere is fraught with expectation, for we see it all
through the youthful sensibility of a boy eager to meet and absorb
the fullness of life. The boy's older brother, Krikor, comes home
one day with a cactus plant and imparts the news that their valley
was once a desert, with cactus growing everywhere. The boy tries
to imagine "our valley without people and streets and houses" and
thinks it "very strange, very irregular." Krikor plants the cactus
and in a couple of years the desert plant produces "splendid red

blossoms and a fruit no one knew how to eat; and it was taller than a tall man."

The word "splendid" appears again and again, as if echoing one of Hemingway's favorite words, though Saroyan's "splendour" involves much simpler things. There is, for instance, the memorable visit of his uncle Vahan, the lawyer, who comes down from San Francisco with a brand-new Apperson roadster, the *only* red one of eleven Appersons in America. It is this small distinction that allows the boys to feel superior to their neighbor Rouben, whose uncle has only a Cadillac that runs sixty miles an hour:

> "Yes," I said "but is it red?" . . . There is only one red Apperson in America. . . . It was like saying that one's great-grandfather had seen Lincoln or that one's ancestors had come over on the *Mayflower*; only it was more impressive.

The boy connects this rarity with his Armenian background: "I felt, there is a lawyer in our family and he has a red Apperson. We are an enterprising people." Rouben is invited to take a ride with the boys in Uncle Vahan's car, and when they return his mother serves watermelons, "and we all sat in the parlor, eating watermelon and talking." Though they are hot and perspiring, "it was a clear moment of our lives."

Though Uncle Vahan speaks Armenian with his sister (the boys' mother), he is very much an American. "We do not know," he tells the children, "how fortunate we are to be in such a country as this. Opportunities are unlimited here. Every man is free and he can go as far as he is able." When the uncle broaches the question of Krikor's career, the boy, in embarrassment, gobbles up his watermelon and discreetly avoids revealing that his brother's secret ambition is to become a musician.

The whole family is musically inclined. The older sister, Lucy, having taken lessons, plays Chopin, Liszt, and Mozart. The younger Naomi plays popular songs like "There's a Long, Long Trail" and "I Love You, California." And the boy "beats the keys of the piano" as if "half crazy." He feels impelled to play, to fill the time. "We were all living and it seemed to me that something should happen." Reality remains remote in the presence of small, unexpected interruptions.

One day Krikor comes home with a black satchel containing a cornet. After explaining the nature of the instrument to his mother, he announces that he will learn to play "Barcarolle" by Christmas. But Krikor does not have the making of a musician. "Do you think," he asks his brother, "it's because this horn is so old or is it just that I haven't any talent for cornet playing?" The boy has no answer. He only knows that

> there is something to be done, something perfect and precise and grace-
> ful, but we hadn't found out what it was.

At this point, the desire for "something perfect and precise and graceful," the transcendence of art—which Saroyan would seek as an antidote to mortality—is beyond the children's grasp. Not to be daunted, however, Krikor gives up one challenge for another. The next thing he brings home is a bicycle so large for him that he can only ride it from under the bar. He has bought it to please the merchant selling it. His mother hides it in a closet until he promises to return it for a smaller one. But the smaller size leads to fights between the brothers over who is to use it. Finally, they set out together to the deserted county fairgrounds, where they ride the dirt track feeling "it was finer and more private and we had lots of fun being alone." They are impressed by "the quiet and the enormity of the place, the strangeness of the empty grandstands," and they take turns riding around the mile track.

When the bicycle breaks down under the weight of their growing bodies, they walk home silently, as if "coming out of an endless dream." However "trivial the occurrence," they feel it was "a vast and a vital thing." "Bewildered and frantically awake," it becomes a symbol of something ending. The boy thinks, "only the fork of our bicycle had broken but we knew that everything was not the same." It seems to him that they had forgotten their lives, "that now . . . we were remembering all the little details that marked the stages of our growth."

The boy is sensitive and reflective without being neurotic. In swift flashbacks, he remembers how he nearly drowned some years ago and he heard his brother's voice calling him in Armenian; he remembers his sister sobbing over the loss of her job at Woolworth's, the other sister's struggle with pneumonia and their prayers for her; he remembers Krikor bringing home a small phonograph and two records, "Barcarolle" and "O Sole Mio." But the incident of the broken wheel mainly brings back the day Uncle Vahan goes off to war and his mother's tears as she sees him off at the train station. As a newsboy shouting headlines, he remembers coming home "sick in my soul because it was all over and my uncle Vahan was out there dead," and the time he had walked alone, "seeing things and being alive . . . and suddenly burst into tears because life was so bright and clean and fierce." The boy's direct response to life remains intact even after his exposure to tragic events. For, along with their own pain, they have learned of the "pain and the dying in the old country," as their mother reads to them about it in the Armenian papers.

In the end, it is the saving grace of humor that chases insecurity and fear. When their mother and sisters burst into laughter over the broken bicycle wheel, the boys feel "as if everything in our world was all right and that we had nothing to feel sad about." There is therapeutic reassurance in their laughter and immediate consolation in the knowledge that "we were still living together in our house and we still had our trees."

But this is not in the end a Chekhovian world, with its eye on the past, and even though, as in Chekhov, small distractions have the power to dissipate tragedy, the boy's feelings are deepened.

> I felt that at last I was part of life, that at last I knew how all things ended. A strange, desolating sadness swept through the earth and for the first time in my life I was feeling it definitely, personally. It seemed as if I had just been born, that I had at that moment become aware of the earth, and the pain, the joy and the fear and the ugliness.

For the first time he finds meaning in his habit of pounding on the piano keys, of his fighting with his brother, of their laughing together. He is momentarily pacified by his mother's stoic words: "It is no use to cry," she says in Armenian. "We have always had our disappointments and hardships and we have always come out of them and always shall."

The last scene in the story establishes Saroyan's eagerness to confront life. The boy gets out of bed and opens the door to the parlor where he sees his mother crying over a picture of her dead brother. "I could see her swaying her head from side to side the way people from the old country do." The story ends there, but what is left unsaid is the boy's awakening to the pain of others.

The third "Sirak Goryan" story, "The Barber's Apprentice,"[16] published four months later in two installments, strikes altogether a different note: again in this allegorical tale, the ethnic atmosphere is muted and derives from character and precept rather than overt customs and manners. The staying power of the family has its counterpart in the irrepressible free spirit of the national Armenian hero, David of Sassoon, the mountain giant whose spirit of excess, like that of the Irish epic hero, Sweeney, verges on inspired madness. Unlike Sweeney, however, David is a peasant, a man of the people. It is significant that Markar, the town's drunken fool in Saroyan's story, is nothing more than a barber's apprentice, unwillingly being "tutored in the art of shaving, cutting hair and extracting teeth." Always jolly and good-humored, always drunk and sleeping when he should work, he lives by his own laws. In the old city of Moush, he is the eternal drifter, who belongs to "no village, no city, no nation, no race," and is "the product of no era." Markar has decided that

All [men] are his brothers; all are weak, miserable, pathetic. All pursue the same chimeric fantasies of perfection, heaven on earth, everlasting bliss. . . . [They] demand more of life than it has to give.

This being the case, he concludes, "Why should not each heart burn with the fire of fluid, the soul sing with its warmth?" Markar has all the commonness of everyman made *un*common by excess:

Markar slept as soundly as the sultan, and snored as vigorously as the judge on his bench. His dream, however, was purer than that of the prophet: he dreamt of God.

A descendant of "tipplers, poets, singers and dancers," at nineteen he is the soul of eloquence as he stalks through the hills, knocking at doors to deliver the message of joy and goodwill. In the name of St. Garabed, patron of the poor and the humble, he outsings the birds, outroars the lions and outlaughs the hyena "who broke down in despair and wept." In his exalted state, "his impatient soul" "spurred forward by drink," he feels "his flesh was stronger than the trunks of great trees." Only when he finally collapses and is led home by a child does he become repentant and promises never to touch drink again.

The narrator of the story (the author) shows no more scorn for Markar than Shakespeare for Falstaff. "He is life's prodigal. . . . [T]he prodigal is the favorite of his father, the most beloved of his brothers." With all his faults, "he is loved by all men . . . and out of his bountiful pity God himself smiles down on him."

"The Barber's Apprentice" is Saroyan's earliest celebration of "the simple man, the good man" who believes that "the world is good, . . . life is pleasant, . . . [and] God is kind." In his role as the free and happy fool, Markar enters the exalted climate of the poet and dreamer. But Barber and Apprentice both have their place: While one plods at his trade, patiently waiting for "one beard to shave, one head of hair to trim, one rotten tooth to pull," the other spreads the word of unalloyed joy and goodwill.

Of the other four "Sirak Goryan" stories published that same year, "The Moment of Life" is worth noting at some length not only for the significant biographical details it contains but for the particular emphasis it places on them.[17] The family scene on Santa Clara Street in this short, lyrical, evocative story is more uniformly somber than in "The Broken Wheel," with reality suspended in the aftermath of the father's death. References to poverty, hardship, dislocation, and insecurity are only obliquely made, in the unfolding of the *real* story, which is the boy's gradual assimilation of his father's death and the sudden recognition of immortality that follows it.

The dead father is known to the small child only through a framed photograph over the piano in their parlor. Standing on a chair to get a closer view of his face, he sees "a young man with a solemn expression and an old style mustache with the ends curled up," and though he has no remembrance of him, "I did not feel his being dead had ended his life or at least the meaning of it for me."

The boy can imagine an abstraction of death, "an empty universe a void without substance and life and light," but "he could not understand how something that had life could be no longer alive." Having no firsthand memory of his father, he has reconstructed his life from family conversations, and so vivid is their remembrance that the child "believed that he would somehow come walking up the street and casually enter our house." The need "to see him and be in his presence" becomes linked "with an incredible longing for a time and a place which seemed forever lost."

The boy cannot yet connect with the lost dimension of the past that contains his father's short life, so he merely recounts what he has heard: that his father had been born in Van in 1876 had had an American education and had become an itinerant teacher; that he had been arrested and jailed for teaching the peasants to be prepared for the revolution that was to come, and that he later escaped to Russia, returning finally to his native land to be married. Then comes the decision to make a new life in America, but once settled in Carmel, California, he has disappointments. The scholar turned farmer is heartbroken when the chickens on the farm begin to die. He tries to be an inventor, but the new top he invents that whistles as it spins does not help to feed the family, and finally, though he wins an essay-writing contest, he fails to get the cash reward.

When he dies in his mid thirties, the father leaves behind "two frock coats of very fine cloth and a half a dozen books, four in English and two in Armenian." Among these are *Gulliver's Travels,*

The Beauties of Shakespeare, and the first volume of Edgar Allan Poe's works containing "The Philosophy of Composition," "The Poetic Principle," and "Poems." These the boy will eventually read, but the books in Armenian, "with their strange, ornamental print," will always haunt him: as he grows up he becomes pleased that he cannot read them

> because I came to see gradually that its symbols had become for me symbols of the vast and eloquent silence of my father, and every page of Armenian print seemed a communion with him beyond articulation and beyond language.

The story veers briefly to the family's daily life: The cow his father had bought them and that has sustained them with the wholesome nourishment of the Armenian *mazoon* (yogurt) and *tanabour* (yogurt soup) is stolen, and the mother is too proud to accept the gift of another cow from her husband's kindly younger brother Mikel (who "looked something like the photograph of his father"). "They do not look hungry, do they?" she retorts. But soon afterward she goes to work for the Guggenheim's Packing House, and the boy acknowledges they began to eat "more substantial food."

All this is told in a very matter-of-fact way, though the boy does not miss what is salient in this little drama—the characteristic qualities of both his mother and his uncle, one very proud and self-reliant, the other generous and compassionate.

Sometime after, when the boy has "acquired a rich store of memories and felt therefore definitely alive," he has his moment of illumination. One fall evening as he stands before a crackling fire of dried leaves with his brother Krikor, he sees his uncle Mikel coming toward them in the dusk and feels "something so intensely and ineffably real about the moment . . . that I believed there could never be death among us, that my father was not dead, and that every moment we chose to live vividly could be made to survive forever." It is an intimation of immortality:

> Standing together about the fire, in an alien land, and yet the same land of our earth, it seemed that all the past and future had met perfectly and become perpetuated in this moment of our consciousness. . . . Our religion was life and the awareness of it. We lived and because we were aware, we could not die and this awareness in us made immortal all who lived finally within and through us, my father, and his father, and the family of our whole people.

Published in the same two issues that contained "The Moment of Life" was a short sketch, "Noneh," Saroyan's first effort in characterizing with the long arm of extravagant detail verging on the humorous.[18] In the portrait of his maternal grandmother, Lucy, he introduces a member of his family who will subsequently appear in many short stories and plays. A commonsensical, determined, and outspoken lady, eager to dispense her fount of intuitive wisdom, Lucy will play a large role in orienting the young Saroyan to the earthy, life-worshipping breed of Armenians who stand in sharp contrast to his idealistic and impractical father.

A bundle of contradictions, Lucy is scornful of hypocritical churchgoers, while herself believing "savagely in a personal God." When praying at the table "in a loud and angry voice," she says "*Im Ahstvots* (My God) and never God alone." She is ever-solicitous of the health of her family, old and young, but is quick to pick a quarrel with any of them, feeling that "such things were proper among people who really loved one another." Though she has had no schooling and does not read even her own language, she is tuned in to the outside world:

> She had an uncanny talent for getting the latest news and seemed to perceive the truth of any given state of affairs without being thoroughly familiar with its details.

She likes gossip and is full of song and laughter, but she is silent and moody for hours "remembering the old country and the quiet life there that had been mangled and slaughtered and violated."

In her twice-yearly visit with the Saroyans, she creates an Armenian ambience that leaves deep traces. Saroyan's portrait of Lucy is never condescending or mocking, but grows out of sympathetic attention:

> Winter or summer, she was in the habit of rising before daybreak and making noise. Through our morning sleep, when we were half-awake, we could hear her going about the dark house, sweeping, bringing in firewood, cooking, shouting at the cat, and singing. . . . [S]he sang in a mocking tone of voice the sad love songs of the old country, as if she were criticizing people for believing in such nonsense. But when she sang a religious song she would be passionately serious and she would seem to be very angry at the same time.

Lucy's greatest gift to the Saroyans was probably the hours she spent recounting folktales to them, tales "which she related with the accuracy of a post." Most of her repertoire consisted of stories she had heard from her grandmother and aunts, but the ones she especially enjoyed telling were those she invented herself, told in her own style, and which contained her own philosophy. "In her way she was an artist," Saroyan remembers. The stories she told had morals:

> They were designed to teach young people to have courage, to be honorable, honest and gentle, to help the poor, to have no fear of evil, to be industrious, thrifty, intellectually awake, and above all things skeptical. The world swarmed with minds scheming to rob from innocent souls their virtue, their peace of mind, and their money.

"It was not good to have too much faith in man; it was better to have faith in God," she counseled the children.

It is the last of the 1934 "Sirak Goryan" stories, "Yea and Amen," that explains and explores the role that "faith in God" played in those childhood years.[19] In this forerunner of the boyhood stories in *My Name is Aram,* Saroyan is not yet writing strictly from within the child's world but rather from an adult retrospect that seeks spiritual replenishment from the wisdom of childhood. Though the story becomes overwhelmed by an amalgam of essay, sermon, and impressionistic prose, its psychological insights are so delicate and acute that it leaves an indelible impression. Moreover, the story's ontological perception is essential to an understanding of the Saroyan canon and its inevitable break with the material realism of his contemporaries.

The story is a simple one. An unnamed small boy observes a maimed bird crawling under a car and rescues it; it is a chicken with a broken wing, and feeling sorry for it, the child takes it home. On his way, he imagines its sadness and "almost mortal loneliness," and tries to comfort it, talking to it in his native Armenian. At home, he shows it off to his family, and as he watches it strutting around the room, imagines it "listening to us laughing." All that night he and his brother and sisters feel they have "a distinguished guest at our house." The following day his brother Krikor builds a small house with a coop. They put the hen in the coop and wait for it to hatch, not just any egg but "the *egg,* our egg." When it finally happens, they are deeply awed, and in their eyes the egg becomes "a statue of grace, sealed and solid and whole." A miracle, "repudiating the ugliness of all broken and decayed things."

The story's real meaning is hidden in its preamble and is revealed through the narrator's recollection of a deeply impressionable childhood experience. His memory is linked backward to a primordial time: "We had God, and above all things," the story begins, "blessedness, belief, and the longing for precision." The story's first two paragraphs, like those that begin "The Daring Young Man on the Flying Trapeze," are a pastiche of an imagined prehistoric world, of

> vast and unseen things, oceanic, the swelling of unseen seas, . . . the roar of deep rivers of the soul, canyons of mind, tall ageless trees.

That world abounds in a surge of inevitable human life—

> God within us, and the wailing of babes, and the oratory of mighty men, the stride of mobs within us, the surge of history, turning in us, squirming to unworded language, the first of all things mortal and the last.

—along with the inevitable human deeds:

> the glamor of wars, the ache of bleeding men, and God, our face in the light of the sun, and the face of man everywhere, and the swift life in us, our godliness.

The vision of a world without end, where "the word was the word of all men, of all life," is suddenly transported to the child's world, where God's immanence is fixed and unquestioned:

> We had vision [the narrator recalls] and stance and touch, and the earth was beneath our feet and we stood upon it, and over us was the firmament, and beneath the touch of our hands was the texture of living things and things that stood without life, of leaf and fruit, rock and earth, fire and water, and within us, our God.

Because everything derives from God, truth is indivisible—"silence and sound, motion and immobility, good, evil, wholeness"—and the child readily accepts God as "the author of our fable . . . the fact of my father who was no more of our earth, and of my brother Krikor, and of my mother and my sisters." The child sees God as the source of "the meaning of us, the very shape and the rhythm of our living . . . the fountain of our laughter . . . of our grief and gravity."

The children come naturally to the concept of belonging:

> We used to pray. [the narrator continues] To be related to all things, to have relationship with things living and things dead.

Life stretches to infinitude, backward and forward in an endur-ing "circle":

> We were an end and a beginning and we used to pray to be related to the coming and going of men, to the appearance and disappearance of the faces and forms in all regions of the earth.

They feel a compulsion "to be a part of every act of man, the good and the evil, all things performed, all thoughts and hopes and griefs, all joys and pains." Intuitively, they absorb the lesson of evolution "from small living things, unthinking yet with the grace of God," and its inevitable consequence, the notion of perfectibility. First "the form of man," then "the form of God in us." Divinity is, thus, not only "given" but achieved through an evolving effort toward perfection: "to be precise yet universal, to be immediate yet eter-nal." In retrospect, the narrator sees danger in this concurrence of the human and the divine: "There was evil in us along with the good, and it was the evil of man and of godliness." It is in the knowledge of his failure to be godlike that man learns to destroy.

> There was a wish in us to destroy, to bring things to an end, and it would make us frantic, because alongside of this wish, there was an even stronger wish in us to build.

The boys want "to create new things, to make new shapes, new meanings," but in fact "we broke things, smashed them, and we swore at them, and *it was the same as praying.*" (The italics are mine.) Swearing at their failed humanity was a form of praying to be like the God they wanted to emulate and couldn't. But they try. They construct a lamp and fix a broken alarm clock, which they ultimately break in a fit of frustration:

> We had made nothing. . . . We asked one another if there was some-thing wonderful we could make. And the answer was always yes. Cer-tainly there were splendid things to come, and we would think a long time about those splendid unknown things, . . . but we would never be able to devise a new shape, and we knew we had to do *something,* so we destroyed.

When Krikor cannot fix the clock, he hurls it against the barn wall. "Everything I do is like this," he cries out in despair. Saro-yan's immediate concern here is to imagine a child's gradual loss of his sense of connection with divinity, but the story's message goes beyond that to suggest as a source of evil in the world man's alienation from his own godliness.

By almost uncanny reconstruction of the child's understanding of reality, Saroyan gives shape to his meandering story with a final incident that challenges our concept of entropy, of a purely physical universe condemned to decline:

> The shape of things [the narrator remembers] were holy to us, the mere shapes and outlines man had given to reality and to God, the designs with which man had graced the world.

He recalls their sadness before Levi's Junk Yard, "the cemetery of objects, broken-down wagons, old automobiles." They would visit the place as "mourners visit a grave, . . . ruins of our time, our own Babylon." In contrast, the most commonplace things in their own home were objects of veneration, like the old-style kitchen stove with the name Excelsior, Troy:

> Those shapes, those swift straight lines, the sudden curves, the round lids, the oven doors on hinges, and the whole mass of it, . . . the tables, the small things, the plain objects, visions of God . . . the shape of reality.

With a child's special kind of sight they not only looked at things, they "saw in them the unity and the eternality of God." In contrast, they saw at Levi's Junk Yard "the disgrace of age and inutility, . . . the substance that was without life and grace." It affords a fundamental lesson: "to know the yea and the nay, the whole idea of man and reality, . . . the ugliness of sin and death." Saddened, they turn away, looking about "for the everlasting thing, the object with shape that could never be destroyed."

And by accident they find it one day. The little broken-winged hen that will lay "the *egg, our egg.*" As he waits, the boy wants to know how the shape of the shell could be so fine and precise:

> My brother Krikor said that he did not know. It happened. It was impossible to explain how. It was like everything, like leaves and flowers and man, miraculous but simple and effortless.

When the egg is finally hatched, their sense of immanence is validated:

> It was a marvelous thing. . . . There in the nest was God, the beginning, and everything seemed splendid and precise in the world, and every-

thing was definite and graceful like the egg, and it was a thing to admire and worship.

When Krikor holds the chick in his hand and smiles on it, it is "as if all the errors of man were here corrected":

> And it was God, and it was artlessness that was greater than the greatest art of man. . . . The things men made could end, they could decay and break and fall to pieces, but this, this oval whiteness could never end.

In this newfound spiritually enclosed universe, Krikor continues smiling "because the egg had made him whole, because it had sealed him inwardly, . . . restored him to piety and faith, returned him to God, yea and amen."

"Yea and Amen," (which was reprinted in Saroyan's second volume of stories, *Inhale and Exhale*) is perhaps as Christian a fable as Saroyan has written, but what makes it much more than a simple statement of faith is the care it takes to implant the piety within a child's perceptions, while at the same time implying a larger reality than most adults intuit. In this early example of Saroyan's use of the dual vision, there is a marked absence of esthetic cohesion; the story becomes both essay and narrative, both straightforward and impressionistic in the telling. It has a philosophic pretension in that it tries to establish a basis for humanistic faith, with its source in a concept of good and evil that is not strictly Biblical. In our reach toward "godliness," Saroyan sees a Promethean pride that is both man's glory and his self-destruction. There is surely no false idealism in the recognition that good and evil are opposite sides of the same coin of man's nature as it vacillates between the best and the worst in it.

One reads this story, finally, for an important clue to the writer's literary ambition, to the quest for the fabric or style with which to clothe his faith. Through the teleological premise behind this simple story about childhood Saroyan would learn to cope with the esthetic tension created by the opposing claims of idealism and realism on his writing.

This bears examining at the outset. The wish of the children in "Yea and Amen" to be "precise yet universal, to be immediate yet eternal," involves an intuition of closeness between the physical and immaterial worlds: "The shape of things were holy to us, the mere shapes," is how the children felt, "the designs with which man had graced the void." The subjective element does not obscure what is concretely within the spectrum of vision. Things are more than their "thingness," however, since they are perceived as "holy," created by God, just as each of us is "holy," being the largest of all his manifestations. In this sense, nature becomes synonymous to Saroyan with reality, and as sacred and wondrous as it ever was for Emerson, rejoicing in "the universal Mind" or for Poe, who saw the universe as "the plot of God."

It is in this intuitively grasped idealism that Saroyan parts company from a writer like Sherwood Anderson, to whom he has often been compared and whom Saroyan has indeed regarded as his mentor. "His writing made you say, I can do that," Saroyan wrote in an essay about Anderson titled "His Collaborators."[20] "We were his collaborators." The realist in Saroyan seeking "accuracy and truth" invariably responded to Anderson's dictate that "imagination must feed on reality or starve,"[21] but Saroyan hinted at a limit to his influence when he acknowledged Anderson as having "set up a school whose doorway was anywhere we happened to be, and we all walked in and out whenever we pleased." Saroyan notes in his same essay that while Anderson was searching for something, "he never wanted to take it over or look at it sharply—he wanted to pretend that it was really what he wanted it to be—wonderful." What, in the end, made Saroyan uneasy was that Anderson "seemed to feel that American life was not what it should be, and mentioned people as though they had failed him."

Like Anderson, Saroyan wanted life to be "wonderful," but he did not, like Anderson, include in that concept the idea of the "strange" and the "grotesque." God's art would not permit anything less than "whole" or "precise." One might speculate that Saroyan wrote "Yea and Amen" to negate Anderson's 1921 story, the much anthologized "The Egg," in which an enterprising farmer turned inventor tries to outdo nature by hatching a five-legged hen, hoping thereby to exploit its grotesqueness because "people liked to look at the strange and wonderful." "The Egg" is essentially an awesome tale that perverts an expected affirmation of life with a twist of the absurd. Anderson's characters have no sense of the "holy," and if the commonplaceness of life is there, the palpable reality of sights and sounds, erratic commotion and babble of talk are missing. The effect in this and other works of Anderson is, as Lionel Trilling has so aptly observed, that of "quite negating life, making it gray, empty and devoid of meaning."[22]

To sustain the element of the commonplace without at the same time missing the inner light in all living things would involve for Saroyan walking into the "doorway" Anderson had opened and walking out of it at the same time. The commingling of reality and dream could only materialize through the continued watchfulness of a prescient self who would place in perspective the "reality" of the moment. This is what Saroyan implies in the quote at the beginning of this chapter: "The fact is that I am always speaking and thinking of the place and the time of the place, and that I myself am included in the thought because it is inevitable. It is not a question of pride, but a question of accuracy and truth." Or, as Saroyan in his preface to the Modern Library edition of *The Daring Young Man on the Flying Trapeze and Other Stories* put it some six years after its publication, "I wanted the material to be everyday material, and I wanted to illustrate that all you needed was a writer."

Saroyan must have sensed that this authorial presence would lend his writing an additional value by adding to it an endemic American flavor. Thus he continues in that brashly worded preface: "American expression has one basic defect. It lacks freedom. It doesn't move easily. This first book was intended to introduce a little freedom into whatever future American expression might seek in the short story form." There is no hedging here by a reticent newcomer. He wants to show, among other things

> a few of the kinds of stories it was possible to write, and to suggest the limitless potentialities of the form, provided the form had a writer to go with it. Ease is what I wanted to introduce.

"Seventy Thousand Assyrians," the second story in this volume, is his initial experiment with this new "ease," and without making extravagant claims for Saroyan on this score, one has to concede that even Mark Twain or Ring Lardner (two of his most likely progenitors in the use of the open-ended demotic style) had never placed their story line in so precarious a balance. Along with this stylistic boldness, Saroyan makes the story serve as an apologia for the kind of stories he proposes to write, and in so doing minces no words to show his clear-cut departure from such popular contemporaries as Hemingway, Anderson, and Michael Arlen.

As in most of the stories in his first volume, it is the down-and-out writer as narrator who dominates the action (such as it is), but unlike the dying hero of "The Daring Young Man on the Flying Trapeze," he becomes, here, less the actor than the perceiver, moving the story along through a flow of free association, pausing at those intersections where his own identity meets and merges with the identities of his "creations." Though couched in lighthearted humor and teasing irony, the voice is essentially one of personal protest, of humanistic concern about inequities, that for all its broad references does not allow the claim of the individual to become an abstraction. Saroyan's characters in this, and in most of his subsequent works, are people you meet every day, often in chance encounters that contain the possibility of significant change. Just as the flow of life admits so much that is unpremeditated, so Saroyan's stories attempt to *seem to be* uncontrived.

The story's initial, ironic strategy is in the choice of a barbershop for its setting, for despite the opening stabs at offhand humor ("I hadn't had a haircut in forty days and forty nights and was beginning to look like several violinists out of work.") we know we are not in for a Lardneresque takeoff.[23] If the story's title hasn't succeeded in giving us a clue, the writer wastes no time in informing his reader, in parenthesis, "I am writing a very serious story, perhaps one of the most serious I shall write. That is why I am flippant. Readers of Sherwood Anderson will understand. . . . [T]hey will know that my laughter is rather sad." Here is fair warning that he is not only bypassing Lardner but perhaps even Anderson.

In Saroyan's particular barbershop on San Francisco's Third Street where haircuts may be had for fifteen cents, the narrator waits in line with a sixteen-year-old drifter: "He looked Iowa: splendid potentially, a solid American, but down, greatly down in the mouth." With the strategy of realism, Saroyan connects the boy with the mood of the scene itself:

Third Street below Howard is a district; think of the Bowery in New York, Main Street in Los Angeles; think of old men and boys, out of work, hanging around, smoking Bull Durham, talking about the government, waiting for something to turn up, simply waiting.

The briefest exchange reveals Iowa's hopelessness and as the writer envisages his imminent death, he has bitter thoughts:

At the same time all the theatres in America were showing over and over again, an animated film cartoon in which there was a song called "Who's Afraid of the Big Bad Wolf?" and that's what it amounts to; people with money laughing at the death that is crawling slyly into boys like young Iowa, pretending it isn't there.

In the same voice of democratic concern, the writer turns his attention to the apprentice Japanese barber who is fastidiously cutting the hair of a tramp, holding back his nose all the while. The scene reminds him of his own unwilling stint at his uncle's vineyard in the San Joaquin Valley; the feeling the writer senses they share is in the wish to be somewhere else. But Saroyan's only comment here is a mocking one emphasizing (strategically) his seeming lack of contrivance:

> A trivial point in a story, a bit of data with no place in a work of art, nevertheless I put it down. A young writer is always wanting to put in everything he sees.

The writer tries to connect with the Japanese boy by reciting the names of Japanese workers he knows from his uncle's vineyard, but the young barber remains involved in his work, his racial past confined to a few remembered names.

It is in the third and final encounter, with Theodor Badal, the Assyrian barber, that Saroyan breaks down the barriers and allows himself to walk out of Anderson's "doorway" to his own particular literary arena. But not before he has struck a blow against conventional storywriting:

> I want you to know that I am deeply interested in what people remember. A young writer goes out to places and talks to people. He tries to find out what they remember. I am not using great material for a short story. Nothing is going to happen in this work. I am not fabricating a fancy plot. I am not creating memorable characters. I am not using a slick style of writing.

Now, finally, he states his "mission." If he does not seek fame through publication in *The Saturday Evening Post* or aspire to "the Pulitzer Prize or Nobel Prize or any other prize," it is because all he wants to do is write "a letter to common people, telling them in simple language things they already know." His wish expands to a still larger ambition: "If I have any desire at all, it is to show the brotherhood of man." If the statement makes sophisticated people laugh, let them: "That's what sophistication is for." And so he goes on, unabashed, to declare the underlying premise of his work:

> I do not believe in races. I do not believe in governments. I see life as one life at one time, so many millions simultaneously over the earth.

And because language creates a barrier between people, he vows that

If I want to do anything, I want to speak a more universal language. The heart of man, the unwritten part of man, that which is eternal and common to all races.

The writer stops short, as if suddenly aware that he has been sermonizing and losing the thread of his story, when in fact—strategically again—he has been preparing us for its real theme. The tone changes, and there is the mere suggestion of apology: "an ordinary journalist would have been able to put the whole business into a three-word caption. Man is man he would have said. Something clever with any number of implications." This is clearly said to highlight the purpose he now reveals behind his circuitous style:

I want to use language that will create a single implication. I want the meaning to be precise, and perhaps that is why the language is imprecise. I am walking around my subject, and the impression I want to make, and I am trying to see it from all angles, so that I will have a whole picture, a picture of wholeness. *It is the heart of man I am trying to imply in this work.*

I have emphasized the last sentence because it is so uniquely Saroyan's idea—that in looking with the modernist's multi-vision, one might at the same time capture what draws everything together—the center, or the heart of man.

At this point in the story, Saroyan attempts to reenter Anderson's doorway to resume the "story" part of the story: "Let me try again. . . . This is what happened. It doesn't make much of a story, and the reason is that I have left out the barber, the young man who gave me the haircut." Once more he circumvents:

"That name," I said, "Badal. Are you an Armenian?" People look at me and begin to wonder, so I come right out and tell them. "I am an Armenian." It is a meaningless remark. . . . I have no idea what it is like to be an Armenian or what it is like to be an Englishman or a Japanese or anything else.

If all this seems by the way, it is nonetheless doubly motivated: it leads him to reiterate his chief "concern," as he puts it, "to be alive," while ironically relating himself to a famous contemporary. "[Being alive] is the only thing that interests me. This and tennis." This ludicrous juxtaposition, with its correlative that he "hopes someday to write a great philosophical work on tennis, something on the order of 'Death in the Afternoon,'" is again a mocking reference to Hemingway's pretensions as a thinker: "It is a finer philosophy [meaning not much better] than that of Will Durant and Walter Pitkin. . . . Hemingway tells you what actually takes place [meaning he is a good reporter] and he doesn't allow the speed of occurrence to make his exposition of it hasty"—meaning he goes on much too long about unimportant things.

When he returns to his story it is almost as if he were perversely mimicking the style of the writer he just mocked. In an offhand way, he reduces the loss and suffering of his own Armenian people to a statistical matter—the imbalance between their high birthrate and low population count. "We begin to imagine how rapidly we will increase if we are left alone a quarter of a century and we feel pretty happy," he observes in the tight-lipped manner of the writer he has parodied. Then, in his own gentler vein of humor, he describes his uncle's desperate oratorical efforts to raise money for the dying Armenians—dying now not because of "the enemy" (who is not named) but because of an earthquake. Away from the platform, the emotional man privately laments,

> Man won't let us alone. God won't let us alone. . . . What is our sin? I am disgusted with God. Jesus Christ, have we done something?

The matter-of-fact Assyrian, Badal, has no such reproaches to make of God. The dialogue that ensues reveals that despair need not be the only response to misfortune—if one can project into the future. "We are trying to forget Assyria, . . . want to get over it," Badal tells the writer, dryly. "We were a great people once. . . . Now we are a topic in ancient history."

The writer—as reporter—interjects: "I am repeating his words precisely, putting nothing of my own." Badal continues:

> Why should I learn the language? We have no writers, we have no news—well, there is a little news: once in a while the English encourage the Arabs to massacre us, that's all. It is an old story, we know all about it.

Piercing the argument to give it perspective, the writer says, "It is much the same with us. We [Armenians], too, are old. We still have a few writers." He names two. But Badal continues, rationalizing,

> We went in for the wrong things. We went in for the simple things, peace and quiet and families. We didn't go in for machinery and conquest and militarism. . . . There is no use being disappointed.

The narrator is intransigent: "There is no Armenian living who does not dream of an independent Armenia." But Badal's people can no longer even dream. "Seventy thousand, that is all. Seventy thousand Assyrians in the world and the Arabs are still killing us." In a pithy coda, Badal reads the death warrant of his race: "My father reads a paper that comes from New York, but he is an old man. He will be dead soon."

The story ends there, but not the writer's thoughts:

> Why don't I make up plots and write beautiful love stories that can be made into motion pictures? . . . Well, I'm an Armenian. Michael Arlen is an Armenian, too. He is pleasing the public. I have great admiration for him, . . . but I don't want to write about the people he likes to write about. . . . These people were dead to begin with.

He prefers to write about Iowa, the Japanese barber, Theodor Badal because they are "the stuff that is eternal in man."

> You find them where I found them, and they will be there forever, the race of man, the part of man, of Assyria as much as of England, that cannot be destroyed, the part that massacre does not destroy, the part that earthquake and war and famine and madness and everything else cannot destroy.

What has begun on a note of lighthearted banter within a commonplace setting, involving transient people, ends in a tone of intense personal engagement and compassion:

> I am thinking of seventy thousand Assyrians, one at a time, alive, a great race, . . . and Theodor Badal himself, Assyrian and man, standing in a barber shop, in San Francisco, in 1933, and being, still, himself, the whole race.

To contemporary readers the high-flown rhetoric of this ending may well mar the story's loaded human message. We no longer say things quite so plainly, nor do we want to take matters of this import at face value—we must be shown. But in the propaganda-dominated 1930s, declamation was tolerated in serious prose in much the way it is accepted in today's commercial advertising. In this widely anthologized story, Saroyan for the first time displayed a characteristic gift he would develop for combining a youthful earnestness with a virtuosity of style that is far from guileless. In words that are plain yet resonant, he would hit his target precisely and memorably while at the same time deflating what was too easily accepted as true.

Although in all these stories he moves from one style to another under various literary influences, the one guiding principle remains his awareness that the stories have universality and must reach a varied audience. His submissions are only partly to well-known magazines. They include the lightweight and obscure ones as well, like *Aperitif, Inland Topics, Pasadena Junior College,* and *College Humor.*

Whether in the Armenian magazines and newspapers or in insignificant minor journals, what he is trying to do is to establish the Saroyan voice, which makes the presence of the writer within the fiction he creates ever evident. This involves the elaboration of what I have stated in the preface as the double vision as well as the creation of a technique that suggests the storyteller as ventriloquist. Under the rebellion there lies a still vaguely understood artistic purpose. He also reveals an idiosyncratic understanding of realism, open-ended with an infinite potential. He is also unabashed to use nonliterary language to express everyday life material. The democratic sense of equality in Saroyan does not need to equalize human beings and hence to have them conform to a standard pattern. His cast of characters commingles familiar and unfamiliar figures and qualities—the exotic Armenian with the average immigrant, the boy next door with the romantic prostitute, and most of all the childlike in the grown man. The voice is frequently melancholy, but the optimism inherent in it makes possible the general overtone of humor and hope.

Apart from Mark Twain in his ironically humorous stories and Ring Lardner in his wisecracking tales of 1920s urbanites, there had never been so insistent and self-assertive a voice in American fiction as this young writer's—a voice eager rather than shy about being "different," even while assuming the stance of a spokesman for humankind. His realistic details are minimal, yet by his selection of them he captures the essential features of the social scene that interest him. Whether the details are intuitively found or deliberately sought, it is hard to tell. What does appear deliberate is the attempt to arrive at a new meaning of "realism," by isolating a new American type—the disaffiliated ethnic whom he associates with the socially marginal man.

There are also the beginnings here of Saroyan's special use of humor—its strategic role (later so widely expanded in another direction by the black humorists) in allowing for a "painless" revelation of deeply serious matters. In this early stage of his career, it serves also to buffer an essential "innocence," thereby avoiding undue embarrassment to himself and to all but the most sophisticated reader. More important in terms of his stated purpose, Saroyan is able to tell his story with himself as an involved witness, holding center stage to bring about a balance between a realistic subject and an idealistic perspective: The alternating currents of wistful despair and intense hopefulness that emanated from him would be especially welcome as the decade drew to a close amid fast-encroaching violence and disaster.

Yet if the critics of Saroyan's day recognized his new "voice," they were less ready to accept his method. Form and unity have traditionally been the sine qua non of art, the means by which the artist achieves coherence and meaning. Saroyan's brashness in eschewing uniformity of tone and consistence in style made him at once suspect. A tragicomic stance might work for a master of the short story like Chekhov, whose characters experience historic reverberations, but Saroyan's trapezelike reversals from light to dark and vice versa seemed to involve nothing beyond the mundane present. In truth, though, Saroyan was looking for a substitute for unity in its accepted sense, and finding it in its very opposite— fragmentation and discontinuity. His awareness of the sudden reversals in modern life, its general unpredictability, would lead him to a kind of coherence that form could obscure.

Modern writers long before Saroyan have evaded form and structure for the very purpose of conveying chaos and meaninglessness. Saroyan's avoidance of structure would hold to no such purpose, if only because chaos would be warded off through an authorial self that interpreted life at the very instant it was lived, unfettered by unfeasible, preordained designs. "Who touches this book, touches man," Whitman had proclaimed of his *Leaves of Grass*. But the difficulty of Saroyan's task would be compounded by the realization that the self he represented was essentially no more worthy of being singled out than the persons he would draw out of anonymity.

3

The Story as Discursive Dialogue: The Emergence of "A New Kind of Artist"

"THE short story form, as such, never appealed to me especially, and for years I couldn't do a thing with it," wrote Saroyan in 1950 in a preface to his twelfth volume of published short stories, *The Assyrian and Other Stories*. If the admission, on the face of it, sounded like Saroyanesque teasing, his elaboration on the subject left little doubt as to what he really meant: The short story in his hands had to take a new turn. And he made it quite plain what it was he would avoid:

> I didn't want to describe a room or a house or a city or a street or a sky or a hill or a valley or anything else. I wanted to say something about myself, and something about the effect people I happened to run into, including my family, had on me.

He knew he wasn't "educated enough" to write essays like Max Beerbohm or George Santayana, but essays in general left him cold, being based merely on the "possession of certain facts, generally about something . . . tiresome."

> Between the essay and the short story, though, it seemed to me there existed a form or formlessness which would permit me to write. I didn't make a decision about this, however. I didn't need to.

He determined to do the best he could, even if at first it seemed quite "hopeless." He was comparing his writing with what was then being published, and "no matter how bad the thing was I compared my writing with, my writing seemed worse." At last he decided that "either I myself was the beginning and end of the matter, or there was no matter at all."

Saroyan's self-analysis, however acute, leaves out one important matter. Though frequently straying from the old style of the short story, he remained faithful to the genre itself; it was the only genre, perhaps, that would allow him to discover his art while discovering himself, since the two were linked intrinsically. He could say with some finality in 1950 that a Saroyan story would not exist without Saroyan, but it is a fact that only after years of practice (much of it conducted in public) did the Saroyan story as such make its mark: "It takes a lot of rehearsing for a man to become himself," a Saroyan character has aptly remarked. If Saroyan's progress through a succession of short-story collections from 1934 to 1939 reveals no clear-cut line of development in the accepted sense of the word, one can nonetheless observe in the profusion of styles and approaches a certain continuum to forestall the propagation of one more "tiresome" mold. It explains at the same time why, despite his serious foray into the theater in 1939, Saroyan never abandoned the short story.

The tale of Saroyan's meteoric rise to fame with his first book, *The Daring Young Man on the Flying Trapeze and Other Stories,* has eclipsed the much less glamorous account of his apprenticeship years. Though somewhat unreliable and confused, current commentators on the early Saroyan years are uncovering facts and events that should prove of considerable interest to future biographers;[1] of special pertinence is the material dealing with the years between 1922 to 1933 when Saroyan was in serious pursuit of a literary career. But the subject here is not pure biography. Saroyan's struggle for survival carries implications outside and beyond his personal experience. For the literary historian, the Saroyan story all but attests to the presence of forces in our society that if properly tapped can spark and direct individual talent. It is not a simple matter of surmounting hardships and obstacles; it is discovering and manipulating a seemingly rigid set of circumstances for the benefit of one's own growth. Only the latter makes a significant difference to literature.

Assuming that the young Saroyan had an abundance of confidence in himself from his days as a rebellious schoolboy at Emerson High School, the gap between his aspiration and the possibility of its fulfillment was large enough to daunt an egomaniac. His determined indifference to being "educated" by teachers he considered essentially his inferiors did little or nothing to enhance him in the eyes of those who might have been supportive of his gifts. His verbal facility, manifested orally at first and subsequently in his schoolboy writings, had not gone unnoticed even by those who held his "foreignness" against him. For the son of an immigrant to keep body and soul together while harboring and sustaining a distant goal called for no great physical hardship, especially for someone so abundantly energetic and inured to work as the boy Saroyan seems to have been. What required greater agility was countering the unreasonableness of a society that placed so little faith in the will of the individual to rise above his given milieu to remake the world for himself.

The initial area of resistance had been school, which he left prematurely. The next opposition came from his family. In the accepted Armenian tradition, it was not enough to be a steady breadwinner—and indeed the boy had, by moving on from selling newspapers to working as a telegraph messenger boy, later landing a job in the vineyards and still later doing a stint as office boy in his uncle's law firm. One was expected, if one had the brains, to succeed in a respectable profession or in business. Saroyan's Uncle Aram was a successful lawyer, his Uncle Mihran was in business; both were landowners, capable of lending a helping hand to their nephew had the young Saroyan shown interest in some rewarding field of endeavor. It is important to point out that worldly members of the clan, like Uncle Aram, mocked his extravagant ambition out of ignorance rather than cruelty. There had, of course, been no demonstration of cruelty from either William's mother or his brother Henry in the years when the struggling writer moved from one job to another while clinging irrationally to his dream.

Nor was ignorance the sole defense. The general attitude was rooted in something larger—in the indifference of society to aspirations connected with the arts. And, for Saroyan at first, that indifference seemed endemic to Fresno, his hometown. He could not get away from it soon enough. First to Los Angeles, then San Francisco, finally New York. But once there, working for a short period at the local branch of the Postal Telegraph office, while gathering a pocketful of rejection slips, he was overpowered by nostalgia, and he headed back West to settle into the new "home" set up by Henry in San Francisco.

In Saroyan's initial effort to get published, San Francisco was to play a major role. There, in the city of Jack London and Ambrose Bierce, he holed up with his typewriter for long months at a time, his large vision precariously fed by his meager savings. It was San Francisco that would provide the background for the stories that dealt with the more somber aspects of life, standing in sharp contrast to the free and easy ambiance of the Fresno vineyards. In 1928 a local magazine, *Out West Magazine,* published his first "story" with the eye-catching title "Preface to a Book Not Yet Written." Here Saroyan announced his predilection for brevity, while at the same time circumlocuting (à la G. B. Shaw) to make his point:

> I thank the Lord that there are no scenes to prefaces or I would never commence this book. I did not like scenes in literature, and if it is ever going to be necessary for me to describe anything whatsoever in the following pages I am going to find the shortest distance between a couple of points.[2]

He further warned that if people wanted scenes, "lakes or gardens or city streets," they could go out and take a look at them for themselves. As for himself, he preferred prefaces to books any day.

Six years before the publication of his first book, Saroyan was striking a rebellious, nonconformist note. Inevitably, he was being turned down by national magazines like *The Atlantic Monthly, Scribner's, American Mercury,* and *Harper's Magazine.* He wrote his cousin, Archie Minasian, on the last day of 1930, "I am having a tough time. The only magazine that prints my stuff pays so damn little that it hardly covers postage, and the others send rejection slips only."[3] And by 1933, even though his name appeared regularly in *Hairenik* (a publication scarcely read outside a limited ethnic group), he would still characterize himself as "the best unpublished writer in America."

It would have been quite possible for a writer with the singular and solemn aims of Saroyan to have gone unnoticed by the literary world of the thirties for a much longer period had he not seized on the one avenue that seemed ready-made for him. Saroyan's special association with *Story* magazine, the important role that it played in launching his career, is an oft-told tale that hardly needs repeating here in any detail.[4] What needs to be done, however, is to place it in its proper perspective. In rescuing Saroyan from prolonged obscurity, the enterprising team of Martha Foley and Whit Burnett was at the same time rescuing the literary story from a precipitating decline. The lifeline would prove to be mutual. Without *Story,* Saroyan might have succumbed to the currently commercial product; he was a learner who could have developed the skill for turning out stories in the familiar mold; and being a self-styled humanitarian, he might have turned to writing the proletarian fiction then so much in vogue.

Story, without Saroyan, on the other hand, might not have forged into a magazine of "discovery" from which so much of its prestige derived. This tiny magazine, begun on a shoestring in Vienna in 1931 by two American journalists looking for a magazine in which to publish their own stories, would in three years' time evolve into a magic cauldron from which much distinguished American short fiction would emerge. As it expanded in the ensuing two years, *Story* introduced the best short work of such writers as Faulkner, Caldwell, Anderson, Aiken, Boyle, and Lowry, and, finally, in February 1934, the fledgling work of an unknown writer from Fresno, California—the purest testimony, perhaps, of the magazine's stated purpose, to welcome "short narratives of significance by no matter whom and coming from no matter where."

In a letter to the editors, a grateful Saroyan wrote,

> We are most at home in the short story form. . . . I am sure no one will disagree that except for *Story* the American short story as it is being published in every variety of magazine . . . would not be the healthy and natural thing it is today.

And, Saroyan went on, whether or not the editors of *Cosmopolitan* or *The Saturday Evening Post* realized it,

> their stories are being written by contributors to *Story* who very seldom get a hundred dollars for a story, and usually get around twenty-five, and gladly.[5]

Saroyan had been quick to grasp that a magazine that contained nothing but short stories allowed the writer a freedom he could find nowhere else. Not so readily apparent to him, or to anyone else it would seem, was the fact that *Story* served at the same time to bring back the short story as a viable and even lucrative literary genre. It was *Story*'s connection with the new publishing firm of Random House that would make possible the publication, in that same year, of Saroyan's first book, *The Daring Young Man on the Flying Trapeze and Other Stories.*[6] In more than one sense, Saroyan's book became a publishing landmark, establishing a precedent for first books of short stories.

Later, in the 1980s, we would be experiencing a period when collections of literary stories are often making money for both writers and publishers. But from the very beginnings of American literature, it was the exceptions—Washington Irving, Edgar Allan Poe, and Mark Twain—who could call themselves story writers. Hawthorne, Melville, and Henry James also wrote memorable stories, but they thought of themselves chiefly as novelists. Faulkner and Steinbeck were initially story writers but soon turned to longer fiction, establishing their reputations ultimately through their novels.

One would not be off the mark in claiming that until the recent past, volumes of short stories by a single author were regarded with misgiving by most publishers. To this day they are approached with some condescension by literary critics. No one has rushed to write a critical study of J. D. Salinger (who has only one major novel), or to deal with the intricacies of the short prose written by James Thurber, Dorothy Parker, or E. B. White. Much has been written about Saroyan the man, much less about Saroyan the dramatist, and least of all about Saroyan the short-story writer. Eudora Welty's short stories—her major contribution to fiction— did not initially receive the critical attention of her subsequent novels, one of which won her the Pulitzer Prize. A tradition has prevailed in America that considers the literary story an inferior form, a form, moreover, commercially unviable and, like poetry, written for a specialized audience.

Yet the short story began as our most popular form, encouraged by the spread of journalism and intended for a mass (not a special) audience. In newspapers and magazines at the end of the last century, it fell into the hands of amateurs and remained there for a long time, becoming a stepping stone to "better things," i.e., full-length novels. Not surprisingly, now and then a "masterpiece" would turn up—to use the words of the literary historian, Fred L. Pattee—"in the rubbish heap of forgotten periodicals." For even writers of the stature of Dreiser and Norris might turn out a story to make a quick buck. "The journalization of the short story," as Professor Pattee puts it, eventually produced typically American writers like O. Henry and Jack London (both self-taught) who focused on the "news" element of a tale—the extravagant, singular adventure told in a terse style that masked the author's individual voice while making a social or moral comment.[7] In its diluted form, it would become the "feature story" of our day. All too few writers in the first decade of this century departed from this convention to become aware that the short story had an art of its own. Sherwood Anderson, with his quiet, gentle awareness of anonymous human beings, and Ring Lardner with an exceptional wit and virtuosity that ranged over a variety of worldly matters, were among the few Americans who gave a new permanence to the short story, and doing so paved the way in our day for writers following in the footsteps of William Saroyan, Eudora Welty, J. D. Salinger, and Flannery O'Connor.

If the short story came to flourish as a popular genre, it was because it had the potential for being a "people's literature." More easily than novels, it could deal with topical matters and the dailiness of life in narrative that was succinct and direct. It was a form of writing that came naturally from the writer who was often "of the people," self-educated, familiar with the life of the common man, if not directly a part of it. Naturally, the wider the distance between the writer's world and his subjects' the more difficult it became to bring a semblance of reality to commonplace scenes. Yet the likelihood of bridging that gap would at best have to be minimal, since writing is a verbal gift not given to all and usable only after long and serious application, involving no small amount of book learning. Even then, there remained the problem of how to support that gift. (The National Endowment for the Arts and writing colonies like Yaddo and the McDowell are of recent vintage.) In the event that the writer took on a drab and steady job, there was the danger that it would drain the source of his inspiration, distracting him at the same time from what is close at hand and grist for his mill. Though a writer like Sherwood Anderson remained productive through many years of a mundane job schedule, one would have to concede that this was not an ideal situation for a writer who sought to penetrate the common life: reading his stories today, one detects a shadow between the writer and his "ordinary" characters, and it is just this distance between them that makes them appear outside the norm and, as he himself described them, "grotesque."

In Saroyan's case, the disparity that existed between himself and his characters or at least the disparity that he wished to recognize, was strictly one of a moral nature as he showed from his earliest stories, the "disadvantaged" background that he shared with his subjects made a basic identification with them possible, but his humanistic ideal of social progress implied a scale of values that allowed the exceptional person (that is, the morally strong person) to reach for the advantages he lacked. If circumstances had made him a breadwinner at the age of eleven, that did not prevent him from indulging in innate curiosity by spending long hours at the public library, while at the same time keeping an eye on the hurly-burly of life around him. From this dual activity would come his initial recognition of the natural wisdom of the man in the street and the ease with which he was able to remain "one of the boys" to the end of his days—not without the risk of often being cut down to size. Unlike Sherwood Anderson, Saroyan would not be found sitting humbly at the feet of the literati, basking in the aura of their approval, while imbibing the "literary" ambience of his day. In his initial encounters with writers in San Francisco, Hollywood, and New York, Saroyan had been put off by what he saw as an effete, exclusive fraternity that drew attention to his own unworldliness. And future encounters were only to reinforce his unwillingness to be "the artist above all else." In later years he would admit that being in their company had encouraged his "arrogance or leg-pulling on my part; the dead-pan references to myself as a genius, for instance." It would not, however, rule out "what [I] fancied would turn out to be a new kind of artist."[8]

In the absence of a literary mentor in his apprenticeship years, survival became of the essence. It is no mere legend that Saroyan barraged editors of literary magazines with endless submissions in the early 1930s, until one bright day he caught the attention of Martha Foley and her husband Whit Burnett. It was the speed with which Saroyan's discovery happened that was to make literary history. Within a year of receiving honor rating for a Sirak Goryan story from *Hairenik* in Edward J. O'Brien's annual *Best Short Stories,* Saroyan not only published three stories in *Story* magazine but landed a contract with Random House. To cap it all, when his book was published on 15 October 1934, it was heralded by rave reviews throughout the country. There is no strict logical explanation for this phenomenon beyond the known fact that Saroyan had been practicing his trade for a number of years and that he had developed an extraordinary rate of productivity (he would claim that he turned out a story in less than six hours, and would do this on a daily basis). The drive behind it all was his determination (however naive) to live by his writing, since everything else—so he said—bored him, including making money for its own sake.

It was the novelty of his writing—that mixture of moral intensity and genial lightheartedness—that immediately appealed to reviewers and readers alike. As Budd Schulberg testified in one of the most vivid evocations of Saroyan's early years (in an essay, "Ease and Unease on the Flying Trapeze"), "It didn't read like Hemingway or Morley Callighan or Daniel Cornel De Jong. . . . It was absolutely its own voice. It was imprudent, it was audacious, it was true." Reading Saroyan in the pages of *Story* magazine, Schulberg was attracted to stories

> of the vigorous peasantry of the California valleys and autobiographical tales of a penniless, irrepressible country boy coming of age in the streets of San Francisco, peddling papers and a crazy love for the world.

This "in a day when hope bore a Marxist, a New Deal, or a Union label." Meeting Saroyan in Hollywood, Schulberg was further struck by how the man matched his work:

When he said, Who is Hemingway and how can anybody possibly compare his stuff with Saroyan? you could not fault him for an enlarged ego or overconceit, for this was not adult fantasy but a rare and delicious childlike exuberance. It was Look, no hands! I'm the greatest bike rider in the whole world! Every word he put down was a holy miracle to him, the son of an immigrant Armenian vineyard worker, who could not only talk the adopted language but use words to make beautiful American sentences![9]

From the beginning, the legendary aura surrounding Saroyan had a double edge. Himself a kind of myth (or anomaly), he set out to carve an ideal, mythic world in his writing. Myth? In modern America? In a society committed to diversity, change, and progress? The concept seems far-fetched until we remember that this was Depression America, with its social barriers unhinged, making the country fertile ground again for the unity, cohesiveness, and assurance that are the promises of myth. "Myths," the critic Frank Kermode has observed, "are agents of stability," calling for "absolute . . . assent."[10] In a relativist society, when economic distress is added to metaphysical anxiety, the undeterminable nature of myth becomes suddenly attractive, a voice of hope in a time of darkness. As Saroyan's very presence on the literary scene became a source of optimism, the writer's affirmation of "community" in the land would open up a larger arena of action—America itself as myth, as the eluding dream.

But if, in terms of the audience, the terrain was ideal for Saroyan, it was less than propitious in terms of critical acceptance once the flurry of the novelty wore off. The spontaneity and open-ended structure that are the essence of a Saroyan story became alienating factors for those who judge literature by strictly traditional standards. Many of the initial commentators of Saroyan's work assumed that his spontaneity was accidental, the result of an untutored, unsophisticated artlessness. There being no subtlety, it required no interpretation. Other influential critics discounted the freshness and originality as tricky affectation; the ease of the style itself provided an excuse for condescension. Louis Kronenberger, who reviewed Saroyan's first book for both *The New York Times Book Review* and *The Nation*, complained that Saroyan was "an exhibitionist, a verbalist, a poseur, a nose thumber, a prima donna, a victim of genius mania. . . . He is most of the things a serious artist is not."[11] Hershel Brickell would later write in *The New York Post* that Saroyan's "trick was to put paper into the typewriter and let the words flow."[12] Still others dismissed Saroyan as "a romantic," "a narcissist" who revealed "precious little outside Mr. Saroyan."[13] In flight from reality, with nothing much to say, he represented at best "the raw material of genius."[14] But the most cutting remark of all came from a fellow writer, Ernest Hemingway: "You want to watch yourself, Mr. Saroyan, that you don't get so bright that you don't learn."[15] Only the English writer H. E. Bates (much later) would recognize Saroyan as a catalyst who opened up the short story to new possibilities—though even he would state flatly at the same time that "after eight volumes the Saroyan method shows no sign of change and appears to be incapable of further development."[16]

If I highlight these negative remarks over the many favorable comments that circulated about Saroyan's stories in 1934 and after, it is because these criticisms, which dogged Saroyan's career to the end, were repeated almost automatically after a while by critics who had barely read him. It was because of the proliferation of these views that for a long time scarcely anyone troubled to take a close look at his work as a whole. It is legitimate to quarrel with a writer for repeating his message to a point of surfeit, but it is also valid to point out that a story can be made unforgettable as much by how it is told as what it actually tells: A poetic composer like Chopin will rarely depart from his essential combination of motifs, but it is through the play of variations that the music is able to make its statement memorable. The early critics of Saroyan (and even later ones) often wrote off as mere self-dramatization what was in fact Saroyan's original device for carrying on a discursive dialogue between himself and his characters; he failed only when the ventriloquist's mechanism broke down and his own voice became indistinguishable from that of his characters. But whether or not he succeeded thereby in creating tension, the discursive dialogue drew attention to what mattered most to Saroyan: the story as a means of self-discovery or self-creation. The close reader of Saroyan will find ample proof that he valued this device and used it to better advantage when he turned to the theater: There, the Saroyan voice would resound without occupying the entire stage.

If there is a suggestion of insincerity, of "fraud" in some of the early writing, there are facts to support the view that the effect was more accidental than deliberate. On the eve of the publication of *The Daring Young Man on the Flying Trapeze*, Saroyan was exhibiting all the anxieties of a young writer with a high mission and minimal financial means. When Random House accepted his volume of stories, he was living a hand-to-mouth existence in San

Francisco, getting little or no remuneration at best from *Hairenik* and twenty-five dollars each for three stories published in *Story* magazine. The most he made as a short story writer in those days was one hundred dollars for the story, "Myself Upon the Earth," which *American Mercury* published. Yet, rather than take an advance from his publisher, he asked permission to have some of the stories from the book appear in magazines prior to publication. In a revealing exchange of letters between author and publisher, we find his young editor, Bennett Cerf, insisting that Saroyan take his advance of one hundred dollars nonetheless "as a token of our good-will."[17] Mindful of his emerging gambling habit, Saroyan agrees, but only if the money is doled out to him—fifteen dollars per week—for such necessities as cigarettes, stamps, and paper. With the advance soon spent, Saroyan timorously queries Cerf's partner, Donald Klopfer, "Any chance after the book is printed I will owe you money?" Anticipating this possibility, he had enclosed in his letter half of his fee from the sale of "Myself Upon the Earth" to the *American Mercury*. To which Klopfer, returning the money, replies, "Go out and get drunk." It is hard to see a "poseur" or "exhibitionist" lurking behind this display of humble dependence on sponsors who had still to rise above the status of "little press."

Again, in this exchange of letters, "the genius mania" (to go back to Kronenberger's phrase) manifests itself only when Saroyan wants to impress his editors with his versatility. He writes to Klopfer,

> Most prose is stodgy, hard to wade through unless one sleeps along with it, and this is a time in the world when the mind is nervously alive, and writing of this work is the writing of this nervousness, the swiftness, the lack of artifice, that driving toward what is pertinent, the omission of what is not: i.e. *the faking, which is so much a part of most writing* (my italics).

And again to Cerf, he excuses himself from the writing of a novel (which is expected of him), by emphasizing his superiority in the story form:

> At the present time, it appears as if the story form is my form; I mean that which I can compose swiftly, in one time of effort, and be done with it.

He is ingenious, if anything, about "the defects in my writing." He is aware of them, he writes, but "they are a result of wanting to get below the surface and use language in a fresh way." Nor will he easily compromise: "I can write slickly, but so can everybody else. I am not, of course, satisfied with what I've written: therefore I go on writing."

At this early stage in his career, Saroyan is fearful of falling into a groove:

> One thing I plan to avoid: getting into too much of one style of writing: The Seventy Thousand Assyrians-style. I mean the easy going way, which I *could* overdo, and seem to be. I plan to do some more objective things for a while, . . . some more legitimate experimenting again. Jesus Christ, writing is swell: I mean, there are so many fine things to be done yet. Limitless: an endless variety of decent kinds of writing!

What some of these "limitless" kinds of writing are that he would like to do the impassioned young writer suggests in a letter to *Story*'s editor, Martha Foley, a letter that begins by describing the trouble he is having writing while freezing in a cold-water room in San Francisco: "The thing that amazes me is that my typewriter hasn't clogged. . . . If the machine will work, I tell myself, then you've got to work with it."[18] And he bares his ambition:

> Think of America. . . . The whole thing. The cities, all the houses, all the people, the coming and going . . . the movement, the talk, the sound of machinery. . . . Remember the great machines, the wheels turning . . . the newspapers and moving picture theatres and everything that is part of this life. Let this be your purpose: to suggest this great country.

Up to this point in the letter, there is the echo of Thomas Wolfe. But in his next paragraph, Saroyan veers sharply from the Wolfian stance:

> Then turn to the specific. Go out to some simple person and dwell with him, within him, lovingly, seeking to understand the miracle of his being. . . . Go with him to his secret and speak of it gently, showing that it is the secret of man. Do not deceive. Do not make up lies for the sake of pleasing any one.

In the rest of the letter, Saroyan formulates a writer's credo, which if strictly adhered to would have all but revolutionized American fiction, making it possible for the writer to transcribe life with a vision as opaque and unadorned as Emerson's famous "transparent eyeball":

> The man you write of need not do some heroic or monstrous deed in order to make your prose great. Let him do what he has always done,

day in and day out, continuing to live. Let him walk and talk and think and sleep and dream and awaken and walk again and talk again and move and be alive. It is enough. There is nothing else to write about.

Detaching "literature" from life, he goes on,

You have never seen a short story in life. The events of life have never fallen into the form of the short story, or the form of the poem, or into any other form. Your own consciousness is the only form you need. Your own awareness is the only action you need. Speak of this man. Recognize his existence. Speak of man.

But the closing words of his letter reveal (unconsciously perhaps) what would make the credo no easy achievement for Saroyan—or anyone else. "Early this morning," he writes, "when I was warm with coffee, I had this great story in my mind, ready to get into print, but it got away from me."

The moment of illumination must be caught and recorded in the instant it is felt, lest it dissolve. In the pause required to shape it, the experience—which is the "story"—would depart. By stating *"your consciousness is the only form you need. Your own awareness the only action you need,"* Saroyan is dissociating the most exacting achievement of the artist from dependence on technique and rules of the craft and envisioning an art that links reality with revelation. Yet, unlike a later generation of so-called surfiction writers, Saroyan is not abjuring the link between the "real" and the revealed. (Hence the discursive dialogue.) He would learn later that "form"—without which art cannot exist—need not be restrictive (it could be free-flowing) and that "action" could enhance revelation. One can see that the false steps were the result of ambition and zeal.

Saroyan's ambition to "think of America. . . . The whole thing," lent itself inevitably to the impressionist style, for him a kind of amalgam of Dos Passos's newsreels and Thomas Wolfe's romantic and prolix lyricism. Indeed, even the archetypal Depression story, "The Daring Young Man on a Flying Trapeze" switches back and forth between evocations of cosmic surreality—juxtaposing sleep and wakefulness—and the young writer's urgency in warding off starvation. If in retrospect, one detects a note of affectation (a young writer showing himself in tune with "modernism"), it must be said he is already proficient in the use of stylistic effect to emphasize a dichotomy of vision, setting the temporal and the concrete against the eternal and universal from which a deeper meaning may be derived. Thus sleep and wakefulness are complementary within the young man's consciousness, and the two states of being are expressed in a manner appropriate to each.

In another story from the first volume, "Big Valley Vineyard," the stylistic experimentation is less successful but again suggestive of his purpose. It begins in a collage of impressions that tries to mingle the abstract world of art and books with the earthy existence of works in a vineyard, where the writer/narrator has worked "fraternally with peons from Mexico." Here, in the attempt to cross the ephemeral with the timeless, Saroyan lapses into an Eliotic shorthand to evolve the quasi-portentous eruptions of the postwar era: "Jew Stravinsky, the nose and mouth in the aquarium, swimming, and Russian Diaghilev, seated with legs crossed, sending the girls up on their dancing toes. . . . Tender Cocteau. . . . And Satie, bearded like a pawnshop ghost gone broke." Impressionism (a synonym for artistic refinement) becomes a part of the story.

> It was argued . . . that impressionism was dead . . . along with the soldier and along with the half a dozen decent ideas about civilization. . . . It was determined that . . . because we were soft, it did not necessarily follow that we were civilized. . . . Barbarians were needed. . . . Facts shall be substituted.

Without lapsing into a stream of consciousness, the narrator moves from snide remarks about Mr. Morgan and his associates, sitting "quietly consuming the public, men, women and children," to "the great fiction room of the public library," where the writer sits daily running his fingers over the pages of Zola and Balzac, even as he thinks back on his days in the vineyard and how "the vines stood in their places in the great warm valley of my awakening."

With the meagerest suggestion of a storyline or exposition, he juxtaposes the commonplace experience of "instant pleasure" with "the lonely harlot whose sad room overlooked the alley between Mariposa and Tulare Streets" with his rememberance of how when he "clipped off a good twig, a twig which would have borne fruit," he would feel "guilty of a spiritual misdemeanor, and would therefore ask the vine to forgive him." Throughout, there is the suggestion of a lost innocence which, nonetheless, he guards in his memory. The same consciousness thus bears both the cynical, ironic truth and the less clearly measurable poetic reality, as when he recalls "all the Armenians . . . going in their automobiles to the vineyards and gathering the tenderest leaves" because "to Armenians the taste is the very taste of Armenia," and by eating them each spring they "declare to God and Armenia that they have remained loyal." Gathering the grape leaves is for them "not purely an affair of the table."

This self-consciously literary story ends nonetheless with a moral explicitness: a young man's fear of a new "dawn of experimentation" that will make man "a document, the subject of bad poems." With a writer's eye he sees that "Drama is impossible because everyone is interested in himself, as an experiment," and he foresees a future in which "the blurring of specific character among universal precepts is whole, and man, the individualist, is a lie for the next generation."

In the end, the muted irony rises to a pitch of protest; in a materialistic America "there is no dignity anywhere, not even among peasants." Vineyard workers no longer talk about "eternal things"—since they fear nothing more than starvation, they can think of nothing but food. But the young writer, hungry also for self-cultivation, continues his visits to the public library, his sustenance being (as he explains to the peons) "bread and print."

From these two early examples of stylistic experiment, we see that Saroyan's interest in recording the simultaneity of experience and the overlapping of areas of consciousness is not altogether in line with the ontological perception at the root of James Joyce's or Virginia Woolf's fiction. Even at his most fantastical (as in his later plays), Saroyan never sees his characters apart from the world in which they have their being. His method, and I believe it is a conscious one, is to tease the reader into accepting the presence of two opposing claims to reality—the palpable and the ulterior—and being prepared to leap from one to the other, and sometimes reconciling the two. If the predominant tone in his first book is one of irony, it is because he will not let go of the lyric strain: that separation can only come when humor takes over, as it does in works that follow. Plot or "story" is still of secondary concern, and characters still function as if balanced on a ventriloquist's knee.

The central character—in different guises—is the young man (Saroyan) who wants to see "eternal things," whose enchantment with life gives a romantic glow to suffering itself. But contrary to the impression of those who have never closely read the stories in *The Daring Young Man on the Flying Trapeze,* the book is not meant to uplift the reader or promote an easy sense of well-being. In story after story, there is an acute recognition of injustice and prevailing alienation that originate as much from within the characters themselves as from the social order. The young man is not always glued to his seat in the public library. He has the urge, as he has written to Martha Foley, to "go out to some simple person and dwell within him. Thus, in a story titled "Among the Lost," he is a roamer at night in San Francisco, mingling with a group of ethnic gamblers and drifters (he refers to them as "the Jew," "the Irish," "the Russian"), trying to learn "how it feels to be out of things, to have no present, no future, to belong nowhere, to be suspended between day and night, waiting." The impulse involves more than idle curiosity. At midnight, he decides to "go with this boy to that waiting-room and try to sleep in a chair, Smithy shouting. Seat here for a player . . . one more seat."

More dispassionately, the narrator in "Sleep in Unheavenly Peace" observes that the rich also suffer "the sickness of frustration." He watches

the people emerging from the theatres, smoking cigarettes and looking desperate, wanting much, the precision, the glory, all the loveliness of life; wanting what is finest and getting nothing. It is saddening to see them, but there is mockery in the heart: one walks among them, laughing at oneself and at them, their midnight staring.

At three in the morning, he speaks to a thirty-five-year-old man who says his name is Jones:

He said he walked at night and rested during the day, standing up. He said it was easy; he had been doing it for years. He was not a Communist. I asked and he said he was not. He was more afraid of me than I of him. . . . My question startled him, and his mouth fell open, increasing the horror of his face, the dirty beard, the haunted eyes, the filth, and the very long lower teeth. I felt great love for him, even though he was ugly with the vilest ugliness of man, ghastly sexual ugliness: anger, amazement, and the desire to kill or rape, in his eyes.

There is an almost Dostoyevskian identification with the dispossessed who "were born of women, . . . have names . . . [and] belong to the family of man." And there is no sentimentality when he later observes that "[N]ot any of the girls are trivial. . . . It is impossible to be trivial, being so close to the secret of man." It is a physiological truth, not wishful thinking, that finally dissipates the young man's dark thoughts. The girls must sleep—work ends for them at three A.M., "no NRA codes of regulations." "They sleep soundly," he notes, "in unheavenly peace in the stillness and hush of the time of man."

From his earliest stories on, Saroyan was never to be without an acute awareness of the role that metamorphosis—both physical and metaphysical—played in human existence. A perception of change that is both dramatic and inevitable suffuses the ironic play between sleep and wakefulness in the title story of his first book; it is embedded in the melancholic apprehension of his dead father's presence watching over him from a photograph on his wall, altering his knowledge of himself; most poignantly, it is in the self-realizations of his adolescents. And, less expectedly, it is behind his attempt to associate mortality with humor. "If you will remember," he writes in his earliest preface, "that living people are as good as dead, you will be able to perceive much that is very funny in their conduct." Death, the final metamorphosis, can be grasped most vividly through the perspective of humor.

Because his humor is not yet much in evidence in this first volume, Saroyan relies heavily on his sensibility to capture transcendent moments in rites of passage. The child's open trust counterposed against youth's awakening to an impenetrable world occupied Saroyan from his first autobiographical stories for *Hairenik,* and he elaborated on this theme with increasing assurance, proceeding from the mere articulation of the experience to portrayals that aim at larger implications. To take the best example from this volume, "And Man," the metamorphosis begins with its physical manifestation in a boy who has just turned fifteen and wakes up one morning thinking "something was going to happen." All through a sleepless night, he feels the effects of the summer's "hurried growth," the turning inside him of

> some swift and wordless thought, on the verge of articulation, some vast remembrance out of time, a fresh fullness, a new solidity, a graceful rhythm of motion.

The reference to genealogical continuity—"some vast remembrance of time"—adds a metaphysical dimension to the concept of growth. There's both wonder and anxiety in the boy's realization that he has changed overnight from "a small and sullen boy . . . wanting desperately to know the meaning [of life] and never being able to do so" to "a vaster form of myself as a man, and to the vaster meaning of myself as something specific and alive."

It is this leap into the meaning of an inner growth that makes the substance of the story. In contrast to this physical ugliness—the large nose, for instance, that becomes the butt of family jokes—comes the boy's recognition of "another face, a finer, a more subtle and dignified expression" that no mirror will reveal.

The real growth was going on inside, not simply within the boundaries of my physical form, but outward through the mind and through the imagination to the real largeness of being, the limitless largeness of consciousness, of knowing and feeling and remembering.

The true nature of his transformation is brought home when he realizes that the girl in school he's loved from afar will never be able to see him as he really is. Yet the personal pain does not interfere with a larger apprehension: how far, he wants to know, would the transformation go?

What it was in me that was static and permanent and endurable, what it was that belonged not to myself alone but to the body of man, to his legend, to the truth of his motion over the earth, moment after moment, century after century.

Suddenly aware of his physical powers, he revels in his isolation: in the early morning light, he leaps over fire hydrants, walks into town, seeing it as if for the first time, "with all its meaning, giving it its real truth, like the truth of my hidden face." Like everyone else, he is alone, a stranger even to his own family, but he exults in the knowledge that he can perceive something beyond the literalness of his being.

In prose that is heavily impressionistic and overcharged with lyricism, the story goes on to describe the boy's defiance of school authority. Conceding that he played hookey because he felt like walking in the vineyards, he stoically accepts a whipping, sobbing only when he suddenly realizes the existence of "incredible blindness everywhere." Another writer might have ended the story there, but not Saroyan, whose purpose is to draw an analogy between the physical metamorphosis of child into adolescence and the endless transformation of man in eternity:

I have seen it thus, the whole universe, quietly there in the mind of man, motionless and dark and lost, waiting for man, for the thought of man, and I felt the stirring of inanimate substance in the earth, and in myself like the swift growth of the summer, life emerging from time, the germ of man springing from the rock and the fire, and the fluid to the face of man, and to the form, to the motion and the thought, suddenly in the emptiness, the thought of man, stirring there. And I was man, and this was the truth I had brought out of the emptiness, walking alone through the vineyards.

At the heart of this impassioned humanistic statement (of a kind Saroyan will make again and again) is the notion of a fundamental unity and continuum that postulates for every individual a place in the scheme of things. He will say it with less verbiage and greater clarity when he has replaced the lyric sensibility that overstates with the more direct perception that dramatic distance allows. But not before he has used up a huge backlog of unpublished or uncollected work.

His next volume of stories, published two years after the first, *Inhale and Exhale,* is even more generally strewed with large pronouncements and gives only occasional proof that he is ready for the "disciplined" writing the critics were demanding of him. Once more it is the autobiographical element that stands out for the critic Harold Strauss in a curiously superficial review in *The New York Times Book Review:* "The more easily Saroyan himself can be substituted for the protagonist of the story," he writes, "the better that story is likely to be."[19] Not accounted for is the fact that much of the material in this hefty and uneven volume was anterior to that in his first book, containing as it did many pieces from the *Hairenik* years. The versatility of style and approach were the result of Saroyan's abundant productivity which allowed him to tap publications as various as *Yale Review, Story, Esquire, The New Masses, London Mercury,* and *Redbook.* Indeed, even in the light of the kind of unity he sought, some of the selections might better have been weeded out. Random House, now emerging as a major firm that published Proust, Gertrude Stein, and Joyce's unabridged *Ulysses,* had, in fact, advised Saroyan to cut the book in half, after receiving his proposal for a nine-hundred-page book. This thoroughly unsettled the young writer who proceeded to explain that there was method behind his seeming self-indulgence.

In the previously mentioned exchange of letters between Saroyan and his publisher/editors, the writer makes no bones about his strong belief in himself or of his intransigence in upholding his intentions as a writer. Declaring himself "at least potentially" as important a writer as Thomas Wolfe or James Joyce, he asks Donald Klopfer if he would ever think of cutting those writers' works to one-third or one-fourth. What would have happened, he asks, if their publishers had been "cautious and fearful"? Outlining the book's contents to Bennett Cerf, he writes,

The idea is to imply through the title, the meaning of the words involved . . . and through the way in which the title is printed, these things: the inseparability of all opposites in the living, in the world, the universe, and everywhere else, including nowhere: life & death (inhale & exhale),

growth and decay, good and evil, William & the world, Cerf and
Klopfer, Jesus Christ this is a great title.

What Saroyan insists upon is the inclusion of "the experimental
stuff, . . . especially writing about experimental writing and what
it means and what the idea is, etc." In doing this, he points out,
he will be "the first writer in the world to criticize his own stuff
exactly as it should be criticized." And he will try to show "it isn't
enough to know technique, to use it effectively."[20]
But the publisher does not take kindly to Saroyan's proposal to
include "The Slot Machine" (part of which had been printed as a
section of a novel in *transition* magazine), and still later, a Sirak
Goryan "novel" titled *American Glory*. In this instance, Saroyan
can only defend their inclusion by the irrational fiat that "the good
goes with the lousy. . . . And also: the bad is not so bad because
it is the work of the same man who wrote the good." Conceding
that he is no novelist, Saroyan writes,

> I'm not even a short story writer. I've accepted no forms, but have
> made them; and this is so even to the form of the Book . . . not a book
> of stories, not a novel, but a work of writing by a writer.

It is Saroyan's way of saying that he is a writer in the process
of evolving into a new kind of writer. He ends the letter on a note
of rebelliousness, saying it would be dangerous for him as a writer
to change his attitude: "I should forever after be at the mercy of
others, and I would rather be completely unpublished than that."[21]
A month later, having settled for a book of 438 pages, Saroyan
appears pacified as he writes to Cerf,

> What it has . . . is variety: and I mean the best and only kind; solemnity
> and mirth: dignity without pomposity; tempo; ease, everything. . . .
> This God damn book is twice as important as any novel published in
> America in the last decade, with the exception of maybe one or two.[22]

In *Inhale and Exhale* Saroyan's subject is still himself, in the
sense that Harold Strauss pointed out, but the circumference of
the contemplating eye now enfolds a spectrum of varied human
beings: "the unmerciful panorama of America, and everything that
is taking place," is how the author puts it in one story. If it is still
very much part and parcel of a single atom of consciousness, there
is always the underlying faith of indivisibility to bolster its viability.
Now or later, Saroyan will never leave the scene long enough to
"select his material carefully."

It is easy to dismiss *Inhale and Exhale* unmercifully as Clifton Fadiman did in his *New Yorker* review, as "a hodge podge" of "monologues, prayers, jokes, conversations, lectures, sermonettes, travel sketches, anecdotes, [and] diary extracts" by a writer whose "mind, fresh, agile, and acrobatic, darts about like a waterbug . . . and lives on surface tension." Fadiman is troubled by what he sees as "the Whitman manner. . . . [H]e's simply crazy about Life. . . . Life, folks, is better than death." And he mocks Saroyan further by composing an Aesopian fable in which "a Wolfe" [Thomas] warns Saroyan to "keep off my territory."[23] But to dismiss the book out of hand is to risk missing not only some of the best early work of this writer but an important key to his evolving short-story technique.

I use the word *technique* in full awareness that both Saroyan and his readers over the years have denied the existence of anything so deliberate and studied for his kind of stories. But artistic intention invariably involves manipulation of raw reality, and if nothing else, the fragments of correspondence just quoted offer proof that his "experiments" were not wholly accidental. It is also clear from these letters that it was not Saroyan but the publishers who were resisting the introduction of new and untried facets of the writer's talent; far from succumbing to the temptation to coast on his initial success and reproduce a succession of stories in the original mold, Saroyan was ready at one point to withdraw the book rather than risk his freedom to choose what it would contain. And to a degree he had his way. The 438-page volume did include a large number of pieces in which he tried out new styles (though at times with little or no success) or in which he moved away from his established stance of affirmation. True, Clifton Fadiman could not have foreseen that the Whitman "manner" would trail off in Saroyan's future work, but an attentive reading of even a third of *Inhale and Exhale* should have revealed to him the distance that Saroyan had already traveled in terms of subject matter alone from the great poet's orotund celebrations.

Beyond the simple nostalgia that was always its burden, memory has assumed a new function for Saroyan; at times it flirts with Eliotic irony (contrasting what was once grand with what is now tawdry) but at its most suggestive, it lingers at the edges of reality, ready to reverse its course and transform it. Where once reality and fantasy were at odds, they are now juxtaposed through the presence of memory:

> Everything begins with inhale and exhale, and never ends, moment after moment, yourself inhaling and exhaling, seeing, hearing, smelling,

touching, tasting, moving, sleeping, waking, day after day after year after year, until it is now, this moment of your being, the last moment which is saddest and most glorious. It is because we remember.

Thus begins "Resurrection of a Life," a story that experiments with the melding power of memory. Seen side by side through a succession of scenes from a semi-fictive life, is the boy he once was (now long dead) selling newspapers, "like an alley cat prowling all over the place" through city streets, avid for experience and "another boy alive on earth" (the young man he has become) "seeking the essential truth of the scene, . . . the static and precise beneath that which is in motion and which is imprecise." Memory becomes the connective tissue that binds the discrete, lost moments flowing by, revealing what belongs to oneself alone with a larger, continuous reality. *"It is because we remember"* that we exist at all, Saroyan implies.

In Saroyan's articulation of Proust's *temps perdu,* what is salvaged of the past becomes not the stuff of art alone (although the young man, the narrator, knows that only what is "static and precise" can endure as art), but the very substance and meaning of a life. One remembers the "self" that one chooses to resurrect: thus, what stands out in his remembrance of the boy he was—wandering with his load of paper into drab buildings, saloons, and whorehouses, watching "the faces of old whores, and the way they talked, and the smell of all the ugly places"—is a certain invulnerability; no matter that he felt resentful or angry or disgusted staring "at rich people sitting at tables in hightone restaurants, eating dishes of ice cream," or studying "the fat man who slept in a chair all summer" at the Crystal Bar, what memory uncovers is how he always remained an observer of the city "seeing this place with a clean eye, . . . looking for whatever it was that was there and that nobody else was trying to see."

The recollections are not necessarily associative in the Joycean stream-of-consciousness sense; they are rather intuited, and only because observer and observed, create a dual vision in which the child and the young writer interact. Thus, memory goes on to resurrect moments at the movies, when he searched in the "falsity of pictures of man in motion the truth of his own city, and of himself," or, walking alone from the theater when he becomes "insane with the passion to live." In yet another "still" from childhood, the schoolboy tells his teachers, "Don't try to tell me anything, I'm getting it direct, straight from the pit, the ugliness with the loveliness." Memory moves from the textbook heroism of Daniel

Boone learned in school to the quiet nobility of the baker from whom the child buys chicken bread every morning, pretending it is for the chickens they raise, when in fact it is for himself and his impoverished family who can afford nothing better. What he sifts from the recollection is the fact that "the important man" (the baker) always smiled and kept up the pretense: "he always picked out the best loaves" for him to take home. The words the boy spoke then are played back to him now: "We know we're poor. When the wind comes up, our house shakes, but we don't tremble. . . . [W]e are all there, all of us alive."

Poverty—as memory reveals—does not obliterate the sense of beauty, and sees again in his mind "the fig tree he loved: of all graceful things it was the most graceful." Climbing it, the boy would eat "the soft fat figs, the flowering of the lovely white woman, his lips kissing." He remembers how it stirred the Old World roots he idealized: "of the other earth, the older and lovelier earth, solid and quiet and of godly trace," and how he felt himself expand knowing he was a part of it.

"The moment of my time calls me back," says the narrator, and once again he returns to the newsboy now shouting that ten thousand Huns have been destroyed. It is 1918, and the news is being greeted with cheers; it is a devastating moment for the child who sees war as "a large and monstrous thing for each man involved"; it is, as the narrator puts it, the dying of "one man at a time, . . . gasping for breath, to go on inhaling and exhaling, living and dying."

Nothing now can fully restore the child's faith, not even church on Sunday mornings and the songs about Jesus who "loves thee best." "He could not believe and he could not disbelieve." It just made no sense:

But glory? There was an abundance of it. Everywhere. Madly everywhere. The crazy birds vomiting song. Those vast trees. . . . And clouds. And Sun. And night.

The story ends on a note of acceptance—or quiescence—of an earth "unaware of us, unaware of our cities, our dreams." And out of it all the assurance that

I am alive and glad to be, . . . somehow glad that I can remember the boy climbing the fig tree, unpraying but religious with joy, somehow of the earth, of the time of earth, somehow everlastingly of life, nothingness, blessed or unblessed, somehow deathless, insanely glad to be here, and so it is true, there is no death, somehow there is no death, and can never be.

Reality has now absorbed the dream: "all that I know is that we are somehow alive, all of us in the light, making shadows, the sun overhead, space all around us, inhaling, exhaling."

If Saroyan puts it all too bluntly and lyrically here, what he has tried to do through his technically imperfect story has more than passing importance as a measure of the writer's ambition to bring artistic distance to an evanescent experience.

Much more perfectly realized as a story is the second one in the volume, "Five Ripe Pears," which tells how a six-year-old boy was suddenly impelled to pluck five ripe pears from a neighbor's tree during recess in second grade, fully aware that it would involve an adventure, though not one he wishes to identify as "stealing," even as he recollects it years later. He directs his reminiscence to "old man Pollard," the principal, "because I want him to know I am not a thief and never have been." Nor had he lied, because the branches on which the pears had grown fell beyond the spike fence that protected the tree. "I was six, but a logician. A fence, I reasoned, can protect only that which it encloses."

Saroyan is discovering the humorous strain that will anchor his stories in reality while allowing the sentiment he wishes to explore to find its metaphor. If the story is not essentially humorous, there are many moments of humor; one such, tinged with irony, is when the boy proudly rushes to school to show off his pears only to find himself identified as a thief; or when he gobbles up the pears one after the other to hide the evidence from the principal who has threatened to give him a licking; and again when the unflinching honesty of his response intensifies the unreasonableness of the punishment he is made to suffer.

What the boy wants to convey but cannot—knowing nothing about the laws of private property—is that his desire for the pears involved harm to no one: "I hadn't stolen the pears because I had created them," is how in hindsight he interprets his youthful escapade. The gentle irony laced throughout the story catches up with the reader when the narrator recalls that although the

licking with the leather strap . . . didn't hurt so much, . . . I *had* to cry because it seemed very strange to me that no one else could even faintly understand why I picked five pears and carried four of them to class when I could have eaten them instead and made up a lie about helping a stranger find a street, or something like that.

By couching a teasing humor inside a simple adventure story of childhood, Saroyan not only suggests how irrational the concept of private property can be but shows how insensitive and inconsistent adults often are when faced with the innocent psyche of the child.

Inhale and Exhale contains other childhood reminiscences, dating mostly from the *Hairenik* period—"Yea and Amen," "The Death of Children," and "The Broken Wheel" among them—stories deeply intertwined with his Armenian heritage as we have discussed it. Touching and moving as these are, they do not reflect the venturesomeness of the author that the volume as a whole sets out to reveal.

Of particular interest in this respect is a story in the second section (titled, with Wolfean overtones, "World Wilderness of Time Lost'), "Two Days Wasted in Kansas City." The tone is anything but Wolfean here, as Saroyan begins the accumulation of prototypes that will serve his future work, especially the plays in which the discursive style will yield to the specificity of characters, and early recollections will become the clay from which he will mold his encounters with the outside world. This slight but substantial story is written in a manner that Saroyan will learn to make his own: beginning with the familiar and ordinary and ending with an unexpected departure from the norm. With hardly a nod to local detail, he moves in full authority to the rhythm and pace of small-town gamblers, evoking their world directly through their speech patterns: "I put the dice into the cup and laughed at the man with the rake," is the narrator's opening line, and he goes on to say: "You don't know what kind of luck I have. Watch me make that number."

He rattles the cup and laughs and tells the man with the rake he will keep on playing in one city or another "until I die." But this same freewheeling "touch guy" notices "the door [opening] very slowly and a little girl [coming] in smoking a cigarette." It is the archetypal Saroyan heroine, the vulnerable small-town girl in the big city about to lose her dreams. As in future Saroyan works, the little girl with the cigarette (a prostitute in the making) is momentarily drawn to the modern knight-errant who cannot tolerate the destruction of innocence.

The young gambler sees the girl at first as an emblem of his luck: "the girl was nobody. He could send her away and break down the whole arrangement. He didn't though." Of the five spectators, only he "was aware of what was going on."

At this point, without departing from the distinctive vernacular he has established, Saroyan switches gears—as if he had turned the narrator's psyche around, and from then on the story unfolds with the indirection of a poem. This instant "metamorphosis" happens when the girl starts to leave the gambling joint: at that moment only does the young man realize why he wanted so much to win. He has lost before: in Seattle, he remembers, "I had nothing to win but money, and nothing to lose but money, and I always lost." Even now what he wanted the money for is not quite clear: he vaguely connects her departure with the loss of his luck. But once she is gone and he imagines her "lost in the world," he becomes frantic in the sudden knowledge that he has somehow missed his cue. To have "saved" her with his money would have confirmed his innate faith in "everything in the whole boundless universe, . . . in the goodness of all things organic and inorganic."

Thus, what had started as a lighthearted Lardneresque story about two down-and-out gamblers turns into a story about self-revelation that is uncommonly sure in its handling of a demotic articulation (or semiarticulation) and at the same time subtle and humane in its implication. What takes place here is no sanctimonious turnabout: Saroyan is careful to present this sudden psychic deflection as the surfacing of an unsuspected impulse in a simple character who, even as he thinks about it, is astonished at his insight.

"I wasted two days in Kansas City, hoping to find her," he says at the end, "I only wanted to tell her I made my number because I knew how it was with her and wanted her to have the money so she could go being alive the way she wanted to be alive." He imagines that for a moment

> we had the whole world and the whole universe and every idea of God on our side, and I wish to Christ she hadn't gone away and left me only a lot of lousy money in my pocket *instead of the real rich winning I had made.*

I emphasize the last phrase because it is deliberately ambiguous. Using the imagery of gambling, the young man indirectly acknowledges the worthlessness of money in and of itself, while at the same time recognizing that the real "winning" lay in his impulse—arising from his better self—to salvage another person's dream.

"Think of America," Saroyan had written Martha Foley, "the pain in America and the fear and the deep inward longing of all things alive." And in the process of "de-composing" the conventional short story to arrive at its core, "where everything begins, inhale and exhale," he seeks to evoke sharp and poignant images of contemporary America. As William Floan has pointed out, the book is organized according to Saroyan's own life, beginning with his boyhood in a small town, then his manhood in the big city (San Francisco), and finally travel abroad (including his ancestral Armenia). But what is most striking in our first encounter with this mammoth volume is how heavily it is strewed with odd and snappy titles, such as "A Hat Tipped to a Lamp Post," "With a Hey Nonny Nonny," "The Great Unwritten American Novel," and "Ah-ha." For Saroyan it is more than an obvious device to entice the reader. It serves to dissipate an underlying solemnity, and as such the device will become a Saroyan trademark.

In *Inhale and Exhale,* the solemnity is thicker perhaps than it will ever be again, for the author's task is nothing less than that of saving the anonymous from anonymity. A varied lot they are, with small needs and large desires, their individual outlines diverging from what would normally be expected of them. "The Oranges," for instance, is a Depression story that moves the attention away from desperate poverty to consider its indirect effect on a sensitive child. A sad little boy, Luke, is pressed by his immigrant uncle to smile as he sells oranges for five cents apiece to people riding in rich automobiles by the roadside because "in America you've got to make people like you." Luke smiles and smiles until his cheeks begin to ache and is finally seized with great anguish *because no one smiles back:*

> For all he cared, the whole world could just fall into the darkness and end . . . and there could be nobody anywhere, not even . . . one empty street or one dark window or one shut door because they didn't want to buy oranges and they wouldn't smile at him, and the whole world could end.

The story thus ends in the language of a child's feelings.

In another, less successful story, "With a Hey Nonny Nonny," Saroyan uses the tragic consequences of a labor strike to point up the disparity between the private dream of a young Mexican worker in the valley and the violent actions which are forced upon him. Saroyan never underestimates the simple man's capacity to dream: against "the sharp certainty of his life," with its "gladness of inward smiling" and a vision of an ideal love, the young peasant discloses a moral commitment:

> Deeper within than his smiling is his bitterness about his people, laboring in the valley, . . . his violent hatred for that in life which made his people suffer.

Saroyan imagines the young man praying, "using the vocabulary of simple souls, the wordless language of being, and each intake of breath was the equivalent of a pious exclamation, devotion to God." The young man's inarticulateness does not numb his sensibility, and as he stands at the entrance of the Hollywood Picture House listening to the player piano, the music comes to him as

> a universal sadness in the heart of man, a strange yearning for the precise and ineffable, a melancholy longing for the grace of a solid and more precise life, for love and truth and dignity.

In the words of the piano player's foolish and glorious song, "With a hey nonny nonny and a ha-cha-cha," he hears "the inevitable ugliness of the event [that] that would mar his dream, perhaps destroy it." And on the eve of the strike that will victimize him, he identifies with the song: "knowing that the whole thing would end foolishly, in some foolish waste of strength, and blood, and life and dream, . . . something almost glorious, but like the American music foolish." At the end, his death has the pathos of another anonymous Saroyan character, the starving writer of "The Daring Young Man on the Flying Trapeze;" for like him there is stoic acceptance as he faces being torn from his dream, from all he wanted of life—"the meadow, the sky, the tree, fire, air, water."

Saroyan's technical problem in this and other stories in this volume is not difficult to pinpoint: the author's voice intrudes too often to allow the protagonist's character (here the Mexican worker) to emerge. Even when he uses mood-conveying phrases to express deep feelings, it is hard to separate the lofty inner voice of the young man from the violent actions in which he is to become involved. But there is boldness in what Saroyan is trying to do: namely, to find a kind of "objective correlative" for the *wordless language of being,* whether it be that of the child or of an untutored laborer. What is potentially fruitful here—something on which he will later build—is the connection he makes with music, for unlike language, music's meaning, however intense, has to be diffuse and imprecise.

In *Inhale and Exhale* Saroyan has also begun to shift away from the individual to the archetype, his hope being to reveal the character of the period and, beyond it, the American ethos itself. It is in this exchange that the solemnity and lyricism begin to give way to a new tenor of bemusement, teasing humor, and even ridicule, which enables him to enlarge the meaning of "Saroyanesque." There are eccentrics and oddballs but no "outcasts" in his large cast of characters—among them drunkards, gamblers and prostitutes, incipient Communists and agnostics, wrestlers, vineyard workers, actors, bartenders, soldiers and sailors, do-gooders, and—always—the unemployed. And although they are not individualized, they almost never come across as stereotypes. They are all dreamers of one sort or another, their laughter a source of their strength, their moments of despair supported by a tenacious belief in life.

"International Harvester" begins like a harsh inventory of America: "Noise and vibration. Steel traffic whistle steam cement. The beggar, the blind musician, the lonely soldier, the hooker. Rugged reliability. Demonstration."

But in the next paragraph, the harshness begins to dissipate, as he points out that "the beggar is not lame," he walks. He has a name. "Alfred Garth. Age 27. Talented." He is an actor, not a beggar, because "he performs, acting hunger and need, performing the truth of his life, playing the part twice, once for himself, once for the stranger in the street." "His soul is saved," the author concludes. "There are ways to be humiliated."

Also in the inventory is "James Fagode with the violin. . . . His eyes cannot see at all, but his other senses recreate the world about him. . . . It is a world of endless light." When a dime is dropped in the cup, the violinist laughs to himself. In a sardonic aside to the reader, the author observes: "The truth will be gladly explained. . . . Sit back and be comforted." "He laughs because his song is the song of death and desolation on earth."

And, there's the barber, Nick the Greek, who is ready for the Revolution: "Comrade, said Nick, . . . when the revolution comes I will cut you so badly you will die laughing." When he gets a dollar tip, he calls his customer "a lousy capitalist." To which the narrator responds, "[T]his is known as affirmation of faith. Belief in man. Belief in God, Stalin, Heaven, Earth, Russia, Germany. . . . This is known as humble piety." Withal, the narrator concludes, people buck their destiny:

> Ten million unemployed continue law-abiding. No riots, no trouble, no multi-millionaire cooked and served with cranberry sauce. . . . And so it goes. One thing and another on every street in every city all over the country.

The archetypes derive from their locale in almost every case. In "The Drinkers," a loquacious drunkard sings praise to Al Capone and streetwalkers and finds excuses for the man who tried to kill Roosevelt. In this early prototype of the San Francisco bar that is the setting for "The Time of Your Life," there are tipsy young girls, middle-aged fops, dozing sailors, and a reflective barkeeper who tries to figure out why "crazy nuts" come to his place. "Crazy people need a lot of the stuff," he muses, "but what I want to know is, how do they get that way?"

> They tell me people haven't enough to eat, no place to sleep, no clothes, no money, but that's a lot of hooey. These people *can't* eat. . . . I'll tell you what they want. They want *everything*, and they want it in a big hurry.

But in "Little Miss Universe," where the cast is composed of racehorse gamblers, there's something beside greed or the need to allay frustration at work. As the narrator—new on the scene— observes of the three representative "authorities" on horses at the Kentucky Pool Room:

> Gambling, betting on horses, among other things, is a way of life. The manner in which a man chooses to gamble indicates his character or his lack of it. In short, gambling is a game, a philosophy, just as in Spain bull-fighting is these things, as Mr. Hemingway has pointed out in 500 pages.

Of the three "authorities" Saroyan focuses on Willie, "himself a superior by nature," who "disliked superior horses and cherished fondly those who most bettors despised." Willie becomes a comic figure in his conflicting needs to develop a "system" while irrationally rooting for the underdog. Miss Universe for him was "not just another horse. She was something more subtle, more mystical," and he develops "an alibi for each of her miserable performances. Also: The name was beautiful. It was poetry." Midway in the story—which has more atmosphere and "inside" details than plot—the narrator/writer undercuts Hemingway, Kipling, et al., by declaring his refusal to "manufacture an outcome, a climax. . . . [to] reveal . . . [a] profound truth." "About these men I cannot make pastry," for

> nothing ever happens at the Kentucky Pool Room. Bets are made, a few lucky fellows collect, but in the long run everybody loses.

When the results of the race come in, the story is over: "There you have it: the story. Nothing added, nothing taken away, like pure mayonnaise." It's the comic figure of Willie, collapsing with disappointment, who appears in the final clip, as the narrator, with pockets empty, ruminates on Little Miss Universe: "What a beautiful name! If I have one slice of bread twice a day and a cup of coffee for breakfast—well, I can make it, I suppose." However cockeyed his "system," it is Willie's philosophy that will ultimately turn the young man into a true gambler.

Saroyan moves from drawing attention to the existence of the "underdog" itself to its possibility as a general theme, characteristically American in two stories that are in other respects not alike. The first of these, "Our Little Brown Brothers the Filipinos," considers the plight of the 250-pound Filipino champion wrestler, Romano Internationale, who is asked to fake a defeat to the Russian "rock crusher." The problem is not that Romano is honest and unwilling to "play the game according to the rules" (as his manager explains) but that he's proud—too proud—when faced with the eventuality of "losing" to the Russian. His sudden determination to throw the "rules" aside is bolstered by the overwhelming presence of his countrymen who have come to watch the fight,

> all the little Filipinos, not one of them more than a hundred and ten pounds in weight, but every one of them dressed in purple and red and green clothes, every one of them smoking a long panetela cigar.

And each has bet money on their magnificent compatriot.

Chaos reigns in the Dreamland auditorium where Romano Internationale demands to be declared the winner, even as the police try to capture him. From all over, people have come to watch the power play, for as the narrator observes, "[P]eople love to see one man, especially dark-complected, challenging the whole world, and nine times out of ten they are for him." This fast-moving story, verging on the absurd, is among Saroyan's least discursive, with the least intrusion by the author. As Howard Floan has observed, Saroyan "was much better at the kind of story Ben Hecht was then making popular." But beyond "the fine sense of the ridiculous" that Floan detected, what stays with the reader is the spectacle of sweet victory for the "powerlessness," most especially for the fifty loyal "little Filipinos," rooting for their intransigent hero as they fight off the police in their own crafty way.

The impulse to identify with the disadvantaged presumes more than average softness of heart. Saroyan's so-called sentimentality would always be connected with his characters' extravagant and gratuitous acts of benevolence. That there was a philosophical basis behind this may be surmised from a letter Saroyan wrote in November 1938 to James Laughlin, who had published Saroyan in the *New Directions Anthology* of 1937:[24]

> There is little interest in new directions in living, so it is natural that there shall be still less in N. D. in writing . . . to us, no doubt, there can be no decent living without decent writing. . . . [W]e ourselves, however, are several thousand light years from the truth, from a decent reality.

Going on to expound the difference between good and evil, Saroyan continues:

> evil is that which disintegrates the Man, that's all; good is that which integrates; the world disintegrates man first: we reported what the world had done, and because what it had done was so vast and tragic our reporting was, in a sense at least, great.

But the works of Joyce, Lawrence, Miller, and others, he adds, were not conclusive:

> These men were or will be burned by the enormity of the task and will die, or have died, before they will have reached the light, and balanced the labor, given it dimension; inhaled and exhaled; and put the good over the evil.

There are many instances in *Inhale and Exhale* that show Saroyan reaching for this exalted conviction, but the story that perhaps embodies it best and is Saroyan at his most wistful is "The Mother." In it an idealistic young man confronts and tries to help a new neighbor he hardly knows—an unwed mother-to-be, cast off by her lover; he does so in full awareness that his extravagant overtures (which includes renting an apartment for her) will seem inappropriate and even silly: "he knew he didn't love the girl. Sure, he didn't but that wasn't the point. . . . [I]t was a question of letting her have her baby." He imagines from observing the woman's shining eyes that she is nourishing a dream of motherhood, and he is determined that she will not feel compelled by the pressures of society to destroy that dream.

Here, as in "Two Days Wasted in Kansas City," the young man's impulse toward an inner "winning" doesn't escape the reader, but in this instance the hero's feelings are tinged with self-mockery: "he had to be a swell guy," he tells himself in a moment of unease before the girl. Saroyan is consciously skirting sentimentality, while exploring the craggy landscape of sentiment. True to the story's realistic vein, the young man's idealism misfires—though not in the expected way, and as nearly always in Saroyan's hands, not in an *absolute* sense. When the young girl walks out of his life, without a word of recognition, much less gratitude, the young man turns away in defeat (like the grieving boy in "The Oranges")—feeling "the place where they had stood together in the city was for a moment one of the most desolate places on the earth." There is no wryly happy O. Henry ending here, but neither is there a hard cynicism in the way Saroyan sums it all up: the abortion of the baby (the loss of a dream) is pitted against the thwarting of a spontaneous will to goodness.

Saroyan's recasting of realism involves a stretching of the imagination to accommodate, along with what is immediately visible and patently true, what is yet to be experienced and revealed as the truth. (Had he read Hegel—and one cannot rule out that this voracious reader had not—he could hardly have come closer to that philosopher's dialectical vision of reality.) By searching his memory, he has found a way to fuse the disconnected strands of experience, and when he comes to "resurrecting" a life—seeing it whole—cause and effect no longer seem to operate with any finality. Although Saroyan favors an impressionistic style (common among literary prose writers of the period), he does not really see through the impressionist's misty lense. The Proustian concept of human change as a gradual and inevitable process that often ends in painful alienation has nothing in common with the spontaneous and unpredictable transformations that so often surface in Saroyan's characters. For along with the usually cited "influences" on the formation of character, Saroyan adds the combined and cumulative experiences of our common humanity, which contain the ethos of a particular "tribe" or culture. Human nature is seen as irreversibly built-in but succumbing to "the winds of change" in a number of ways, and only if so willed by the subject.

None of this is directly articulated in *Inhale and Exhale,* but now and then he is poised at the edge of a philosophical statement in support of this view. What stands out in the early stages of his career is his repeated efforts to reinforce the metamorphic concept over the purely organic. The impressionistic style, ideally suited to conveying mood, cannot serve Saroyan's deeper purpose of placing emotion at the center of his story. And just as Impressionist painters would move on from their initial involvement with *visual* realism to a post-Impressionism in which the *expression* of feeling absorbed the transitory, accidental aspects of a scene, so Saroyan would venture on to a less "realistic" yet more direct style of narration.

In keeping with his gift for availing himself of blessings at hand, Saroyan had paid close attention to his earliest encounters with the unsophisticated adults of his immediate circle, those wise, transplanted folk figures untaught in the skills of articulation with which we tend to coat the inmost part of the "self." At the same time, the vivid remembrances of his own childhood allowed him to see how similar were the responses of these grown-up men and women to those of the still unspoiled child. In both feeling was predominant, its scope and intensity varying according to the degree of felt experience. Words are the writer's trade, feeling the tools of musicians and visual artists. Saroyan had to translate feelings into words if he was to reach an ulterior level of consciousness where the sense of selfhood originates. One is surprised how often the anonymous inarticulate human beings who act out the Saroyan "experiment" in these pages are able to hold our attention and interest despite their inchoate thoughts and feelings. But it is not the characters or even the stories in themselves that mark the originality of *Inhale and Exhale*. It is rather one's awareness of the continuous presence of a creative mind groping for a new literary dynamic with which to perceive art in relation to the mundane realities of existence. In the 1930s it was still a problem for a writer to persuade readers that the short story could be something else.

"Pardon me," the writer/narrator remarks at the beginning of "Panorama Unmerciful," "these are great days, these days of going down and coming up, and going down again." There is a note of prophecy in this announcement that "it is time for us to begin making things over, from the beginning." But the voice here is not the jeremiad of *The New Masses*. Things are not totally hopeless, because we do laugh still,

> [but] right now this mess we are in makes it impossible for me to give a damn about art. I have said it before and will say it again in print: *to hell with art*. To hell with the idea of letting the rest of the world go by.

An Emersonian strain surfaces as he sets forth his aim:

> To make man aware of himself, aware of the greatness that is within him, if he will only stop being timid, if he will only stop letting things bully him; at least to *want* to.

He reminds his reader, with an overabundant exuberance that will become wholly his own, that there are blessings in just being "able to draw breath, to have energy and motion, . . to walk and talk and read and sleep and be alive." And he singles out as the peak of these blessings a crate of peaches in a store window while he ruminates on "what their presence in the world again means: the return of the strong sun to the fields of California, the winter labor of simple man, pruning trees." He buys a peach, "tasting the sweet juice, knowing that I am alive" and contemplates writing a study about it, even if "the critics will rule it out as a story." But he decides "these are not the days to write about peaches." He will not, in fact, write anything at all until he can say "the right thing." It is not enough to be "just another writer." What he wants is to "move in prose directly to the center of our greatness, revealing it to itself." That center, he decides, is the laughter of the homeless and the half-starved: here is the true subject of "The Great American Novel." He becomes manic in his obsession:

> Listen young Dreiser, listen young Balzac, young Dostovesky, get this through that thick skull of yours: this is it, this: *this splendid defiant laughter.* [italics mine]

Now that he knows this secret about America, he has no fear he will lack a subject. He is in no hurry to create a plot.

> It will keep because it is everywhere, all plots and all characters. . . .
> I will not even have to try; the whole thing will fall in place by itself, effortlessly, all the rhythms of it, all the sound and all the meaning.

We see prefigured here the use that Saroyan will make of humor in his work and why it is often bittersweet even as he mocks the absurdity of the world around him. He already knows that his brand of humor will only be possible when he has established its affinity with something profound. The sense of eternity which pursued "the daring young man" to a noble death has retained its hold on Saroyan and it has become a self-reflexive response that is best conveyed, I think, by Northrop Frye's phrase "the definitive experience of poetry." That Saroyan's humor will become embedded in the experience is not hard to surmise from another story in the volume, 'Poem, Story, Novel." Here the narrator speaks of literary forms in relation to the natural world; he defines the poem as something "wholly of unduration and it is uninvolved, being out of both time and space. . . . [A] poem does not occur like history;

it occurs like the sun, uncritically, . . . rather quietly, as the coming of the sun." The story, too, is "not this man did this thing and this was the consequence." It is

> an effortless growth, as of a tree coming up from the earth and rising solidly in a specific place, standing solidly in a specific place, because of the sun, from which there is no escape.

He goes on to describe, with no pretention to subtlety, an idea that is nonetheless subtle—the effect that writing such a story can have on the writer:

> The important thing is to remember that you may if you try hard enough become a form of yourself which can endure a rather long time, and a form of yourself which was not an inevitability when you began to be. In other words, the important thing is to remember that it is possible: that the finest occurrences are possible, and you have only to perceive the possibility of your wildest dreams. Dream not, though of possessing large automobiles or large women: this is current triviality and it is not of the sun.

In their hyperbolic formulations and epigrammatic passages, their insights and their endeavor to move into larger areas of human consciousness, Saroyan's essay-stories take on at times the prophetic ring of a modern Nietzsche. But lest his own idea of the "over-man" become identified with the godlessness that implies, *Inhale and Exhale* adds to the concluding section a piece called "Psalms," which mockingly suggests *Thus Spake Zarathustra*. Beginning with "Who can laugh, Lord, when the earth is a place of loneliness?," the narrator goes on to bemoan the modern world where there are no faces that bear God's divinity, "none here who dwell in the limitless universe of the animal body; none, Lord, who rise above the flesh." But this prophet will not turn away from man as he exists because, like the mountain, he endures "after civilization." He will wait for what is still to be made visible to us. Reverting to transcendence, he rejects the creation of a new tablet to discover the revelations of the old:

> I seek the new, which is no more than the unknown, since all things have timeless existence in probability. He who seeks finds. Creation is impossible. All things *are*. I seek forms which are and are yet not revealed.

The over-man this young prophet awaits does not imply redoing, but rather restoration or accretion.

There is little to say if one seeks the ultimate word, since the word is silence. But there is much to say if one is satisfied to be no more than mortal. The variety of living is infinite, and it is my opinion that we have not yet begun to be mortal.

Saroyan's subsequent work will increasingly involve the impulse to such dynamic conversions in our everyday life. We shall realize that for him "the human comedy" is not Balzac's universe mirroring man's inhumanity to man, but one that contains the possibility of the reverse.

4

The Art of the Saroyan Story

Without humor there is no hope, and man could no more live
without hope than he could without the earth under-foot.
—Saroyan

THE REALITY PRINCIPLE

ALTHOUGH Saroyan had denied the importance of "form" as such,
saying "Any form I achieve in art is form I have already achieved
in myself," there is revelation in some of his best volumes—*My
Name is Aram, The Trouble with Tigers, Razzle-Dazzle* (which
introduces the short play), *The Whole Voyald,* and *Assyrian and
Other Stories*—of how "form" has been given to his unconventional short story. One important point that stands out in these
volumes is that he no longer identifies with all his creations and
that some of the views they express are not his own but merely
the foil for his continuing dialogue between himself and the world.
He is indirectly making an effort to dislodge the impression of total
subjectivity by distributing varying points of view among his
characters.

Another point that becomes evident in this series is that Saroyan
has a more basic humanistic concern than most writers of proletarian works that handle a similar level of humanity. Contributing to
this unflinching faith in the intrinsic goodness of all human crea-
tures are certain forces of his background: the Armenian heritage,
the religious influences (his father had been a Protestant preacher),
the American legacy of Emerson, and other literary influences
such as those of Maupassant, Sherwood Anderson, and Whitman.
Perhaps most important was Saroyan's faith in man's creativity, in
art that confirms what Northrop Frye called "the world of definitive
experience" where life and the imagination meet.

From the point of view of the short story, *Inhale and Exhale* had

111

been an act of rebellion, and one not easy to follow. Practically speaking, the book did nothing to augment Saroyan's fame or reputation. If anything it cast ripples of doubt about his much-touted "genius" even among his earliest fans. Its diversity of styles and mood—from lyrical to bombastic—failed to create the kind of authorial identity the first book had achieved. Clifton Fadiman's harsh verdict that it was a "hodge-podge," written by a writer whose mind "darts about like a waterbug," was countered by other critics only mildly supportive of the new voice from the West with its declarations of faith in the goodness and dignity of man.[1] But even as his once-exuberant editor Bennett Cerf was delivering the bad news of the book's slow sales, Saroyan's confidence in himself and his book remained unshaken. As he would put it in a letter to Cerf, "It's a book that's not going to be dismissed by time. It's damned near the *Ulysses* of the American short story."[2]

While the analogy is obviously an exaggeration, it served Saroyan's purpose in conveying the book's unorthodoxy as a volume of stories. In one important sense *Inhale and Exhale* was exceptional: For the first time perhaps since Mark Twain a book had given expression to the "sound" of America and the common life seen from within a previously unknowledged and invisible cosmos.

Like Twain, Saroyan had aimed for the vernacular, the demotic and, like Twain too, his humor, when it surfaced, was grounded in a philosophical gravity. The "yea" side of the American stance to which he was attuned did not readily admit to a judgmental view, and his freewheeling, generous acceptance of human variety and human foibles created a warm, genial atmosphere that would become labelled "Saroyanesque." In this respect, Saroyan's contention that his book was "experimental" was not totally out of line. In revealing the life of "everyman" he was presenting him neither as a Sherwood Anderson grotesque to be psychologically explained, nor as a Twain creation fixed for all time. He wished, rather, to deliver the "news" that was everyone's concern, while suggesting the various ways people had of coping with it. As to "strategy," if he subscribed to any such thing consciously, it was to entertain and to edify at the same time, or, as he put it in "Panorama Unmerciful," "To move in prose directly at the center of our greatness." What he saw as a corollary to the center of that greatness was "the splendid defiant laughter of the American people." All of it finally hinged on the discovery that "the finest occurrence is possible, and you have only to perceive your wildest dreams."[3]

In the next four years, with six additional volumes of stories, culminating in *My Name is Aram*, Saroyan would not always strictly follow this perceived path, but he would come as close as any writer since Twain or Lardner to invading the highly restricted region of the humorous story that indirectly contained a commentary of the social scene.

Short-story volumes, unlike novels, are not meant to be cohesive wholes, and one critic's observation that the two subsequent Saroyan books, *Three Times Three* (1936) and *Little Children* (1937), lacked unity and consistency[4] needs also to be viewed in the light of the literary situation facing a writer like Saroyan whose income up to 1936 derived solely from the publication of short stories. What magazines other than *Story* were receptive to his kind of writing? As revealed by his acknowledgments, there was a large variety, ranging from the obscure to the sophisticated and the popular: *Aperitif, Bystander, College Humor, Esquire, Hairenik, Harper's Bazaar, Literary America, New Directions* (Annual), *Pacific Weekly, Pasadena Junior College Magazine, San Francisco Tide, Script, Scribner's Magazine, The London Evening Standard, The New Statesman* and *Nation, The New Republic, The New Yorker, The North American Review, The Olympian,* and the *Peninsulan,* among others. With so many magazines to choose from, the short-story writers who resisted slickness and standardized, formula-type writing invariably learned to widen the range of his material. One could, of course, turn that statement around and say that because Saroyan was so versatile he was able to publish in a large variety of magazines; but success did not always accompany each publication, and the independent direction his writing was taking became apparent with the publication of his next work. If none of the books up to *My Name is Aram* lacked the distinction of his first volume, each nonetheless revealed a new facet to be explored in assembling "the world of William Saroyan." It would evolve even as he himself did.

Novelty, the sine qua non of quick fame, would wear thin with Saroyan's subsequent books—as novelty always does—and it was this awareness on the part of his publishers that Saroyan had to meet head-on. In no way could he repeat the kind of acclaim that greeted the publication of *The Daring Young Man on the Flying Trapeze,* and Random House, now comfortably established, could forego the risk-sharing that the new writer presents. In hindsight, however, the risk was worth taking. For if anything, *Inhale and Exhale* had shown that Saroyan had more than one string to his bow. The novelty had been partly in himself—the image he had projected of a new kind of unlettered, natively gifted American writer; yet beyond this, there was something solid and lastingly creative that needed only time to surface and mature, that he learn his craft—though not necessarily in the terms critics were proposing. For Saroyan, it was rather a matter of deepening his experience and its absorption or reabsorption into his grasping imagination.

For a while Saroyan's material would have to run thin, and there was the possibility of tedium setting in as he covered a paucity of human encounters by his everlasting presence in work, forever enticing the reader to live a better life and to become a better human being. What remained in his favor, however, was the feeling of community his writing generated (which went a long way in the Depression years); no ethnic barriers kept his oddball Armenians from hobnobbing with plain American Joes and Sams, and the impulse to happiness and reconciliation insured that the reader would see the humor or feel the poetry of everyday existence. Just as the Depression era had responded to his natural buoyancy, a certain wistfulness (the other side of the coin) would find an echo in the pre-World War II climate of impending disaster. But irrespective of the conditions to which his talents were attuned (or which he exploited, as some critics would have it), the durability of his writing would in the end be determined by his artistic seriousness.

No one was more aware of this than Saroyan, as his dealings with his publisher reveal: It was not fortuitous, for instance, that when Bennett Cerf, in exceedingly harsh terms, turned down his next book of stories, *Little Children,* Saroyan countered by breaking off with Random House. Masking injured pride with bravado, Saroyan wrote to Cerf, "I don't want to make money on a book. . . . I just want to be published in the public libraries."[4] The break came during his momentary success as scriptwriter in Hollywood for Budd Schulberg's father, "B. P.," as he was called. Barely settled in, Saroyan became disillusioned with the industry that sparked his childhood dreams, seeing in its crassness the death knell of the artist. Now he announced to Cerf that with what he had saved from not gambling and with the help of four college undergraduates from UCLA, he was going into self-publishing. His book, *Three Times Three,* would be the first of the Conference Press books. "It will get more publicity than my other books," he went on, "It's an item for collectors. The first edition 1,500, is almost sold out—mostly to wise booksellers and college kids." The profits, he added, would go to the poor. "We are dedicated to the idea of not making money."[5]

No press could survive such a lofty aim, and after the publication of the Saroyan book was dissolved. But *Three Times Three* put Saroyan back on the map. The defiant attitude surrounding this project bore a novelty authentic to the original image, and reviewers like Lewis Gannett filled a column in *The New York Herald-Tribune* with a facetious and essentially inaccurate account of the venture. The good-humored retort it promptly drew from the author filled the reviewer's subsequent column. Setting the record straight, Saroyan stated, "I was not patronized by capital." He took the opportunity to describe the evolution of the project:

> I put up $100 cash; paid $75 for 100 copies of the book for friends and public libraries. . . . The book is almost out of the red. No chance for a financial profit, though. The kids are tickled to death. . . . I liked their earnestness and believed we could have a lot of fun. All I wanted was another book this year to go on record.[6]

Much of this kind of self-advertisement mars the opening pages of *Three Times Three,* and Saroyan's flippant, chip-on-the-shoulder tone in his remarks about "book critics, professors of English, lousy writers and backward children . . . who want to know how I do my stuff, why, when and where" does less than justice to the reflections on literary art that follow. It is this separate essay, "Life and Letters," that more than anything else in this volume justifies the book's publication.

Saroyan's understanding of the connection between life and literary art has surfaced before this in casual asides in his narratives, but this is the first time that he elaborates on it with a degree of explictness not generally characteristic. The essay nonetheless bears the marks of his conversational flair, and it is possible, when measured by today's standards of articulation on such topics, to dismiss it as naive and platitudinous. (Indeed, even in 1936 no significant note was taken of it as far as I can determine.) Yet those who had followed Saroyan up to this point with any degree of seriousness were bound to find one of the most significant statements here of the writer's artistic intent—one that would reach into the heart of his future work. With hindsight, it also explains the limits he himself placed on the development of his "craft," of "technique."

The reader of this essay is well advised to begin with the second paragraph, avoiding Saroyan's verbose introductory note in which he retells the circumstances of his writing the piece for which the *Book Collector's Journal* in Chicago paid him ten dollars.

I was gambling at the time and having very poor luck. . . . I was putting down all this stuff about writing and circumstances surrounding the writing of a piece because I figure nothing is more remarkable than the difference between the way a writer is feeling at a given time and the way the writing turns out, and the way his writing goes.

The Steinesque mode takes over here in the fear that he is becoming solemn. But in fact he has gotten ahead of the reader, who will know better what all this signifies after reading his self-imposed inquest into the raison d'être of his writing:

I daresay . . . that after a writer *is* a writer, after the world has decided to let him be a writer, he still wonders what the hell he is supposed to be doing and why. . . . I daresay he ought to wonder, because I daresay there has never been any such thing in the world as a writer because writing, I daresay, mind you, is essentially living.

"Living," however, has a connotation other than the one associated with routine, "going and coming . . . meaninglessness . . . absence of direction . . . entanglements in the props of time." "Living" for the writer is rather "equilibrium, or an essay at it, and it is poetry, emerging . . . from events and conditions largely unpoetic except for the fool whose equipment makes him seek and find poetry everywhere." He goes on to enumerate all the things that "living" comes to mean for the creative writer: among them, humor, grace, truth ("one of the million varieties of it—magic, pity, compassion"). These remain with the writer only while he is doing his work, for time is something the writer can no more escape in his ordinary day by day living than the man who has no dealing with art or letters. But time, so precisely doled out in life, is far more various and efflorescent in letters:

Time in letters is not daybreak, day, noon, afternoon, evening and night. In letters time is altogether an inexplicable and magnificent thing, and so small a thing as a mere short story can become so tremendous an intensification of experience that the reader, God bless him and keep his eyes anastigmatic, will have lived more richly, more greatly, more swiftly, more meaningfully and more magnificently than he could ever have had the wit or daring or madness to live in the light of day, in the world.

The artist may have "a burning impulse to bring life and letters into holy wedlock," but, says Saroyan, unless he is prepared to "run away . . . into the hills" and renounce "the good and crazy world," he is not likely to succeed in his quest. The only possibility that remains, in his view, is that a writer's concept of everyday living become transformed, so that there is

> an inward progression of an inward time, an inward growth of an inward world or universe, an inward purification of the inward identity, and an inward strengthening of the inward body.

It is in this sense, he concludes, that "life and letters are the same, but only for the writer." But do such writers exist, he asks?

> There are not many writers around anywhere. . . . [T]here are mobs of dopes who piddle around with words and horse around with what they call characters and situations and plots and atmosphere and all that crap, but these babies aren't writers.

For this reason, the public can no longer recognize "great writing" when it comes along. If nonetheless he remains optimistic it is because real writers do not write for the public but for that in themselves which exists in others:

> They seek in themselves the universal and believe that in finding it in themselves, it is found also in all men, and if men are not ready to accept what they have found they certainly will be in a century or two or three, unless Fascism or something else destroys these qualities which is, frankly, out of the question.

What stands out here is Saroyan's faith in the writer's power to address "the highest sensibility in man that he can find in himself," thereby allowing common readers to achieve "a state of reality" that will satisfy their own "instinctive passion for some kind of godliness and immortality." "Letters can wait," he affirms wistfully and also humorously: "maybe [in] more than ten centuries for the ones whose equipment for life is not inferior to beavers, as Henry Miller in Paris says." Momentarily, he envisions (with perhaps the boy Saroyan as his model) the trek to the public library to imbibe the works of "a man who really wrote" and sensing "their own inward lives begin to accelerate as [the writer's] did."

> The old boy who did the writing has pulled a fast one on time, has made himself immortal, started the growth of immortality in another, and nothing short of the end of the world can end the continuance of this everlasting potentiality.

What counts for Saroyan ultimately is not a selfishly sought immortality for the writer but an immortality transferred through the writer to humankind as a whole.

> We can imagine then that if immortality is out of the question in the time of life. . . . Perhaps it is not out of the question in the time of letters which men themselves have made and placed in competition with the time of the universe. . . . We can figure maybe immortality is a swiftly evanescent condition which centuries of inward living swings into reality, and that's as far as any of us can go with the theory.

The transformation of the man into an artist becomes only the beginning of the larger task of transmuting the artist into a new man. We now understand the introductory note, which deals with his discovery that there is no connection with the writer's state of being as he writes and the success or failure of what he produces. A writer can have everything on his side, "be very accurately balanced in himself" and have "the greatest story in the world to tell," but when he goes to work it turns out lousy—while the same writer will be completely broken, bitter, "displeased with God and the world," and produce a masterpiece. This leads him to conclude that "art is a correction of errors, within the artist, in the world, in man, in the universe." So for Saroyan, "if you would be immortal in art, you must be mortal in life." Art and letters belong together, however apart they seem.

Saroyan's self-publication gives him the opportunity to expound his ideas explicitly, and if his "experiment" puts his art at a disadvantage, he appears to derive a perverse kind of satisfaction in being able to avow that "this book is not worth two dollars and fifty cents," while at the same time acknowledging that "the essential value of this book, which cannot be measured in terms of money is as great as that of any book published elsewhere this year." And, indeed, except for the first short story in the volume, "My Heart's in the Highlands," which Saroyan would turn into a play (his first to be performed),[7] *Three Times Three* was like a dare (to Bennett Cerf?) meant to demonstrate the connection between what the market conceives of as "failure" and the "inward progression" an author often makes at a risk.

"I tried too much in this one," he apologizes in the foreword to "Baby," a much longer story; "Here and there it is all right, it is fine, it is great, but without form, and in as much as form is our only truth, our noblest objective in art and life, this piece fails."

Form for Saroyan is, of course, spontaneous and almost inherent—that fortuitous correspondence between an inner vision and its embodiment that unerringly swings a work into being, and when the work doesn't come off it spells "failure" beyond a lapse of technique or skill:

> My idea was to make an American character, the American out of all the lives in our country, our time, and I wanted our land, our cities, our streets, our sky, everything about America, to be part of this American, as these things certainly are part of the great American body and spirit.

It is this vision he seeks to embody, and if he has failed to do so in "Baby" it is because "You always fail when you try too much." Conversely, "you are good . . . when you try enough." He cannot blame the critics for wanting him to tell a little story that is a pleasure to read because it is "whole, and with form," but he feels he is not yet old enough not to want to be a truly great writer. And he thus sums up his ambition:

> I know I shall be very miserable when I no longer wish and need to try to do, in prose, with the word, that which would seem to be impossible to do.

He does not, however, directly explain why "Baby" reveals his inadequacy in terms of his grandiose vision. Earlier, he has casually told us the story was a back number, written "possibly during 1933." In tone and substance—apart from one vignette that stands complete in itself, about the telegram messenger boy who delivers the news to a mother of her son's death—it is a kind of blueprint for future work.[8] Though mainly drunk with words, this youthful voice is different in timbre from Wolfe's or Whitman's or even Anderson's as it tries to encompass "the American magnificence." In a curious blending of poetic feeling and probing eye, it begins by evoking an urban wasteland here redeemed by the power to inspire:

> The furnished room. I am in the heart of Manhattan, August 1928. I am looking for a place to sleep. God Almighty, I never saw so many people alive. The whole thing is a dream. . . . The bridge. I walk across that bridge at nightfall once, Manhattan to Brooklyn, and laughed. To be there on the bridge, alive, walking, Manhattan's million windows glowing, electricity and progress, night and sadness, to Brooklyn. Wherever you are, you are alone.

But being alone is not something to be feared:

> A man is seldom not alone. He is not alone only when God is near by. I used to meet God in many places. In the subways. On Broadway, his

gentle face in a mob of twisted faces, in the weary smile of an overworked stenographer, going wearily to a small furnished room.

A new kind of heroism is communicated to him, and he asks,

I don't know who perish first, the weak or the strong. I think the strong.
Timelessness in them cannot accept contemporary horror. They die.
The weak turn away from themselves and are protected, living two
lives at one time. The surface life and the inward one waiting patiently
for another century. It will come. Horror cannot exist forever. The
inward life will lift its broken body out of the nightmare and breathe.

And that "inward life" somehow does breathe, in the random
examples he places before us. A big mountain girl from the hills
of Sierra Nevada, spending her first day at school at the age of
fourteen: "Neither ashamed nor embarrassed, . . . she talked with
words hewn solidly from substance." And the small Greek boy,
called Socrates, in his home town, Fresno, who "couldn't feel badly
about being caught with stolen raisins [from the packing house] in
his pockets." When stopped, "he would stop speaking in English.
He would answer their questions in Modern Greek. Dumb look.
Greek words." He would say, "They got more raisins in that packing house than all the people in the world can eat. Who the hell do
they think they are?" These Greeks, the writer concludes, "were
natural-born philosophers."
Rebellion for Saroyan has a new face that includes the likes of
"the dancing fool," Caspar,

a black Armenian of the vineyard country, a free slave in America,
busting loose with the glory of his body, . . . his arms strong with the
love of life, hugging the girl, embracing America, the new world, the
loping easy-going world of the west. . . . Black Caspar bending his
beak of Asia Minor over the glowing face of Miss Nebraska.

Black Caspar, like Tom Sawyer, "myself and yourself," will all
take part in the author's effort to "grab hold of this continent . . .
and reveal the bright gem of our mortality." "Only the mind cannot
die," he determines,

and the smiling mind makes an everlasting ripple in the void of the
universe. . . . Laughter is the only thing. Laugh down the cruel. Laugh
down the evil.

He has no time for death. "The races of this earth are many, and
each of us is of every race, and this is a narrative of the living,"
he continues.

Invariably into this narrative comes the eager boy Saroyan remembers himself as being, tearing around town on his bike at daybreak, whistling "all the symphonies Bach and Brahms forgot to
compose."

I dreamed, laughed, wept, waited, watched. I wanted to say something.
I wanted to make. I wanted to bring about equilibrium in all things.
I wanted to shape all essences into one imperishable body of grace
and humor.

To do so, the boy has "wrestled with God and laughed," knowing
that "if one man is pure in heart, the earth is saved." There is
missionary zeal in his determination to "show them God in
themselves."

I will talk to them in the language of revelation. If they are deaf, I will
give them hearing. If they are blind, I will give them sight. If they are
crippled, I will make them whole. If they thieve, I will teach them
charity. If they kill, I will teach them love. . . . Their frowns I will turn
into smiling. Their weeping I will change into laughter. Their envy I
will change into goodwill. . . . I will resurrect the germ of life in them.
    But whence will that power come? "I? Who the hell am I? I am a
small boy always in trouble: Trouble at home, trouble in school, trouble
in my heart."

The answer at hand is one that Saroyan will always seek to
remember:

You must be as children again. The germ is cleanest in the child, in the
child-heart, and the wisdom of the child is the wisdom of God.

And so he asks that we recapture the child's experience of seeing
things for the first time: "An apple is an apple, but for the love of
God look at an apple before you eat it and you will become a man
alive, for a moment a man who cannot die." Like Whitman (or
Robert Burns) he glories in seeing little things alive—"the shy,
secretive gopher of the warm summer prairie. The field mouse . . .
that small eye seeing." But he goes Whitman and Burns one better
by juxtaposing the relationship or man and mouse to the ruling
mechanism of the universe:

To be thus a mouse. In the cosmos, a mouse. By men despised. And
yet with the ferocious instinct of the mice to live. I laughed the splendor
of the lowly despised. . . . If it could be known which of us is most
truly God's, I think it would be you. . . . To breathe I need the poise

of Socrates. You draw breath from the vast lungs of the universe. To stand I need the support of Jesus. The holy pneumatics of time and space and substance fix you lightly at the center of your world. . . . My untutored eye can journey and dwell within the universe of Cezanne, but who knows what microscopic magnitude unfolds itself from grain of sand before your silent stare?

Without the support of the cosmos, man needs faith and hope. And so we dream.

"Baby" ends with a jazzy newsreel, a collage of unsung heroes, "seldom seen, yet always present."

Sang baby O maybe. Sang motors and wheels till Saturday night in America, and a hundred thousand jazz orchestras sang *So come sit by my side if you love me.* . . . In and out, a hundred million faces of man, Big Joe, the great American, the rube from everywhere, weeping baby O maybe. . . . Big Joe, who laid the tracks across the continent . . . and on Saturday night sang baby o maybe. Who shaved his leathery face, put on his Sunday clothes, and went looking for the loosest of men, or a wife. Who fell dead of wounds of war . . . who lived once and never died. . . . This American Big Joe. Yourself and myself.

From this fluid, undefined mix of the dreamed and the dreamer, Saroyan would find the best specimen for metamorphic conversion—the magical children of his later stories and the free spirits that helped shape his "new American theatre."

The notion of life as a balancing act between private dream and the realities of the everyday world had fueled Saroyan's earliest inspiration; in the touching yet ironical story of "The Daring Young Man on the Flying Trapeze" the spiritual acrobatics of his frail hero was at best rewarded by a noble death that affirmed the strength and totality of his humanity. That this search for equilibrium was a principle essential to the highest form of life (and hence of art) was something Saroyan would repeatedly uphold, and indeed it can be traced as a theme throughout most of his work. It carried a special significance in the stories of childhood and childlike adults that comprised his next book, *Little Children,* since it implies how deep-seated is the impulse to meld dream with reality. Deeply distressed that Bennett Cerf had called the book "a juvenile" and "trivial" at that, Saroyan had countered that the stories were "about children and childlike people."[9] And when the book appeared in 1937 under the imprint of Harcourt, Brace & Co., Saroyan was vindicated, though not without reservations of a kind that accompany a facile reading of the book.

His perennial *New York Times* critic, Harold Strauss, for instance, while conceding "an increasing maturity," warned readers that by "arbitrarily circumscribing his point of view by limiting his consciousness . . . to the consciousness of a single human atom," Saroyan was skirting "the obligation of omniscience." The review was, in fact, contradictory, since it pointed out that the stories were more than childhood memories: they contained not only children but

> immigrant Yugoslavs and Greeks and especially Armenians. . . . There is rebellion against monotony and temporary relief in drinking and gambling; and there is the great loneliness in which men live their lives and which invariably brings from Saroyan his deepest notes of compassion.[10]

Strauss's assumption that Saroyan's potential remained unfulfilled in his not writing a novel of total objectivity with "purposive actions through a patterned world"[11] blinds him to the underlying meaning that the book's title itself suggests. Nowhere in this review is there a reference to Saroyan's humor, much less an attempt to define it; nor to the sharp demographic awareness that enables him to reach to the core of ethnic vulnerability; and no mention, finally, of the allegorical thrust that enables the writer to extract from a commonplace situation a universal meaning.

One of the book's most often quoted stories, "The Sunday Zeppelin," broaches the dichotomy between dream and reality on the simplest level. Two small boys, brothers, dreaming of taking off on a world of adventure, save their nickels (meant for the Sunday school plate) to buy a zeppelin advertised for a dollar in *Boys' World,* only to find when it arrives that it is nothing but a small toy made of tissue that crumbles as they try to construct it. Saroyan makes the whole story stand on the pain and frustration of a child's experience with a dream betrayed. Told from the point of view of the younger child, the story is rendered with minimal direct commentary that nonetheless conveys with a teasing humor and arch-social overtones the pitfalls the innocent face. We are witness to the action from the minute that Luke and Mark confess to each other that they are withholding money from the Sunday school plate ("that's a sin, Luke said. I know it, I said. You didn't either.") to their extravagant faith in all possibility ("Two people can go up in [the zepplin], he said. Me and Ernest West.") to the sibling rivalry that threatens the dream of the younger boy ("I ain't a baby, I said. I'm eight and you're ten. . . . Please, Luke, I said, let me go up in the zeppelin. I'll let you go around the world with me in my boat."). The boys bicker over other things and call each other names, but uppermost in their minds is the zeppelin. Mark wakes up at night "thinking about being up in the zeppelin." The more eager his pleas become, the more Luke rejects him, resorting finally to the exclusivity of a made-up language from which the younger boy is barred.

Saroyan's method is greatly altered from the earlier childhood stories in which verbal richness engulfs the actions of his characters and what actually happens in a particular moment is filtered through the writer's memory in its broader contours. Here, the characters are allowed to fend for themselves as if finally severed from the ventriloquist's lap. When, for instance, Miss Valentine, the organist in the Presbyterian church who "played as if she were sore at somebody and wanted to get even" gets up to pray for the missionaries in Africa, reminding the congregation that "we have erred and strayed from Thy ways like lost sheep," Mark typically and impiously adds, "And a lot of other stuff." Mark's impiety directs the reader to the false piety (worse for being adult) surrounding the boys in Sunday school. The fact that the boys went at all was because their father reasoned that "it would do less harm than good. . . . [I]t's good discipline." But Mark is not immune to the pompous Mr. Parker, who tries convincing the boys that the movies are evil so that they will save their money for the church plate. When the children confess their "sin" in withholding the nickels to their father, he counters the teacher by giving the boys a dollar to go see a Tarzan movie with the proviso that they clean up the garage and Mark be allowed to go up in the plane when it arrives. The father's motivation is left unexamined, but the implication in terms of the correction of "discipline" and compassion for the blow he knows will come is unescapable and touching. When the small flat package finally arrives, the boys' responses are also on target: the impetuous Luke faces the end of his dream by running to the barn and turning his anguish into aimless action, nailing boards, while Mark, who has already begun his battle with lost dreams, merely vents his anger verbally at the perpetrators.

There's not only truth here, but reverence for the child's world. Because the child's innocence and his particular brand of humor are never mocked, it becomes easy for most adults to recall with regret a lost dimension of themselves. What Saroyan finally suggests is that childhood is not only a period of life but a location we carry around with us into adulthood, one that surfaces whenever there arises a conflict with what exists and what one desires to have exist. It becomes an important stage in a pilgrim's progress to which we are committed.

In *Little Children* Saroyan is also trying to establish a correspondence between the early dream people carry around with them and the dream or image he sees as endemic to America. As the son of an immigrant, he has learned the hard way to "accommodate" in order to survive, developing along the way a sharp eye for the real thing and its imitation or distortion that spell disaster. His stories are often meant to bring back into focus what is necessary to our well-being. "Laughing Sam" is about a teenager, "some sort of Jew, small and intense," who was always laughing, most of all when he least felt like it. As a newsboy, "he was out to make good." Like the little boy in "The Oranges" who was told to smile so he could sell more oranges, Sam has learned to laugh even when the joke is on him. Undernourished, overworked, foolish-looking, "he is not simply out of place in the press-room, but out of place in the world." And the self-fulfilled prophecy announced in his tragically noble stance dooms him, despite the front he creates. Only when the narrator, a fellow newsboy, probes finally behind it all is it revealed that the laughter was an inverted kind of crying. When he dies in a freak accident, the narrator gives the story a fable-like ending:

> He lived sixteen years in this world and laughed all the time. He wept from the beginning of his life, ten centuries ago, to the end of it, fifteen years ago.

The pathos of Laughing Sam stems from the fact that he has no dream to sustain him: "He was man on earth at his worst. Taking everything and laughing about it." He thus becomes an easy victim to unalterable circumstances, or what we call "reality."

Among these circumstances, here only suggested, is racial prejudice. Confronted by Sam's hidden fear, his boss, Buzz Martin, displays an easy tolerance that hides an ingrained contempt. "Buzz Martin was a great guy," the narrator says somewhat tongue in cheek,

> He was tough. He used to cuff the boys around when they got out of line. . . . He was an American, as we used to call them in my home town, but he wasn't like most Americans: in my home town fifteen years ago an American was an incompetent who despised people of other races because they weren't incompetent. Martin was OK. He took a broader view: he didn't care what you happened to be, just so

you were OK, and if you weren't, he didn't blame it on your race. He just put you in your place with a clout on the ear.

In these stories Saroyan usually deals with prejudice in a covert way, his sense of humor and his delight in the energy and spunk of the larger part of humanity overcoming any bitterness that has seared him in the past. He is amused and charmed by people's capacity to endure and especially by the extravagant reach toward which some aim. In one story that amounts to little more than a demographic sketch, he reveals, for instance, how the eagerness to "make good" or to "amount to something," creates false hopes and veers innocent immigrants from their true dreams. "O Higher Accountancy, O Traffic Management" focuses on the competitive spirit that becomes obsessive in a Santa Clara Valley immigrant family when one of the children turns out to be as smart as the American boy next door. When the mothers got together "they talked about their little boys who were going to be important men in the world some day." The American boy, Toby, hasn't bothered to make up his mind "just how he was going to be great," but Emo, the Slovanian boy, "was going to be a great doctor one day and the next day a great lawyer and the day after a great something else." After their graduation, the boys become celebrities of a sort, "maybe smarter than any two people in the whole valley," but to their parents, they become a source of irritation as they sit on their laurels, oblivious to the demands of job hunting. But the wheel turns—and the boys' sights are lowered as they move from one ordinary job to another. "Toby almost got to be human," the younger brother notes. "He didn't make fun of anything any more." He settles for studying "higher accountancy" by mail (the brother inquires "if he had already studied lower accountancy and he said not to bother him"). Not to be outdone, the Slovak boy studies traffic management, also by mail. The parents sitting on their front porches proudly brag about their respective boys "studying," and though Toby's brother can't quite figure out just what they will do, "I figured it would be something marvelous."

The slightly mocking tone of the story comes through almost in spite of Saroyan's clear-eyed observation of the children's urge to improve their lot, despite their parents' drastically different measure of success. The values may be skewed, Saroyan seems to be saying, but the will and spirit remain unshaken.

If the humor remains muted in most of these stories, there are signs of a new extravagant streak. The direction he chooses comes naturally to a writer consistently caught up with the new American. What is gently exposed as different or odd behavior derives from the juxtaposition of a predominant ethnic trait or stance and the more general prevailing order of things. What Saroyan sees as "Greek" or "Slovak" or even "Armenian" may not actually be unique to those national groups—but it appears to be so because any deviance in behavior is easily identified in a small group and readily affixed to it. The transplanted Greek, Peter Karamakoulos, in "The Only Guy in Town" assumes heroic proportions by virtue of an inherent, obsessive urge to dominate his life's circumstances, such as they are. A man "who had a kind heart but liked to drink," Pete's additional weaknesses are women and the need to prove his physical mettle. "He kept shoving people around and telling them about the athletes of Athens and the runners and warriors." But when he is defeated three times in a wrestling match with a gigantic Yugoslav, Pete's compatriots form a committee to stop him from disgracing "our ancient civilization." An illiterate, Pete gets his news of world events (it's the time of World War I) through the local newsboy, the story's narrator; this eleven-year-old boy teasingly exploits the Greek's delusions of grandeur by allowing him to believe that Greece is making major victories. When the boy's ruse is exposed, Pete chases him for three miles, until the boy recognizes he has good reason to be "sore." "It's not nice to conquer half the world and then find out it's all a dream." Pete's dogged will to run an all-night hamburger parlor single-handed is doomed to failure, as are his many casual encounters with women. But for the narrator he still rates: "Pete was somebody," the boy feels sure. "Nobody in town was somebody the way Pete was." Feared and hated and finally jailed, he somehow makes his escape from the small town to Frisco, "a town his size."

Saroyan's playfulness with his subject allows him on the one hand to sidetrack moralizing, and on the other to keep his eye on the socially vulnerable human quality: Pete's eagerness to break out of the bounds limiting that creative lust for life Saroyan associates with the ancient Greeks.

The excesses of individual ambition so humorously viewed in Pete's case have a darker message in "The Man Who Got Fat," which contrasts the lives of two of the fastest messenger boys at Fresno's telegraph office. On the one hand is the easygoing Armenian boy (the narrator) who scorns big business; on the other, the ambitious Jewish boy from San Francisco, big "roly-poly" Nathan Katz, who rises to the top but dies of food, drink, and too much wealth. The Armenian, it is immediately revealed, is only peripherally concerned about rising up the executive ladder: His more deep-seated concern is being considered intelligent: "In an elevator I always removed my hat." (He prides himself in being "a model young man."):

> I used to help drunkards home. I used to do little favors for young and unhappy men who were unhappy with their sweethearts, their wives, or somebody else's wife. I used to break my neck to be a gentleman. I didn't want any white riff-raff making cracks about the manners of Armenians.

Added to this obsessive rebounding to prejudice is the boy's reservations about "machines that get fat with the time out of the lives of men, with the blood out of their lives." "If the machine makes a lot of money," he muses, "the money belongs to the slaves who *are* the machine." His ambition remains limited to becoming at most the sixteenth vice president of the Postal Telegraph Company.

Not so Nathan Katz, who moves on to the "shipping racket" and gets "busy as hell making money." He ships grapes and peaches and goes on to shipping "everything else that grew." While Katz cleans up, the Armenian, learning "all there was to know about any racket," steps out of them all and moves to Frisco. ("I had a lousy time of it, but I got by," he confesses.) Katz, on the other hand, slowly loses his shift, succumbs to drink, loses sleep, grows fat, and dies. Remembering the vital boy that Katz was, the Armenian was bewildered to learn of his sad end. "What the hell does it all come to?" he despairs. "I've got use for six or seven things in this world, and dying of this sort is all seven of them."

Has Saroyan rolled the dice too heavily against the go-getting Katz? Does an element of moral superiority creep into his comparison of the two nationals—the Armenian and the Jew? Today's ethnic sensitized readers may easily take to this view. But in 1937 the comparison was not without its social validity—Armenians were still low in the social scale as compared to Jews who had forged ahead to amass large fortunes, and Saroyan's sharp-eyed critique aimed at the same time to restore a sort of balance in showing that success hinged on attitude: Though the two boys begin as equals— "the fastest two guys in the world in our fields"—the Armenian's revulsion from the nonhuman aspects of the success game drags him behind the Jew. It also saves him from the tragic end of too much success too soon. All this is implied, never stated. The shorthand narrative style Saroyan has begun to borrow from the fable allows him to edify without becoming polemical.

Midway in the story, in a kind of aside, the narrator establishes the destiny of two ethnic figures within the confines of "the warm valley in the fine little town." There is an ambivalence in the narrator's feelings:

> By God I loved that crazy town. I loved all them fine ordinary people. They didn't want us to move in among them on account of we were Armenians. Our poor friends and neighbors, God Almighty.

Turning ironical, he goes on to reveal the town's prejudice against the dark-skinned Armenians. "Black or white, . . . they didn't like the manners of the Armenians. They didn't like the loud way Armenians laughed" (a laughter Saroyan comes to identify with rebellion in his later stories). Katz's death, which the narrator sees as resulting from an overeagerness to break his bonds in the town, only reinforces the sense of futility about fighting the tide of small-town mentality and values.

Taking the longer view not only softens the impact of resentment, in Saroyan's case it creates an atmosphere of pacification. With all its ingrained bigotry, "the crazy town" of his youth finds it possible to reconcile and bring into close association the shrewd but kindly Armenian rancher (the narrator's Uncle Mihran) and the easygoing but dauntless Mexican fruitworker in "My Uncle and the Mexicans." The latter offers his labor if the rancher will also house his wife, his son, three daughters, a lame cousin, four dogs, a cat, a guitar, pots and pans, etc. The narrator explains that though it breaks their hearts to admit it, the Mexicans want to work for the Armenian rancher. When the uncle protests that he doesn't need help, Juan Cabral amicably but irrationally wants to know how much the work pays. In the end, somewhat absurdly, though humanly—as a result of his exposure to the plight of the family—the uncle agrees to hire the Mexicans at a rate higher than he was paying Japanese workers. "I am honored, said my Uncle," the nephew reports.

> He was all mixed up. It was the dogs mostly [who were prancing around without aim], but it was also the five Mexican children and the Mexicans' magnificent manners.

And although the uncle has no way of knowing that the Mexicans will learn to do the job, he concurs with his nephew that "this Mexican is going to do the trick" and make him solvent this winter.

This story is hard to convey fully in its essence, for it is all in the telling, with the narrator playing an active role as conciliator, drawing on the good will of both negotiators while letting the reader in on the humorous non sequiturs of their actions and conversations. Now and then the narrator throws in a bit of hard social reality, as when the uncle asks archly what the children eat and the nephew replies, "Beans and Mexican bread, . . . stuff that ain't supposed to be good for you." And later, when his uncle fears that the Mexican might steal his tractor, the nephew says, "No, . . . It's much too heavy." (Earlier, the nephew had established that "the stealing they do never amounts to anything.")

Saroyan has said somewhere that his writing "has always been profoundly realistic if not ever superficially so. I don't think it is sentimental either, although it is a very sentimental thing to be a human being." The reality principle and the human principle (I belabor the terms because they are consistently and consciously embraced) are never absent from the stories in *Little Children*. With humor acting as intermediary, these stories are never weighed down by "meaning," but rather send the reader away with a smile, sometimes knowing, but more often wistful, or simply amused.

Another "principle" also operates in *Little Children* and gives proof of the writer's expanding vision. We might call it "the poetic principle" (without in any way suggesting Poe)—something we have sensed from the beginning in Saroyan. But in the past, the narrator's presence was so dominant that the "poetry" had surfaced chiefly in lyrical passages where it depended on language and mood. This led one critic of Saroyan to assume that Saroyan's characters are always "poets of feeling."[12] That assumption would deny the presence of so many different characters in Saroyan's world. It is, rather, that as the writer distanced himself from his characters, he came to see a poetic pattern in life that often escapes the person living it. He now recognizes its presence anywhere— in a child's first day at school, for instance. In "The First Day of School," it is intimated not through the child's consciousness, but through that of the housekeeper, Amy, as she takes the child to school and brings him back home. Amy finds the school building ugly, is intimidated by the halls and rooms with their particular smell; she imagines the boy's fright and despises Mr. Barber, the principal:

> She tried to let [the boy] know how much she loved him and how sorry she was about everything, but couldn't say anything.

When she comes to pick him up, she is amazed that he hasn't changed, that "he wasn't hurt, or perhaps utterly unalive, murdered." Later, when the boy reveals how easily he has adjusted to his new life, the housekeeper's mood changes again: "for some reason tears came to eyes." She has been a witness to the loss of innocence, and she knows there is no turning back. Again, in this story, it is the smallest details—like the boy's mouthing of half-understood, slightly vulgar jokes he has just learned—that draws the story to the poetic center of life as it is experienced by another person.

The poetic principle saves another rather simple demographic story, "Countryman, How Do You Like America?," from simple nostalgic sentimentality or ethnic realism. Sarkis, the melancholic peasant from Gultik, in Armenia, flourishes in California, saves enough to buy a house, marries an immigrant Armenian girl, and manages to successfully educate his children. But instead of feeling proud and happy, he is inconsolable, lonely, and remote from his surroundings. "Ahkh," he complains, "How do I like it? What shall I say? Go; come; and with men known and unknown turn trays. That is all." The poetry that emanates from the longing for home— a feeling so remote from the American—is made both amusing and touching in the brief recital of the man's life, which is told like a fable from the initial "There was a man by the name of Sarkis" to the final repetition of the refrain: "How do I like it? Come, go."

More unexpectedly, perhaps, the poetic principle is revealed in the grace of being and in one's relation to others. In "The Cat," Saroyan brings it down to basics. A little girl strikes up a conversation with a workman repairing a sidewalk. He is introduced to us as a man with

an honest, simple mind and kindly heart, and there was in him the capacity to react youthfully to anything good that came his way.

Without being condescending, the workman filters the world through the child's eyes, responding to her questions about his imaginary cat with wholehearted conviction and empathy. In just an instant, he becomes important to the little girl and to the boy who later joins her. Remembering the workman as "a nice man," they engrave the words "the cat" on the soft cement he has left behind, so they can keep the man with the cat "in [their] memory." While it is hard to imagine this story as a poem, the feeling that it evokes is closer to poetry than so much that one can remember reading in verse.

The Poetic Principle

In the next three volumes of stories, Saroyan repeatedly returns to the poetic principle, though hardly ever at the expense of the reality principle or the inherent comic strain that now brings it all together to create a style that will become his signature. As his troop of characters takes over, the writer himself becomes less visible, or at least less uniformly so. He is now able to assume the artist's privilege of maneuvering a variety of views and voices. It is important to keep this in mind as his discursive dialogues become more studied and self-conscious.

It has been one of Saroyan's misfortunes that his narrators or leading figures have usually been taken as personifications of the author, despite his oft-stated position that he wants "to make an American character, the American out of all the lives of our country." It is especially important to keep this in mind when the stigma of "sentimentality" is raised; though it may take a close reading at times, it is usually possible to distinguish the author's response from that of the archetypal character he has created. Indeed, as he gains in experience of his craft, Saroyan learns the subtle art of using character as a foil for his continuing inner dialectic. Having given himself free reign to discuss the relationship between life and letters in *Three Times Three,* he goes on to show how in fact they fuse in his work.

Though he has persistently denied the need for "form" as such, stating "any form I achieve in art I have already achieved in myself," he is clearly developing a more traditional artistic viability in *The Trouble with Tigers* (1938), *Love, Here Is My Hat* (1938), and *Peace, It's Wonderful* (1939). Though each of these volumes contains ample evidence of "the Saroyan story" as a genre unique into itself, it is in the last book of stories of the pre-World War II years, *My Name is Aram* (1940), that its apotheosis is reached.

"Romance," an element inseparable from the short story since time immemorial, increasingly comes to tempt Saroyan in this period. Sentiment—love—so endemic to this writer, one might think, would be easy for him to handle, but it holds pitfalls for Saroyan, bringing him at times perilously close to what generally passes for "sentimentality." If contemporary readers have little tolerance for an excess of sentiment, the critics of this period, steeped in naturalism, had even less. Called by some "a sentimental romanticist," and by others "a complete romantic," Saroyan in fact reverted to a paradigmatic concept of romance as idealization and dream of unattainable love. The "passion" that transfixes his lovers, from his earliest stories, has less to do with sexuality than with a platonic humanism; in effect no more than an intensification of sentiment felt in any kind of human relationship, love at its apex becomes almost Dantesque in its power to metamorphose the lover. This is not to say that sexuality is missing from the Saroyan story, but when it's there, it is a banal, physical manifestation that takes the form of sheer lust, a momentary satisfaction far removed from "true love." (The idealized harlot, a Saroyan creation, is a social/ human scar that arouses compassion but leaves no tangible residue of relationship behind.)

The polarity of pure and impure love that writers like Carson McCullers and J. D. Salinger would later lift to a quasi-mystical plane has a strong moral connotation for Saroyan, who views love in its widest context—its power to redeem our humanity and bridge the void that separates us from one another.

In some of the early stories, love is a kind of alchemy posed over one's wildest dreams. For Saroyan's adolescents it is synonymous with the adoration of a person of the opposite sex who seems to be an extension of oneself—a schoolboy "crush" that verges on a spiritual quest for self-identity. The fifteen-year-old boy in "And Man," who has discovered overnight "a vaster form of [himself] as a man," imagines that the girl in class whom he loves from afar will understand his transformation because she had infused her being into his:

> She was of me, I had taken her name, her form, the outward one, and I had breathed her into me, joining her meaning into my meaning.

But when she reveals her insensitivity to his uniqueness, the boy is sadly disillusioned; he knows he will not be able to speak to her of his love, of its meaning to him *"and to the earth and the universe and to man"* (italics mine).

And in another story, "Laughter," where memory is still the filter separating the author from his creation, Saroyan injects an ambiguity that allows his boyish illusion a place in the wider context of human connectedness. Ben, a ten-year-old boy of Italian descent, has been disrupting the classroom with his compulsive laughter and is held after school by his young teacher and told to laugh for an hour as his punishment. The boy is puzzled at first, then contrite. He was

> sorry not for himself but for her. . . . She was a young girl, a substitute teacher, and there was that sadness in her, so far away and so hard to understand.

Watching her erase words from the blackboard as they sit in the empty classroom, the boy senses her tenseness and suddenly sees her as a person toward whom he has nothing but goodwill. Bewildered by their antagonistic situation, he thinks about

> the strange feelings of people, the secretiveness, each person hidden within himself, wanting something and always getting something else, wanting to give something and always giving something else.

In order to continue laughing, he imagines "really comical situations everywhere, the whole town, people walking in the streets, trying to look important." Then, suddenly seeing tears in the teacher's eyes, he is filled with a sense of communion: "he wanted to know why or how it was with her, inside, the part that was secret."

With compassion replacing the anger in his laughter, he thinks of "all the pathetic things in the world":

> the things good people cried about, the stray dogs in the streets, the tired horses being whipped, stumbling, the timid people being smashed inwardly by fat and cruel people.

As his laughter becomes the protective coating of his vulnerability, he finds in this perfect stranger a conspirator of love:

> The two of them in the empty class-room, naked in their loneliness and bewilderment, brother and sister, both of wanting the same cleanliness and decency of life, both of them wanting to share the truth of the other, and yet, somehow, both of them alien, remote and alone.

In this moment of illumination in which love is connected with ultimate goodness, Ben sounds like no ten-year-old one is likely to meet in life or literature. Yet the portrait remains affecting because the fragments of truth revealed need no validation—a patent authenticity is irrelevant.

Love that holds a holy quality is inevitably doomed for lovers who must contend with the real world. In the early stories when Saroyan still closely identifies with the lover, love is equated with the unachieveable dream. Even then the effect is more bittersweet than sentimental, as in "At Sundown," which was originally published in *Scribner's Magazine* in 1935 but appeared in *Inhale and Exhale* a year later. The narrator is recollecting a lost love and ruefully explaining to himself how at age twenty he fell in love with a girl named Myrna "who was like nothing else I have seen alive, bird and flower and field and brook, all implied in her strange reality." He is bemused by "the frantic need" he had felt in those days "to know a truth of life more magnificent than any truth I now know," and dreamed of acquiring it through Myrna, when, of course, it was impossible, "since I was mortal, no less than she," and it would end by his buying himself new clothes and leaving him with "a new set of ideas . . . less magnificent."

Reconstructing in his mind the miraculous feelings they had shared without once touching each other, he argues simply that they were "inevitable events of growth, slowly or swiftly pushed aside, as the case may be, since they lead only to most profound sorrows, or to death itself." Like most young men he had expected love to make him "whole," giving him his full identity. But when their love was finally consummated, "it became the same again: as with the others. He wanted life. Here, in this place." Timeless love fades and normal life takes over. Myrna ends up marrying "some young fellow with a good job," while he goes to buy himself a new suit and hat, learning to "forget the whole thing, and stay alive as long as possible, puny and weak and mortal." Unlike the gambler in "Two Days Lost in Kansas City," who is instantly metamorphosed by a fleeting glimpse of an impossible dream, this lover sensibly separates dream from reality, holding at bay the distortions wrought by love.

One looks for a clue in the writer's life to account for any changes or variations in the love stories of his next three books. It was my good fortune to come on such a clue in the winter of 1988. Even though we can only guess at the extent of its importance to Saroyan's life and work, we now have grounds for speculation that he had a serious romantic attachment—lasting at least three years—before he met and married Carol Marcus in 1943.[13] Sanora Babb (Mrs. James Wong Howe) herself attests that Saroyan fell deeply in love with her in 1932 or 1933 (when he was twenty-five or twenty-six and she was twenty-seven or twenty-eight) and asked to marry her. Ms. Babb revealed this to me when I contacted her after I had read the copies of a sheaf of letters Saroyan had written to her in the 1930s. The two had become acquainted through each other's writings at a time when both were seriously involved in their literary careers and were getting published in the little magazines. Because she lived in Los Angeles and he in San Francisco at the time, their friendship began by correspondence, from April 1932 until August 1941, with some bare stretches when they were within each other's reach. It is these Saroyan letters—thirty-four of them—which I was able to see at the Bancroft Library of the University of California at Berkeley, where they have been lodged since 1984. Expressed with full candor and acutely introspective, they reveal, as nothing previously available of that period, the intellectual and emotional depths that were fomenting in the young writer.

Saroyan's letters leave no doubt as to his feelings for Ms. Babb. But because we have no corresponding text from her, we can only surmise her responses to him at the time. None of the letters to him was saved, and feelings of this nature are not to be fully trusted in retrospect. In her eighties, a widow living in Hollywood and still engaged in literary activity, she remembers Saroyan fondly but disclaims having been in love with him—"though I must have responded somewhat to William's declarations," she admits. She recalls that "when we were young, we [herself and Saroyan] were just a couple of free spirits"; but she had already started seeing her future husband, "so I had to tell William this, later." She adds, "I was honest with him . . . so many years ago, I think I was! I can't remember all the details."[14] Thus a dream of "unattainable love"—something not alien to the Saroyan canon—would hang over his life in those early years of his career.

Let me add here, parenthetically, that I bring up this new biographical material with some reservation. This is partly because as a critic I am only mildly committed to the notion of "cause and effect" as a guide to artistic development. But also because in Saroyan's case "cause and effect" are uncommonly reversed. Any outside influence on Saroyan is almost always prompted by a deepseated inclination, so that he seems to be impelling an event or action to justify an attitude or feeling he already entertains. Thus, to assume that a certain love affair altered or tempered his view of love is complicated by the likelihood that the relationship existed and turned out as it did because he so wished it. The value of this discovery to the Saroyan critic is that it now becomes easier to spot a lapse or variant in the writer's stance, and this in turn helps us see more clearly what is essentially unique and original about it.

What remains a puzzle, biographically speaking, is why we find no mention of either Ms. Babb or any other strong romantic attachment in the many scattered accounts of Saroyan's life in the 1930s (his own and others') and why, indeed, to this day no one who claims to have been close to the writer appears to know of Ms. Babb. Of course, there is one simple reason why this has not come up. For a long time it was assumed that Saroyan's love life had but one object: his typewriter. The initial image that he himself created was of a struggling young man, locked in a cold San Francisco flat, furiously and obsessively turning out stories that he couldn't sell. That impression was quickly replaced by the image of a brash, overconfident young "genius" who came to razzle-dazzle fame in 1934. In was easy enough to conclude that the egocentric Saroyan, never absent from the limelight after his first volume of stories was published, remained disengaged, and temporarily at least satisfied to act the playboy in one-night stands.[15] Indeed, no reference is made to a particular woman even in Budd Schulberg's lively account of Saroyan's early years in Hollywood (1936–37), when he was trying his hand at writing film scripts and gambling his earnings away on horse racing. To this enterprising young writer who was now hustling his stories in Stanley Rose's Hollywood Book Store, a permanent love would have been a distraction. Having received no immediate encouragement from Random House for a second volume of his stories, Saroyan got busy aligning his two great admirers, Schulberg and Rose, to act as editor and publisher in a private publishing enterprise. But Saroyan soon wore them out, and the project was dropped. "Saroyan stories did not develop slowly like orchids," Schulberg recalls, "but popped up overnight like dandelions." Before turning away from this euphoric moment in Saroyan's career, Schulberg does make an oblique reference to "Saroyan's girl friend, . . . an attractive young lady in a Beverley Hills bookstore who was much taken with Bill." But the anecdote that follows is told only in support of the image of Saroyan as "a bull-in-the-china-shop ladies' man" who would not hesitate to call a woman acquaintance in the predawn hours to come and keep him company.[16]

A more telling observation of Saroyan in this period is made by Alfred Kazin in his memoir *Starting Out in the Thirties.* When the writer stormed the New York scene soon after he had been fired by Schulberg Sr., he impressed the critic as the personification of "the daring young man on the flying trapeze." What Kazin found "exhilarating" was that Saroyan conveyed "a tower of strength . . . [in] defiance, as he liked to say, of meaninglessness, uselessness, unimportance, insignificance, poverty, enslavement, ill-health, despair, madness." And, he adds significantly: "Though it was an act, it was no act to him."[17] This succinct comment suggests the difficulty Saroyan was facing and would continue to face in adjusting the dramatic identity he had created for himself to the reality of his life. Because the two had become intertwined, it would make a measure of difficulty for his writing as well.

Though we can never be sure whether Ms. Babb's presence in

Saroyan's life affected the tenor of his romantic stories, her "reality" clearly serves to support a view that needs to be emphasized. After the publication of his first book (and I speak only in terms of his fiction), nothing that happened to Saroyan could deflect him from his determined—if not always steady—course of withdrawal from the autobiographical self to a self more integral to his art. "Any form I achieve in art I have already achieved in myself" is how he has tried to explain the equation governing his artistic development.

In the process of "creating" himself—and his art—(the "act" of which Kazin speaks), Saroyan was looking for that special woman who would complement the "truth" of his being. Sanora Babb, who entered his life serendipitously, seemed to fit the bill: a thoughtful, gifted young woman, as he first learned from her writing, she proved on further acquaintance to have a "truth" and independent spirit of her own. Though a declaration of love was long in coming—love expressed in writing has an elastic existence, stretching and collapsing with the verbal facility at the lover's command—the very fact that Saroyan pressed Ms. Babb for as long as he did shows that this was more than mere infatuation. Though their relationship was grounded in an intellectual exchange (his long letters attest that she also played the role of confidante), a sense of urgency and dependence soon gave Saroyan's true feelings away; and when he asserts at last the extreme limit to which his frustration has led him, we are left with no doubt that he has accepted the risk of a permanent love. Yet he is ever realistic, making clear to Sanora that he lacks a visible anchor in his life.

Though at this time he has begun to write a novel (*Trapeze over the Universe*) and has succeeded in selling his short stories, he has no sense of progression. "I feel pretty sick of the falsity of my life," he tells her, "I suppose I am looking in the direction of nowhere."[18] This is expressed in the same letter of May 1934 in which he declares his "humble" love for her. Though in six months' time his first book will make him famous, he cannot hide from her that his faith in himself is fast slipping away.

Nothing in Saroyan's writing of that period gives us reason to believe that Ms. Babb's "unattainableness" in any way reinforced Saroyan's exalted, "literary" ideas of romantic love. Apart from the storybook framework of their meeting, the real-life experience remained down-to-earth—attached to circumstances. "Falling in love" with Sanora had not been something instantaneous and magical but the cumulation of a prolonged exchange of thoughts and feelings; and it had led to the recognition that the loved one was an individual with needs and desires of her own. The suffering he had experienced in the renunciation of this love had also been real for the "autobiographical self," though ironically enough, it had cleared the air for the evolving persona, for the artist who momentarily welcomed a separation from his life.

The love stories Saroyan had written up to now had had a strong element of angst—an agonizing search for a love that would bolster the lover to "find" himself and dissipate his loneliness. As the prolonged period of adolescence came to an end, the halo Saroyan had placed on the head of the opposite sex would fade by exposure to the mundane world. Love, in his 1935 story, "At Sundown," is still dreamy, but in retrospect, the narrator filters his recollection with a worldly-wise awareness that reality will dispel the dream. But the major sea change that comes over the romantic theme from now on is tied in with Saroyan's new experiments with style and tone. When we disengage the new stories from the older ones which he generally includes from a backlog of unpublished work, we are able to see the beginnings of a new stance: a lighthearted sophistication, sharpened by humor that sometimes verges on mockery, and a brand of playful fantasy that is integrated into everyday life.

In *Love, Here Is My Hat,* there are still stories in which love is magical and transforming, but there is also a recognition that "falling in love" is short-lived and the result of "a dream without the dreamer." The title story, written breezily and almost mockingly, is a romantic tale of urban lovers on the run, replete with all the conceits about lovers living on air and water, absurdly spaced out by a numbing passion—that is, until the end, when the story is turned around to say in a tone of dispassionate realism: *being in love is not a normal state*—it is physically devastating. It is

> too good for anything but birds, . . . too splendid for any form of life that's cluttered up with all the crazy things that the human form of life is cluttered up with . . . too fine for creatures which wear clothes, which inhabit the world, who must work, who must earn money, who cannot live on air and water.

Being no "feathered creature," this lover needs nourishment: "rare roast beef at least once a day." "I'm an American," he declares, "fun is fun, but I know the difference between wholesome fun and love, and love is too good for me or anybody like me." Indeed, his love lasts eleven days, after which he gets well, "with nothing spoiled." Both he and she are over it, and they have supper together to celebrate.

> It was the biggest and finest supper we ever had together, and we enjoyed everything. Isn't it wonderful? she said. It certainly is, I said.

The tone here scarcely matches that of the young Saroyan writing to Ms. Babb in April 1934 telling her he felt "like hell" and could not write because he felt so lonesome for her: "I love you, Sanora . . . and I am miserable."[19] Four years later, humor has become a shield for unresolved feelings; and it is clearly an asset worth mining. Through the introduction of humor, Saroyan can give a clearer contour of an *American* psyche he perceives beyond his own; humor also gives a new dramatic edge to his narrative style, breaking through its discursiveness; and best of all it allows him to highlight his natural flair for dialogue and speech patterns, showing at times the influence of his Hollywood apprenticeship.

All of this, unfortunately, escapes the typical hostile critic of Saroyan—Philip Rahv, in *The Nation*—who attributes Saroyan's new comic style to the fact that success has converted "the bohemian trapeze artist into a regular guy."[20] It does make one wonder if Mr. Rahv had read beyond the first story, for in the third story in that volume, "The Trains," Saroyan reverts to his earlier mode of solemn self-examination. (It is interesting to note that this story appeared originally in *Story* magazine, where the writer had his initial acceptance.) The denouement of "The Trains" has a bitter ring: in the epiphany of a moment, the lover, a young artist, discovers that the girl he has met in the park and fallen in love with is not the girl of his dreams. It is significant—and a sign of the author's intrusion—that the expectation of love is made synonymous with the sense of being "home" where one belongs. The twist here is that although he has returned home from his travels, the hero cannot overcome his feelings of homelessness.

> If home were a place, then he was home. But it was not a place. It was a synchronization of a multitude of subtle and constantly changing substances and rhythms and perceptions.

The young man can't decide whether to go or stay. He stares out of the window at the trains going by, and the train's movement becomes a metaphor signaling the unknown future that both lures and frightens him. For, on the one hand, his artist's intuition tells him that the magic was not in the world. It was in a dimension made out of the longings of the inhabitants of the world; and that's where home was, too.

On the other hand, the train's journey "into the outward light" begins to beckon. The die is finally cast in favor of his leaving when the girl fails to give the sign that she shares his feeling of "home":

the going of the spirit which travels ungeographically, signalling absurdly magnificent destinations . . . the essence of all mortality, eternity, God.

Like so many of Saroyan's "romances," "The Trains" has the outer trappings of a fairy tale; the lovers always meet by chance and are at once enamoured. But while the heroine is held up as the prize, it's the hero who gets all the attention. In "The Trains" a direct reversal of the fairy tale occurs when the heroine fails to meet the test of love's permanence—in this case, her inability to see the metaphoric meaning of the trains—and the tale ends in an unexpected disenchantment, with Eros subsumed to the hero's self-conscious spiritual quest.

Again, in "Romance," a story written about the same time for the *New Directions Anthology* (1938) and reprinted in *Peace, It's Wonderful,* Saroyan returns to his more wide-ranging creative self. This time, the would-be lover is not the pining artist merely *watching* the trains go by, but a rider on the rain, a young man looking (as the redcap observes) "like somebody who might at any moment fall in love, without much urging." The young man, though in other respects rather conventional, does not seem immune to the drama of chance encounter, and he confesses to "daydreaming" as he asks the redcap if he forgot to tip him. Though he is happily looking out the window, acknowledging "a wonderful sense of at last beginning to go places," he doesn't fail to notice a girl sitting across the aisle. Even before he strikes up a conversation, he has already considered the possibility of a romance and of his marrying her "and settling down somewhere in a house with . . . two or three offspring." Although they eventually sit side by side and talk randomly about their pasts, nothing happens in the story beyond the young man's silent projection of a dream:

The sun was strong and warm and the girl was wonderful. Unless he was badly mistaken, or unless he got fired Monday morning, or unless America got into a war and he had to become a soldier and go away and get himself killed for no good reason, he had a hunch somehow he would go to work and get acquainted with the girl and marry her and settle down.

Here, in the readiness to fall in love and the belief that it will change reality, Saroyan is plumbing the emblematic American love story. The idea in itself is not new—it is the Hollywood staple of that time—but what the writer sees behind it is innocent generosity of heart that motivates human action in general. In a mood piece like "Romance" it is barely glimpsed. But when it is more fully manifested in his later work, it becomes an important element in the metamorphosis of love—whether romantically or otherwise experienced.

TOWARD AN AMERICAN MODEL

As the thirties era ends, with its social preoccupations, and as Saroyan grows artistically, the style becomes flexible and adopts an antinaturalism that has elements of symbolism, surrealism, expressionism, and the oriental fable. Saroyan's expanding troupe of characters takes over, and as the "ventriloquist" retires, Saroyan merges his voice with the characters to present a tableau of the America he envisions in some of his best volumes: *My Name is Aram, The Trouble with Tigers, Razzle-Dazzle* (which introduces the short play), *The Whole Voyald* and *The Assyrian and Other Stories.* What needs to be noted and has been missed by many of Saroyan's commentators is that he becomes a depictor of the American scene.

It is not surprising that in the years 1938 and 1939 Saroyan begins to relate the romantic story to the social scene, thereby moving closer to an American Zeitgeist. In "The La Salle Hotel in Chicago," he juxtaposes a hungry, unemployed lover and a soapbox anarchist who preaches cynicism but practices an inborn sentimentality. The idealistic young man has fallen in love with a waitress in a hamburger joint; he wants her not "just to have a little fun," but to marry and settle down with her in "a cozy home," something he can't afford. The hardheaded advice the anarchist offers him surprisingly contradicts the blustery stance of his public preaching:

> He believed nothing in the world should stop this boy from getting a job . . . and earning a regular weekly salary . . . and marrying the waitress and moving into a small comfortable apartment with a bath and filing the tub with warm water . . . and putting on new clothes.

He should do this even if it means telling a lie to get himself a job as a bellboy in a luxurious hotel he has recently visited in Chicago.

Though the dialogue is swift, absurdly and wryly humorous and believable in detail, none of the action is predictable. In a brief exchange on the steps of the public library the reasons of the heart prevail.

Throughout the work of this middle period, Saroyan's stories reveal a continuing interest in innovation and experiment. To the lightweight, popular subject he applies an undercurrent of reflection that is no longer simply declaimed but rather revealed. Developing the humorous vein, he listens closely, evokes the tone and idiom of the individual speaker; the verbal patterns he hears characterize not only his region and station in life but his occupation. A frequenter of saloons and gambling bars, Saroyan is never out of hearing reach of the tall story. In "Ever Fall in Love With a Midget?"—the second story in *Love, Here Is My Hat*—a Kit Carson-like character carries on an extravagant monologue in pitch-perfect vernacular that tells us where the strength of the eccentric storyteller originates—the generously believing American listener.

Showing that he has mastered the telling of the tall story in its traditional form, Saroyan goes on to give us examples of eccentrics who have become assimilated into the American scene, their tall stories sometimes being their very lives. Whether he is writing about Gus the drunken gambler who slept two months through in a suite of rooms with a different girl in his bed each night; or of a "lady named Caroline," a kindhearted floozy who dreams of "settling down somewhere where the air is finer than in New York, and the people, too, like out West"; or of Joe Ryan, the black engineer in the Great Northern train who isn't ashamed to be remembered as "Nigger Ryan" for his kind deeds to "men without money," it is all tracked down to "the poor heart," the gullible, vulnerable heart. Then, just in case we've missed the point, one final disenchanted voice declaims

> They tell you Carter's Little Liver Pills are the thing you need, but it ain't the liver, it's the heart. . . . What do the workers want? In addition to better conditions. . . . The workers want what everybody wants and never gets . . . the enormity and abundance that isn't steadily part of this life.

And it ends, archly, "for the heart, all you do is take your time and cultivate the art of telling the truth from the sweet, sorrowful lie."

In the same year that *Love, Here Is My Hat* appeared, Harcourt, Brace & Co. brought out a second book of Saroyan stories, *The Trouble with Tigers,* and as befits a publisher of some reputation, the editors drew a number of stories from more sophisticated sources than usual for Saroyan—*The New Yorker, Harper's Bazaar, New Directions Anthology.* And, while *Story* was also there, not missing from the acknowledgements were the usual parochial ones—*Pacific Weekly, Script, The Peninsulan.* Yet on the whole it was evident that with this book Saroyan was moving into the semicommercial arena, where he was self-consciously aware he must please. As if to apologize for wanting to claim a larger audience, he lay his cards on the table in a half-facetious preamble.

> What I want to do is please you, whoever you are and whatever brings you here. If you find a page that is not what you think it should be, tear it out and throw it away. Forgive me if I bore you; for if I bore you, I forgive you. Happy book, please the ladies and take care of my fame.

The way he knew he would please was by moving away from the lyric mode, keeping his distance from his sentient self. He would never go all the way, as the novelist Milan Kundera has confessed to an interviewer that he had done, gladly destroying— as he put it—"the lyric illusion" for "the art of irony, . . . the perspective of the whole."[21] To do so would mean always looking at life from the outside, something uncongenial to Saroyan's emotional nature. But the personal vision would grow more covert, with his message insinuated rather than declaimed. Starting with *The Trouble with Tigers,* this needs to be understood if we are to be fair to Saroyan's evolving art.

It should be further pointed out in this connection that if Saroyan did not draw the major critics to his work, he was also not served by critics whose misplaced enthusiasms were often based on distortion of his intent. Howard Floan's interpretation of *The Trouble with Tigers* is a case in point. This generally sensitive critic of Saroyan awakens expectations in the reader that the author cannot fulfill when he states that Saroyan "places the emphasis . . . on the value of the moment, especially on the simple, unaffected response of the moment."[22] For this to be true, all the comedic and ironical implications would have to be explained away. What Saroyan—the new Saroyan—more likely wants to say is that "the value of the moment" (so to speak) is the value at the heart of American romanticism—something from which Saroyan does not altogether exclude himself but from which he can now distance himself if he so wishes. The Hollywood experience has had a twofold influence on his writing. As already noted, the script writing has helped him discover the uses of dialogue, and in the city that manufactures dreams, he has been able to view at first hand the American propensity for self-delusion. This last invokes from the impressionable Saroyan a native brand of humor (nearly dormant until now) that thrives on the absurd and gently mocks the pompous. To call the initial story, "The Tiger," "a fantasy on time and death," as Floan does, and claim the book as a whole conveys "a sense of the shortness of life and the vulnerability of the individual," is not only to miss the point but to shortchange the technical skill Saroyan brings to his material.[23]

A crazy quilt of styles, "The Tiger," is in fact the weakest in technique, trying in turn to be fanciful, comic, lyric, and metaphysical. The fact that it was written in 1935 suggests that there was forethought in extracting it from an unending backlog of unpublished work.[24] It is the first time that a metaphor has found its way into Saroyan title—the first at least that can be taken seriously. (*Love, Here Is My Hat* has overtones of a wisecrack.) As the spearhead of a group of stories that have an element of unreality about them, Saroyan here seems to be asking us to take a new look at the concept of fantasy—as a component of everyday American life. This complements the suggestion made earlier that we renew our idea of humor.

The tiger, at best, is a mixed symbol, slippery in its evocation of angst (an echo of a Freud-awakened era) and somewhat perverse in its frivolous use. Mostly "unseen" but often a "presence," the tiger "stalks" those who pursue false dreams; he turns a few gleeful "somersaults" when reason is defeated, and "runs amuck" when complacency takes over at the year's end—or the eleventh hour. All this is achieved with the lightest touch that involves much idle banter and street talk: "By God," "By Jesus" are repeated like a refrain in one passage. Though never heavy-handed, there are endless references to unemployment, world politics, nonconformists, race relations, Hollywood writers, and authors who make so much money they have no time left to enjoy their lives.

At one point in the story Saroyan makes a mockery even of himself as "a dreamer *with* a dream"—"John Brook," he calls his prototype—the unpublished writer "opposed to work" who enters a bar not to deny the world but to "thank God" for it; who, lying on the grass in the park one day, dreams "the earth," while projecting a book that will consist of three words, "God is Love." This is no reincarnated Whitman, however: when Brook lifts his head, the muse he sees is "a divine old lady" ("not my grandmother," he quickly adds) who chides him for his idleness, even as he plunges her into timelessness: "I loved her when she was a girl," he fantasizes, "a beautiful girl who is now an old lady."

To enjoy the story one must appreciate the quixotic inversion Saroyan brings to what he once held as a solemn truth: when the old lady asks if he believes in God, Brook replies, "Could I disbelieve in that which I once was and even now sometimes am?" But the freewheeling manner and iconoclasm don't always work. The story gets bogged down with too many lyric fragments meant to suggest timelessness and illusion. And there are repeated references to "the universe," to "the dream with no dreamer," the lost day, hour, year. We are not always sure these passages are meant to be contrived and platitudinous—are they tongue-in-cheek conceits, or the old Saroyan intruding once again? In the end, one has to believe the former, for while the literary style in the lyric passages reminds one of Thomas Wolfe, the hero of "The Tiger" cannot double for him. Fanciful and down-to-earth, he is most himself when he verges on playful parody:

> When I awakened it was past midnight and the year was very still, the universe hushed, the tiger warm and drowsy. It rose to its feet, stretched its muscles, then roared, while I yawned, groaning.

This mimicry is a sign that Saroyan is weaning himself from "literary" prose as he turns now with humor and empathy to the not always happy results of impulsive, romantic commitment to the moment. In one of his lighter moods, he shows us the young office worker in "Another Summer," whose high spirits on an early summer morning shock an elderly, straightlaced coworker to whom he appears, in turn, "vulgar," "crazy," and "ill"—all because he has called her "lovely" from an excess of exuberance. An excess of energy subsequently impels him to scoot around the office with his foot on a roller chair, and overpowered, finally, with a sense of limitless possibility, he has boldly suggested driving to the country with one of the office help and swimming with her in the nude. The dream is, of course, short-lived. Even before it begins to rain, the young man knows it's all a temporary whim, since he has no car, no money, and no girlfriend. But the impassioned expressions of his desires has momentarily lifted life out of the doldrums, and even the elderly coworker regrets having to return to reality: "She knew he was altogether safe, altogether sane," she muses, "Now everything would be the same."

Saroyan's sympathy generally lies with the individual who seizes the day, but there is a new awareness in these stories that spontaneity often masks an inner void and hopelessness about the future. In "I Could Say Bella, Bella," a frivolous act is revealed as an irresistible longing. In this wistful tale, a young man pretends to be drunk to catch the attention of a beautiful girl waiting at her bus stop; but while his behavior has all the earmarks of a brash movie hero on the make, when the chips are down, the impressionable young man can't follow through the expectations he has aroused in the girl. Touched by her concern for him, he begins to show his insecurity, and the girl feels as ridiculous as the words of the foolish song he has been singing. Full of regret that "the play was over," he wonders as he watches the girl walk away, "Why did he have to change all of a sudden and become ordinary, making her ordinary too, spoiling everything, making her offer to take him home pathetic instead of gay."

But there are other stories in which illusion proves redeeming. In normal times, the romantic hero is impervious to restraints on his imagination—his capacity to project into the future—but in a period of economic duress, when "chance" and "luck" are in short supply, he stands in danger of being mired by his illusions. Some years before Eugene O'Neill wrote his tragicomic play, *The Iceman Cometh*, Saroyan was uncovering varieties of this archetype with whom he shared a fellow feeling as an Armenian of utopian persuasion. His classic Depression story, "The Job," skirts the painful aspects of poverty and insecurity to show, instead, the moral health that comes from perpetuating a certain kind of "lie" about oneself. The story centers on two young men reduced to living the life of hobos, sometimes sleeping on poolroom tables. One of them is an incipient musician who hums Liszt's *Preludes,* "the part where Liszt really got going," as he gives his friend the wondrous news he has found a job. Without in any way sermonizing, Saroyan allows the reader to discover what keeps these impoverished young men in good humor; along with an inherent humor and unwavering sense of solidarity, they have an undiminished capacity to dream about themselves. The would-be musician's self-advertisement before the waitress in the hamburger joint has the ring of a frontier-type tall tale, and like all such tales achieves its goal of boosting the teller's ego. "I have composed three symphonies, two operas, four ballets, seven concertos, eleven tone poems, and forty-six songs," brags the young man who has accepted a reality he cannot change and taken a job as an elevator operator for eight dollars a week. What he refuses to relinquish is the truth of his potential which tells him he *could* become a great composer: "if I could write music, I could be a great composer. It wasn't lying much," he tells his friend in explaining his moment of braggadocio.

Saroyan's most successful efforts in the theater and his later stories will revolve around this form of romantic accommodation and the quiet affirmation to which it leads. But this cannot happen until a certain change takes place in the writer's relationship to the reality principle that he has so steadfastly pursued until now. In the past, the essay-like structure of his stories with their explicit commentaries has made it possible for him to combine realistic narrative with a romantic/philosophical overview. The poetic principle and the precision he sought were never at odds. But once he submits to a consciousness other than his own, the borrowed perception of reality renders explicitness obsolete. The subjective dimension now connects with the created character, while the invisible author takes on the task of mediating between what exists in actual fact and what persists as private myth. Increasingly Saroyan's imagination is pressed into replacing straightfoward verbal expression with metaphor and symbol, and in the earliest experiments a deliberate obliqueness masks a certain ambiguity of intent as well as inadequacy of technique to carry it through.

Along with "The Tiger," two other examples of this stand out in *The Trouble with Tigers*. The first, "The Great Leapfrog Contest," with its suggestion of Mark Twain in the title, places a "tough little Irish kid," Rosie Mahoney, in the position of Twain's frog. In a perverse kind of way, we are shown that within the rules of American competitiveness, the teenager succeeds in establishing her superiority over the Russian, Italian, and Greek immigrant children of the neighborhood. Knowing nothing of her ultimate motivation, we witness in realistic detail how by playing the leapfrog game to its deadliest limit the girl is able to destroy her male opponent, body and soul. An arch tone of mockery creeps into the little postscript about Rosie, who grows up to become "the most beautiful girl in town," marrying "one of the wealthiest young men, . . . Wallace Hadington Finley VI." But the leapfrog contest, like the tiger, remains ubiquitous as a symbol, open to interpretation.

Equally suggestive but even more moot is the inner meaning of "The Acrobats" (another title with a metaphor), which contrasts a child's generous and spontaneous response to an odd circus family passing through the town with the irrational fear and prejudice of a group of her elders. The magical feats of these acrobats, who are a family of midgets, so captivate the child's imagination that she tosses her last coins to them. When the little girl is chided for her deed, she retorts, "you are afraid to see them close . . . afraid they'll look at you or something." An important insight tenuously pervades the story: In the mundane world, risk and fear are connected; but the child's commitment to the fantastic or miraculous protects her from a knowledge of risk and, having no knowledge of failure, she is immune to fear. In many ways this story combines the many appealing qualities of Saroyan's humanistic vision, not the least among these his ability to plumb the heart of a child.

Now that he is barely visible as a participant on the scenes he describes, Saroyan is avid in his pursuit of the multiform experience of American life. He has no trouble inventing situations, since the drama he is out to discover is in the commonplace, the banal: the adolescent boy yearning for an impossible love ("Sweetheart, Sweetheart, Sweetheart"); a grade-school teacher learning about racial prejudice from the children she teaches ("Citizens of the Third Grade"); a couple out of work finding out about the simple joys of life ("Someday I'll Be a Millionaire Myself"); a Hollywood scenario writer unable to connect with his work ("O. K. Baby, This Is the World"); and an idealistic young man wanting to believe in the essential innocence of prostitutes and failing ("My Brothers and the Sisters"). None of these stories builds on relationships. Things happen fast and we catch only fragments of a life, a person. But through it all another phase of the writer's art was being nurtured.

THE EMERGENCE OF A TECHNIQUE

Although, as seen, Saroyan has denied "form," saying "Any form I achieve in art is form I have already achieved in myself," there is a distinct development of form in his unconventional short story in the later volumes. In a letter to Bennett Cerf on March 7, 1938 earlier referred to, he says, "*Inhale and Exhale* is full of experiments of all kinds, which I know are influencing other writers. It is bound to be a source book and a text book of the art of the short story. It is probably the reason it failed with the public: it is a little difficult for the general reader, no less than *Ulysses* was and still is." It is important to note that he no longer identifies directly with his creations and that some of the views they personify are not his own but merely the foil for his continuing dialogue.

"I am sending you herewith probably the first real original piece of writing I've sent you since 'Seventy Thousand Assyrians,'" Saroyan wrote to the editor of *Story* in February 1939, referring to a story that would ultimately be titled "My Witness Witnesseth."[25] In the year that would see productions of his two acclaimed plays, *My Heart's in the Highlands* (April 1939) and *The Time of Your Life* (October 1939), he was filling Whit Burnett's ears with high enthusiasm for a new story he had written which he held up as an example of the kind of writing that would be "shaking up" and extending the "frontiers" of the magazine. "I believe in this piece of mine," he added, "and I think it will have a very good effect both on writers who are now published and who are someday to be published."

This 1939 story (which is virtually an essay) examines the creative process and shows how it is endangered when skill and facility replace the original spark and worldly distractions steer the writer away from his truest impulses. As usual with Saroyan the revelation is first set forth in everyday terms, in this case an experience with deep night thoughts that he has allowed to vanish by dawn. This leads him to the realization that literature in America is failing because writers have lost their way and are merely "taking inventory of mayhem, the arson, the theft, the false witness, . . . telling a story that gets nowhere and means nothing." In a real sense, he concludes, he was a better writer at age twelve than he is now, at thirty,

> except that I did not know how to write then, and now, knowing how, I must say I have lost the way, lost the vision, lost the world I knew must be made real, lost the realm of truth I knew was in myself, except the few odd fragments of the commonplace world which so easily fit themselves into the so-easily written words.

This now recognized "expert" of the short story who has begun to be noticed even by the esoteric, avant-garde magazines, whose books have already been translated into many languages and published abroad, this same writer—William Saroyan—is chastened in 1939 by the thought that something precious has been lost in the process of becoming successful. And a certain apprehension mingles with humility:

> You can write as they write and always have written; you can say everything that means nothing; you can do it expertly; you can make it a pleasure to read; but you can't carry them along to the living they want, you can't take them by the ear to life, you can't move the hour

one second forward from where it was a million years ago; you can't say the word because you've forgotten it.

It was perhaps inevitable that on the threshold of his expanding fame, Saroyan's next published book would be a fictionalized recollection of his childhood and early youth—a work in which he would try to recapture the self-contained world of his transplanted Armenian family in Fresno, California, "the ugly little city containing the large comic world" (as he put it) that had awakened his creativity and nurtured it. Although he had tapped this source many times before, it was with the connected stories in *My Name is Aram* that he would consciously draw from the depths of his memory his earliest vision of life, "the realm of truth" which he wished to guard.

In his prefatory note to *My Name is Aram,* Saroyan acknowledged his gratitude to the two editors who "urged him to buckle down and write this book." They were Edward Weeks of *The Atlantic Monthly,* who had accepted several of the "Aram" stories for the magazine, and Edward J. O'Brien, the editor of *The Best Short Stories* and *The Yearbook of the American Short Story,* who had encouraged him to write more about the Armenians. Thus, for no reason he could have foreseen, Saroyan's own need to retrace his steps to his valley home suddenly seemed to correspond with the needs of the marketplace. In the apocalyptic climate of the day, his stories of an unsophisticated, comically lovable Armenian family (admittedly based on his own) inspired hope; with just the right balance of the familiar and the bizarre, they exuded a wide-eyed faith in a simpler, more wholesome world that offered a welcome relief from chronic despair.[26]

Saroyan now came to be compared to Twain and Tarkington, and one critic announced it was "the most truly American book of the year."[27] Although Aram Garoghlanian's family was a far cry from any recognizable American family, no less an authority than Christopher Morley declared, "Many a heavy tome of history and economics holds less of what America deeply means."[28] A new vein of humor in Saroyan was drawing him closer than he had ever been before to the American temper. For this, he lavishly credited Fresno:

It was . . . as good a town as any in the world for a writer to be born into, being neither too large nor too small, too urban or too rural, too progressive or too backward, too athletic or too lame, too intelligent or too stupid, too arid or too lush, but in all these things . . . so delicately, so nicely, and so delightfully balanced as to give the spirit of the growing writer almost exactly the right proportions of severity and warmth, the firmness and flexibility.

His home town, moreover, had given "the mind a critical and yet compassionate understanding," and much material "rich in the elements of comedy." Indeed, the book had seemed to write itself, "the writer simply wrote the words while his spirit enjoyed their meaning." Fresno—unlike Twain's Hannibal—had clearly not aggravated in Saroyan "a quarrel with mankind."

In a curious sort of way, the "Aram" stories have form. Saroyan's narrator (Aram) no longer meanders, couching his meaning in unlikely juxtapositions or far-fetched analogies. The writer's style has grown swifter, it is more focused. The inward turning has released a new appreciation of his Armenian background. He delves unabashedly into his memory for those colorful exemplars of humanity who had created a special world for him. The memories come in flashes, their meaning held intact within a weblike structure as fragile as a song's.

Unlike his previous ubiquitous narrators, Aram lives on every page in these thematically (though not chronologically) related stories. He is as much a presence as Huck Finn or Tom Sawyer, though with this difference, that he is bound by another kind of ethos. A hyphenated American with an Armenian heritage that modifies and often curiously enhances what is "American" in him, Aram is as willful and independent as Huck and Tom. Like them, he is determined to outwit the authorities, those men and women who try to demean or depress his natural impulses. But, unlike those earlier pranksters, Aram's impulsiveness is checked by a deep sense of family solidarity; indeed, if necessary, he will play the fool to uphold a habit or belief they commonly share. Aram, moreover, even as a child, enjoys the advantage of being both observer and participant; thus he can anticipate the outcome of some folly even as he laps up his role in the "experience." And nowhere in the book is there a harsh word for his relatives' ignorance or lack of knowledge of the ways of the world, and of *this* world in particular.

If Saroyan's humor has less of an edge than Twain's, it succeeds nonetheless in charming us into a new vision of American childhood in which innocence and wisdom seem not too far apart. Aram himself, even at age nine, is attuned to the larger world, but like all real children he is also a captive of *the moment*. And in remembering this childhood immersion into dailiness, he is better able to see "the human race's" capacity for goodness, even as he gears his style to a new comic stance.

Most discussions of *My Name is Aram* (which is often handled as a children's book) begin and end with its ethnic dimension. Both Floan and Calonne have emphasized the book's *remembered* quality, with Floan claiming that Saroyan's turning to his Armenian past "provided him with more than a point of view: it would become his truest subject."[29] True. But one needs to add that it was in the *process* of remembering that Saroyan would discover the components of his faith and style. What had raised these "Armenian stories" above those he had previously written was his more insightful and sophisticated utilization of his early memories.

Memory can be flat, like a documentary, with the retrospective eye guiding and censoring the material into shape. Or it can be, as Saroyan was discovering, the springboard that releases the powder keg of the imagination. Thus, he is not being simply quixotic when he writes at the end of his Note to *My Name is Aram,*

> As to whether or not the writer himself is Aram Garoghlanian, the writer cannot very well say. He will, however, say he is not, certainly *not* Aram Garoghlanian.

What he is saying is that while Aram is in essence himself, he is also his dream of an American childhood. As for the uncles and cousins, he was discovering them "imaginatively" for the first time.

We know from Saroyan's previous stories that Fresno's narrow-minded community of that time provoked the ethnic consciousness Saroyan enjoyed flaunting at school. But outside of a highly articulate grandmother whose memories of the Old Country never seemed to dim, ethnicity did not dominate the Saroyan household. He writes in an article titled "The Impossible Saroyans of Fresno"[30] that his mother had transformed a house they had rented "into not only a home but also a school, a theatre, a forum, a meeting-place and a church of easy-going liberality." He remembers that not only Armenian but Turkish, Kurdish, and English were spoken: "I seldom had a feeling of the existence of a division or at any rate an undesirable division," he writes. Things would disappear in a family trunk: "The idea was to forget as quickly as possible and to get going on the new."

"The easy-going liberality" Saroyan remembers as being the general atmosphere of his home would become part of an invasion of recollections, all suggesting new meanings and new artistic possibilities. Looking back from a new vantage point, in 1939, he saw things he had not observed before.

Depending on one's frame of mind, we seize upon or blot out what we are exposed to, and it is very likely that in the light of another day, the need to be a spokesman for his invisible Armenians either inhibited a direct response to their individuality or limited his interest to what might leave a significant impact on the reader. Now that he had put the Armenians on the map, as it were, and gained some confidence, Saroyan could enter their lives with less solemnity and see in their beauty and strength the comic incongruities that made them *human*. "What you see and what you remember is never literally what it is," Saroyan once told an interviewer, "It's what it is to you." Humor had come to serve him well, both in his personal life (after the painful break with Sanora Babb) and in his new phase of writing. For the moment at least, in the portrait of the successful writer that had emerged, there were all the signs of the man who sees life as a comedy—humor, of course, being equated with truth.

In the evocative opening of the first story, "The Summer of the Beautiful White Horse," Saroyan instantly sets the book's tone:

> One day back there in the good old days when I was nine and the world was full of every imaginable kind of magnificence, and life was still a delightful and mysterious dream, my cousin Mourad, who was considered crazy by everybody who knew him except me, came to my house at four in the morning and woke me up by tapping on the window of my room.

The quick and easy way he gets into the story may make a reader overlook the careful choice of words: "magnificence" to suggest "plentiful" as well as "wonderful" (a poignant word in the Depression years) and "mysterious dream" with its echo of Twain's *The Mysterious Stranger*. There's artfulness, too, in unexpectedness of a name like "Mourad" and at the same time the acknowledgement that "the craziness" of Mourad is quite acceptable to a real child like Aram.

Aram's sense of reality tells him Mourad could not possibly afford the beautiful white horse he had brought to his window, inviting him to ride it. Aram is puzzled: "We were poor. We had no money. Our whole tribe was poverty-stricken." But even before he can reason, he responds to the spectacle before him by noting that his cousin Mourad "enjoyed being alive more than anybody else who had ever fallen into the world by mistake." Mourad, in other words, could hardly be held to account for anything but his mere existence. But something else now troubles Aram, for in the next instant he considers the tribe's honor. "We had been famous for our honesty for something like eleven centuries." He is loath to believe that Mourad has stolen the horse. "No member of the Garoghlanian family could be a thief," he thinks righteously.

But just to set things straight, he asks his cousin, "Where did you steal the horse?" Mourad has no ready answer and Aram quickly switches to a line of reasoning that lets the boy off the hook:

> Well, it seemed to me stealing a horse for a ride was not the same thing as stealing something else, such as money. If you were crazy about horses the way my cousin Mourad and I were, it wasn't stealing. It wouldn't become stealing until we offered to sell the horse, which of course I knew we would never do.

The moral issue is temporarily forgotten as Aram jumps down to the yard and leaps onto the horse behind his cousin. Together they fly through vineyards, orchards, and ditches, with the "feel of the horse running," and Mourad's voice rises into a roar. Then, once again Aram turns narrator, tracing Mourad's "craziness" to Uncle Khosrove, "an enormous man with a powerful head of black hair and the largest mustache in the San Joaquin Valley," whose favorite phrase apropos anything is "It is no harm; pay no attention to it." (The eccentric old man used the phrase once when told his house was on fire and followed it with a roar of laughter.)

The boys' adventure quickly picks up again in a rapid dialogue, which ends with Mourad's promise that Aram may ride the horse alone. Then the trouble begins. Aram's ride proves a disaster; having lost the horse and found it at last, they now face the problem of where to hide it. Mourad confesses to having taken the horse on morning rides, but he won't verify that he has done it more than once. In the event they are found out, he tells Aram, "I don't want both of us to be liars."

There is a long moment of suspense when the horse's owner, the farmer John Byro (whom Aram describes as an Assyrian "who out of loneliness has learned to speak Armenian") visits the Garoghlanians and, after being served coffee by his mother and rolling a cigarette, announces in Uncle Khosrove's presence that his white horse has been missing for a whole month. To which the mad Uncle responds, "It's no harm. What is the loss of a horse? Haven't we lost the homeland?" (Aram, as narrator, does not miss a trick. The madness now discloses its cause.) The conversations gradually reaches an absurd pitch as when the farmer complains that as a result of the horse's loss he has had to walk ten miles, and the uncle shouts, "You have legs." And then the farmer further complains he has lost sixty dollars, at which the Uncle replies "I spit on money."

All of this on the face of it is quite irrelevant to the story, including the mother's compassionate remark after the farmer leaves: "He has a gentle heart. . . . It is simply that he is homesick and such a large man." Irrelevant, and yet not more so than Aram's running over to Mourad's house with the news and finding him sitting under a peach tree trying to repair the broken wing of a robin.

Aram now wants to hold on to the horse until he learns to ride it, but a minor moral matter puts a damper on it; if Mourad keeps the horse for more than six months (which it would take Aram to learn), it would be stealing.

Finally, in what must be the most charming show of trust in all literature, the boys meet the old Assyrian farmer who in the very presence of his horse rejects the thought that the boys have stolen it. After looking inside the horse's mouth, Byro says, "Tooth for tooth. . . . I would swear it is my horse if I didn't know your parents. The fame of your family is well known to me." Without making any admission, the boys return the horse to the farm the next day. Then, in a quick coda that has the feel of poetry, Aram observes, "My cousin put his arms around the horse, pressed his nose into the horse's nose, patted it, and then went away."

If one compares this "Aram" story with earlier stories Saroyan has written about his childhood, what immediately stands out is a new subtlety in his use of the narrator as commentator. The observations are now almost like asides, but are more incisive for their appropriateness within the text, as when Aram draws attention to his mother's gentle understanding of the Assyrian farmer's intense loneliness, and the many instances that reveal Mourad's own gentleness and responsiveness to animals. The dual vision is no longer a strident device for rhetorical persuasion, but a way of insinuating into the readers' minds undercurrents of meaning that will ultimately enlarge their sympathies.

The white horse is clearly a metaphor of the child's remembrance of magic and heroism, but beyond this kind of symbolism, Saroyan has added a still more powerful device for suggestiveness: the associative use of words and phrases that helps to draw significant parallels. One striking example of this is when Uncle Khosrove refers to "the lost homeland" while they are talking about the theft of a horse. Not only does the reference (highly meaningful to the Armenians) serve to explain the uncle's "madness," but it signals the real reason for his presence in the story. He is much more than a picturesque humorous device: as a half-pathetic, half-comical figure, he represents the standards by which the children are motivated—their concern, in this instance, to uphold the established "honesty" of the tribe, of a people who have lost a homeland to preserve their honor.

All this—along with a return to the tone of the fable, now heightened and given a comic turn; the careful selection of detail, swift dialogue and narrative pace—is a sign that Saroyan's literary progress has taken a new direction.

Up to now, the totality of his faith has consumed much of its specificity, so that the recollections had tended to overlap and become indistinguishable from each other. But with the passage of time, a process of idealization has taken place that allows Saroyan to see intrinsic connections. In his mind's eye a gestalt has occurred that flushes out the total entity of these experiences and their essential remoteness from the community in general.

Not implausibly, the job of distilling that entity into a special "world" falls into the hands of "Aram," a boy wise beyond his years who has no trouble assimilating his Armenian family into "delightful and mysterious dream" of his childhood. Whatever their age, "the proud and angry Saroyans" have retained an essential "innocence"; they thrive on instincts honed and cultivated by ancient wisdom. It is the source of their well-being, but also of the comic incongruities their actions generate. They remain unconditionally themselves, not because they are alienated from their environment but because, in fact, they are out to *improve* it, if possible. In one story after another, Aram pays tribute to (even as he gently ribs) the innocent trust and faith that motivates this earthy/spiritual people who have a vested interest in being fully alive, guided without embarrassment by their sometimes "foolish" hearts.

At times, their innocent faith, as in the case of Uncle Melik verges on absurdity. In one of Saroyan's unforgettable "Aram" stories, "The Pomegranate Trees," Aram recalls,

My Uncle Melik was just about the worst farmer that ever lived. He was too imaginative and poetic for his own good. What he wanted was beauty.

The trees he wanted to plant produced an exotic fruit that nobody in America wanted to eat, and to make things further impractical, he wanted to plant them in desert land (680 acres at the foot of the Sierra Nevada mountains) he had acquired. Aram remembers that his was in "the old days of poetry and youth in the world," and he had been chosen to help his uncle in the venture because Uncle Melik "knew I was a poet at heart" and would appreciate "the magnificent impulse that was driving him to glorious ruin." "In the most poetic Armenian anybody ever heard," he had articulated his vision: "Here in this awful desolation a garden shall flower, fountains of cold water shall bubble out of the earth, and all things of beauty shall come into being."

"Yes, sir," the eleven-year-old Aram had assented, but even as he joined his uncle in driving the John Deere tractor, he knew in his heart that "it was all pure aesthetics, not agriculture." The farm would remain a secret from the rest of the family for several years, as Uncle Melik with dogged faith hired Mexican workers to dig for water. This called for cutting down the existing cactus plants, which promptly renewed themselves. Nor did the use of Deere tractors bring about the miracle of water. In final desperation, the uncle called on a water specialist in Texas, who managed to produce a trickle of muddy water, and the planting of the pomegranate trees began. When after a while there appeared a twenty-acre orchard—"the loneliest-looking absurdity imaginable"—the uncle "went out of his head with joy." But Uncle Melik's money ran out and in four years the muddy water produced only blossoms. Three pomegranates finally materialized: the uncle ate one, Aram ate the second, and the third became a showpiece kept in the office. Aram had turned fifteen and grown as tall as his uncle when the trees produced two hundred pieces of fruit, enough to mail to a wholesale produce house. But after long negotiations that reveal his beautiful fruit is unsalable, the eleven boxes are returned express collect. Eventually, the poet-farmer is forced to sell the unproductive land; being still enamored of the trees he asks the new owner if he could take care of what is left of them. But as Aram notes, this was not something easy to explain, especially to a man "who wasn't sympathetic," so the uncle lost both the trees and the land. Years later, Aram joins his uncle for a look at the site; there was nothing now but cactus and desert brush, "exactly the way it had been all the years of the world," Aram notes. "We didn't say anything because there was such an awful lot to say, and no language to say it in."

Uncle Melik's stubborn resistance to reality—a prototypical situation Saroyan would repeatedly exploit in his future work—is affectionately rendered here by the boy Aram, who all along has known better but has had the sensitivity not to destroy a dream.

The "loser" uncle has wanted success on his own terms: the blossoms of the pomegranates are no more beautiful than the blossoms of other fruit trees, but they delight him more and become more beautiful because they are a part of his lost past. Thus, there are undercurrents of meaning in his gently subversive "tall tale."

All along, Aram contrasts his uncle's childlike unworldliness and piety with his businesslike exterior. Melik is a landowner launched on an enterprise that is expected to combine a source of livelihood with beauty and nostalgia. This new American farmer's skin is so thin, however, that when he nearly steps on a horned toad, he feels the need to apologize to the creature; at the same time, he is curious to know if toads can be dangerous. When his nephew assures him that they are totally harmless and do not travel in large numbers, Melik orders the boy to "let the timid thing return to earth. Let us be gentle toward small things which live on the earth with us."

What Saroyan would earlier have seen as a melancholy tale of excessive sentiment is transformed by a teasing humor and new empathy into a fablelike story that stands the American Dream on its head: Uncle Melik's "success" lies, paradoxically, in his very failure. His experience has not embittered him. As Aram helps us to see, the power to dream begins and ends in the quest itself, something that worldly success would only have erased or at best diminished.

But if the Garoghlanian clan has a high quota of poets and dreamers, it also has its family despots. In "The Journey to Hanford," Aram's grandfather harbors no sympathy for his long unemployed son, Jorgi. The foolish and sad fellow is the target of his unequivocal diagnosis:

> When you read in a book that a man sits all day under a tree and plays a zither and sings, believe me, that writer is an impractical man. Money, that's the thing.

His prescription for this irresponsible behavior, however, is short of absurd. He must go on his bicycle (fixed at last) to a village some twenty miles away where there is a job opening: but he must not go alone, since he is not to be trusted. One of the children or grandchildren must go with him, the choice depending on who can cook rice the best. Aram is nominated to go. "Loud-laughing Aram" (secretly beloved of the grandfather) not because Uncle Zorab wishes him to be punished but because Aram, who has been eager to go all along, affirms that he can cook rice that is "sometimes perfect."

Jorgi and Aram promptly settle down in an eleven-room house in Hanford, where the laggard uncle at once makes himself comfortable on the floor with his zither: "it was beautiful," Aram recalls, "It was melancholy sometimes and sometimes funny, but it was always beautiful." They eat the rice the boy cooks and the next day Jorgi grudgingly goes looking for the job, while Aram sits on the front porch for his return, enjoying "a nice region of the world in daylight." To Jorgi's great joy, it turns out there is no job for him—the watermelons have all been harvested. The two free spirits decide to stay on until their money gives out, with Jorgi dancing and singing the time away.

It is the ever ingenious grandmother who saves the day. Being the first to hear the bad news when the two return, she quickly delves into her pants pocket and gives Aram the money Jorgi was meant to earn and bring to his father. The boy promises not to reveal the ruse. Thus the grandfather is fooled. But (as so often happens in a Saroyan story) the old man has a sudden change of heart at seeing his son again. Never at a loss for an aphorism, he first pronounces his displeasure at seeing Jorgi back at the zither: "When you read in a book that a father loves a foolish son more than his wise sons, that writer is a bachelor," he says archly. But, hearing his music again coming from under the almond tree, he is disarmed. Later, Aram finds the old man stretched out on the couch, asleep, and smiling while "Jorgi was singing hallelujah to the universe at the top of his beautiful, melancholy voice."

Told chiefly through a series of dialogues that show Saroyan's increasing mastery in dealing with the absurd in obsessive human behavior, "The Journey to Hanford" is a kind of riposte to the dour Depression syndrome. Jorgi is like the fabled grasshopper that sings and dances the summer long unmindful of the winter ahead, contrary to the ant whose fear of the future makes it unable to enjoy the present moment. The story combines the genial charm of Saroyan's artless simplicity with the new uses he had found for his sense of comedy. More firmly in control of his art, he no longer has to preach. He can simply offer those alternate possibilities of behavior he remembers from his childhood.

Not that the exoticism of the Armenian background is always played up. If Aram has been compared to Tom Sawyer and Huck Finn, it is because, like them, he is a spirited *American* child, whose love of adventure is as intense as theirs, if at times different in effect. Often it is that difference that impels the remembrance.

All bright American children, for instance, would like to have physical prowess (especially if they are under average size), but not all bright American children must contend, like Aram, with a family member who defines power as "those mysterious vital forces in all men waiting to be released." Aram's Uncle Gygo—being himself a student of Oriental philosophy—looks suspiciously at Aram's faith in physical training. The boy's hopes have been raised by a clipping from *Argosy All-Story Magazine* that promises to turn him into a replica of the trainer, Mr. Strongfort, pictured "wearing nothing but a little bit of leopard skin . . . loaded all over with muscle." But the correspondence course will not be free, and when the uncle hears about it, he's even more skeptical than before: "Mohney . . . I tell you, Aram, mohney is nawthing. You cannot bribe God." This makes Aram stop to think:

> My uncle was nowhere near as big as Mr. Strongfort, but neither was Mr. Strongfort as dynamically furious as my uncle. It seemed to me that, at best, Mr. Strongfort, in a match with my uncle, would have a great deal of unfamiliar trouble—I mean with the mysterious vital forces that were always getting released in my uncle, so that very often a swift glance from him would make a big man quail and turn away, or, if he had been speaking, stop quickly.

Unable to summon up his uncle's brand of mysticism, and finally disillusioned by Mr. Strongfort, Aram works out his own "program"—taking it easy and growing powerful "without any trouble or exercise." But the boy's ambition needs an outlet, and he decides to enter the school's competitions. Aram's "continuous meditation on the theme of athletics" becomes so overpowering that he can all but visualize his victory in the fifty-yard dash and all the other jumps. But when he is actually put to the test and it turns out he is nowhere near the winner, he feels "betrayed." Raging with anger, he becomes sick for three days, convinced he would have died but for his grandmother's care.

In the meantime, Uncle Gygo has undergone a metamorphosis. Putting fasting and meditation behind him, he is back again to being "one of the boys around town, drinking, staying up all hours and following women." A much simpler creed has replaced the former Yoga: "I tell you, Aram, . . . we are a great family. We can do *anything*."

At age eleven, Aram's balanced perception is a rarity. He is aware that "betrayal" has more than one face. When, during the course of the race, he fails to release "all the mysterious vital forces" taught by his uncle, he feels "in some strange way I was betrayed." He knows that self-deception is no less real than the deception the world perpetrates on the innocent and gullible.

It is this awareness of misplaced trust as a common human failing that protects Saroyan's story from the censorious humor of a Mark Twain. In showing us a larger truth—two comic paradigms of innocence (a child and a childlike adult)—it creates, instead, an atmosphere of genial amusement that denigrates no one yet is every bit as revealing.

And here lies the challenge of the book and its anomaly as a "memoir" of childhood: the attempt to evoke the healthy, eager, trusting world of the child, while at the same time exposing the pitfalls that inevitably pursue the pure in heart. On the evidence of these stories it is hard to simply regard Saroyan as an ever reverent romantic; a closer look attests that he was too much a child of his era to succumb to glib evasions of reality. No one in the "Aram" stories—least of all himself—has heroic dimensions (though they might thus aspire) and there certainly are "villains" of sorts—though never far from being pardoned once they are exposed. Saroyan's emphasis is on Aram's agility in swinging between what he sees as his own truth and the more complex forms existing outside. It is by keeping the two apart that the boy learns to sustain his fresh and positive outlook, while guarding his hold on the circumstantial world.

In one story after another, we see that Aram is a rebel who has no instinct for violence. High spirits and a quick native mirth keep anger at bay; they are his concealed weapons against negative feelings; it is what makes him know he is a "future poet." In "One of Our Future Poets, You Might Say," Aram tells how he foiled the board of education's program attempting to prove that disadvantaged children were physically as well as mentally inferior. According to statistics, the children of Aram's nighborhood had "badly shaped heads, sunken chests, faulty bone structure, hollow voices, no energy, distemper and six or seven other minor organic defects." Aram, on the other hand, knows for a fact that "these ruffians . . . had well-shaped heads, sound chests, handsome figures, loud voices, too much energy and a continuous compulsion to behave mischievously."

To cap the irony, "certain Presbyterian ministers" were proclaiming their "glorious faith" in the American child; looking into "a sea of faces" they were seeing "the future leaders of America, the future captains of industry, the future statesmen, and I might say, the future poets." The statement made Aram smile, for he knew some of those boys—they were "great baseball players, but by nature idiots. . . . I didn't think they would be apt to develop into captains of industry and neither did they."

To set the record straight, a physical examination is announced for the children in the civic auditorium. And Aram (who has just discovered, at age nine, that he is a future poet) is asked to inhale. When the young "poet" leaps to the stage and appears to be able to go on forever inhaling and exhaling, he is quickly dispatched offstage, and in embarrassment, the board calls off further such examinations. They may have been useful, Aram muses, as far as discovering future "captains of industry," but when it came to the future of poets, the examinations "ran helter-skelter and amuck and nobody knew what to do or think."

Equally revealing of Aram's gently satirical turn of mind is "The Presbyterian Choir Singers," in which, quite accidentally, it is discovered that Aram has "a rare Christian voice," one much "needed by religion." Aram had not, in fact, been baptized until he was thirteen ("What kind of people are you?" the priest had shouted to his family when this was revealed. "To which my people had replied, We have been away."), and the boy cannot recall having felt different afterward. To his grandmother's query, "Do you believe now?" Aram had replied that he couldn't be sure, though he wanted to be a Christian. "Well, just believe, then," the old lady had advised him, "and go about your business."

As it turns out, Aram's business is to sing in the boys' choir at the Presbyterian church (to which he does not belong). For this, he is to receive $1 a week from an elderly lady, Mrs. Balaifal, "a woman of great sensitivity," who reads the poems of Robert Browning and cannot tolerate profane language. After lecturing Aram and his friend, Pandro ("the most uncouth boy in the world," but also "the most courteous and thoughtful"), and offering them pamphlets that she hopes will improve their manners and language, Mrs. Balaifal asks them to help her move her organ from one room to another. This becomes a trap, for she then persuades them to sing hymns with her. This is when Aram's "Christian voice" is discovered, and although Aram is disinclined to become a choir boy, the lady drives a hard bargain: she will even pay Pandro— who has no voice at all and must promise *not* to sing— to make sure that Aram will come to church on Sundays. The pious lady prays for the boys in their presence, but neither of them feels the better for it, and even after a few Sundays of singing in the choir, Aram is not convinced—as Mrs. Balaifal had put it—that he is "deeply religious, although you do not know it yet."

"In this manner," Aram reports, "in the eleventh year of my

life, I became more or less a Presbyterian—at least every Sunday morning." Had Saroyan ended it there, it would have been just another zany little story, but he would have us know that in Aram's life it had an undercurrent of meaning. Having earlier explained that the Armenians have no trouble moving from one religion to another, embracing anyone that comes along, Aram now admits to "growing a little skeptical, as it were, of the whole conventional religious pattern." He is eager to reach "by hook or crook," "an understanding of my own, and come to terms with Omnipotence in my own way." When his voice suddenly changes, he is relieved that he can cancel his contract with Mrs. Balaifal.

Highly comic in detail, the story creates in its portrait of the rigidly pious Mrs. Balaifal the perfect foil for Aram's own liberality. Though the boy's background is Orthodox Armenian, he would have us know that "like most Americans, my faith consists in believing in every religion including my own, but without any ill-will toward anybody, no matter what he believes, just so his personality is good."

This forebearing, easy tolerance of Aram's applies not only to religion but to human behavior in general. A Saroyan character is almost always as eccentric, in one way or another, but hardly ever is presented as a "misfit." Hugging his own truth, Aram has come to accept (if not always approve of) the truth of others. The simple folk of the valley are scarcely touched by common social convention; motivated from within, they add to what they feel instinctively only what ancient tradition has instilled in them. Aram is often found vacillating between the self-reflexive habits of his relatives and the unlimited expansiveness of his curious young mind and imagination. The "poet" in him feels a special affinity to the silent, brooding elders of the clan who are suspicious of the empty flow of words that pass for "education" and wisdom. There is one particularly striking example of this in "My Cousin Dikran, the Orator," one of the best known "Aram" stories.

Aram here focuses on the Old Man (his grandfather), who is "always impatient with any kind of talk, except the most direct and pertinent." He can't understand the fuss that's being made over his eleven-year-old grandchild, "the orator" Dikran, who is to deliver a public speech on why World War I was not fought in vain. Aram, on his part, is not without some reservations of his own:

> About ninety-two per cent of the vineyardists around Fresno, by actual count, believed that any man who could make a speech was a cultured man.

Being themselves limited in self-expression, they are

> profoundly impressed by public speakers who could get up on a plat-
> form, adjust spectacles on their noses, look at their pocket watches,
> cough politely, and, beginning quietly, lift their voices to a roar that
> shook the farmers to the roots and made them know the speaker was
> educated.

But the Old Man was not so disposed; indeed, he regarded speech-
makers as "fools and frauds."

Saroyan's portrait of his grandfather is archetypal: he is a Lear
figure, without the blinders that deceived that "foolish" king:

> He wanted to know what he didn't know, and that was all. He wanted
> no talk for talk's sake. He used to go to all the public meetings, but
> they never failed to sicken him.

When a speaker stopped making sense, the Old Man would give a
signal and the Garoghlanian clan, all thirty-seven of them, "would
rise and walk out, with the Old Man looking about furiously at
the poor farmers and saying, they're carrying the cross again—
let's go."

But, when finally, the family produces its own orator, the Old
Man is put on the spot. Even to Aram's generous eyes, Dikran is
an insufferable "book-reader":

> this boy was one of those very bright boys who have precious little
> real understanding, no humor at all, and the disgraceful and insulting
> attitude that all knowledge comes from the outside

—an outlandish contradiction of the Garoghlanian's ancient belief
that all wisdom comes from within.

When it's all over and the boy's talk is well received, the Old
Man has his say, family pride notwithstanding. He tells Dikran that
much as he applauds his eloquence and ambition in handling such
a large subject as World War I, he can only accept what he has
just heard from the lips of a small boy "who believed what he was
saying." Coming from an older speaker, "the horror of the remark
would be just too much for me to endure." Before turning in, the
Old Man sighs: "These crazy wonderful children of this crazy wonderful world!"

Words are suspect to Aram's grandfather because they so often
mask the truth, and hardly ever reach the feelings that lie beyond
them. Another exemplar of a man who knows the art of silence is

Uncle Khosrove, whom we have met before in "The Summer of the Beautiful White Horse." This "man of furious energy and uncommon sadness" has a friend from the old country, an Arab, "who was as still as a rock inwardly, whose sadness was expressed by brushing a speck of dust from his knee and never speaking." Indeed, he speaks only when he has to, and then "as if he regretted the necessity to do so." Yet he has won the friendship of his uncle and is welcome in Aram's home, where, as Aram notes, nothing counted more "than the charm of a people; the variety; the quality which made them human and worthy of further extension in time." Though Uncle Khosrove is known to be loud and temperamental when aroused in a game of backgammon at the club, when he is with his Arab friend, he can sit silently for hours, sipping the coffee and smoking the cigarettes Aram's mother has brought them. Once when Aram was in the next room, idly riffling through old magazines, he overhead their "silence" and asked his mother about it. She replied, "Some people talk when they have something to say . . . and some people don't." She explains to the child that one can talk without words. But what good, then are words, the boy wants to know. She replies,

> Not good most of the time. Most of the time they're only good to keep back what you really want to say, or something you don't want known.

She can't tell what the men are saying to each other, she adds, because "it isn't in words; but they know."

Once Aram hears his uncle shout at the Arab, "'*Pay no attention to it, I tell you,*' although the Arab had said nothing." And once Aram hears his uncle say under his breath as his friend leaves the house, "the poor and burning orphans." When after a while the Arab's visits stop, the boy questions his uncle about it. Khosrove is silent at first, then suddenly furious, as if his grief had been violated by the boy's questions. Aram wonders if his uncle will ever forgive him. But one day he returns to tell his nephew the Arab's sad story:

> The Arab is dead. He died an orphan in an alien world, six thousand miles from home. He wanted to go home and die. He wanted to see his sons again. He wanted to talk to them again. He wanted to smell them. He wanted to hear them breathing. He had no money. He used to think of them all the time. Now he is dead. Now go away. I love you.

And although his feelings are aroused, Aram goes away, to visit his cousin Mourad: "which must have pleased my Uncle Khosrove very much," he muses, "and him feel there was some hope for me after all."

Essentially a mood piece, "The Poor and Burning Arab" reverts to Saroyan's poetic principle, with the lyric note not only balanced but artfully integrated with touches of gentle humor. Though Aram's empathy exceeds that of the average child, he is not without the chameleonlike flexibility of most children; avid with curiosity and the readiness to move on, his vivid presence dissipates the gloom in which the elders are hopelessly locked, time and again.

What charms and moves us in the end about *My Name is Aram* is how without ever turning his back on the ancient well of loss and silence, the youthful "rebel" in Aram works his way—with hope and humor—into the American mold.

This broadening of perspective and gradually his awareness of form lead him toward the possibilities of the drama and the novel.

5

Toward an American Theater:
A Radical Conversion

I saw drama in everything because there was drama in everything—because there was drama in myself.

—Saroyan

AMERICAN THEATER IN THE 1930S

IN one of her less typically acerb and hard-hitting theater columns
for *Partisan Review* in 1940, Mary McCarthy at once sized up
the sudden arrival of William Saroyan on the theater scene. She
characterized the neophyte playwright who had descended on
Broadway the year before with two plays as a stranger from another planet, as "an innocent on Broadway . . . [whose] strict re-
gime" involved fighting off "Ideas, Movements, Sex and
Commercialism."[1] Showing a generosity rare for her, she went on
to acknowledge that his "well of inspiration, located somewhere in
his early adolescence, has never run dry. He is still able to look at
the world with the eyes of a sensitive newsboy, and to see it eternally brand-new and touched with wonder."

McCarthy admits in retrospect (in her book *Sights and Spectacles*) to "a cocksure, condescending cleverness" in her drama criticism of those years and, truth to tell, she was not altogether lured
by the two plays she was reviewing: "The boundaries of [Saroyan's]
world," she goes on to say, "are the boundaries of the newsboy's
field of vision." Yet when she proceeds to compare *My Heart's in
the Highlands* and *The Time of Your Life* with the plays of Clifford
Odets and John Steinbeck, she acknowledges "the purity of [Saro-
yan's] work is blinding. Puerile and arrogant and sentimental as
he may be, he is never cheap."[2] In contrast to the "autointoxica-
tion" and "fine writing" of those two contemporaries,

Saroyan's writing remains fresh and crisp and never has the look of having been pawed over by the author. . . . Furthermore, . . . you will rarely find a constellation of symbols repeating itself, you will rarely get the same effect warmed up for a second serving.

McCarthy's creative eye seizes at once on the visual appeal of the plays, a fact that clearly announces to her that he is "more naturally at home in the theatre than in fiction." And she recognizes his need for the new medium as having been created by his special world of

ice-cream cones and toys, of bicycles and bugles, and somersaults and shotguns, of hunger and of banquets that tell of distant disasters, of good-hearted grocers and lovable frauds, of drunk fairy princes and pinball games that pay.

Other commentators of the day would make the inevitable connection between Saroyan's "world" and old-time vaudeville, but McCarthy does more, pointing out the appropriateness of popular native form to Saroyan's essentially positive feelings about America. "Saroyan is in love with America and very insistent about it," she observes, though *not* as "the propagandist of the second crusade for democracy." Nor does she see a contradiction in the fact that he shows America both as "an ordinary place" and as "the most wonderful country in the world." For the "literal fact" of the first statement is no more "realistic" than "*the state of mind that the reader is asked to believe in*" (the italics are mine). It is out of this discrepancy that pathos emerges. And she concludes, "The America Saroyan loves is the old America, and the plays he weaves around it are not so much daring innovation as legends."

The astuteness of McCarthy's judgment lies in her recognition that Saroyan's voice has an authentic ring, combining what appears to have an "American" flavor with a viable American viewpoint. Writing dramatic criticism in an era that barely tolerated the genre outside the daily press, this young critic was exceptional in the seriousness with which she approached the new playwrights, and her receptivity to Saroyan was not unreasonable in the light of her general hostility to the topics and values of the prevailing realist school. Herself an aspiring creative writer, she is impatient with the "graceless" prose of Eugene O'Neill who, like Farrell and Dreiser, "cannot write." O'Neill's "lack of verbal gift," she insists, "became a curse to the American stage."[3]

The fact that McCarthy could look favorably on an unschooled playwright from the boondocks, while perversely castigating a dramatist of growing reputation, suggests that a period in the theater was coming to an end, paving the way for new impressions and impulses. Thus, once more, Saroyan would be able to jump on a bandwagon that seemed—for a time at least—expressly prepared for him. But where was the American theater heading if not in the direction of O'Neill, Steinbeck, and Odets at the moment of Saroyan's arrival? A succinct review may help explain.

No critical survey of the American theater in the twentieth century has ever to my knowledge pointed out the uneven, indeed shaky foundation on which the dramatic arts were based in this country—if indeed it could be said that it had one. Though it nourished audiences with serious fare for nearly three decades, the Little Theatre movement in the early part of the century—and one thinks, in particular, of the two most prestigious ones, the Washington Square Players and the Provincetown Players—spawned no more than a handful of promising American playwrights. The Little Theatre's major discovery, of course, was Eugene O'Neill, some of whose best work, along with a slew of short plays, had been produced by both Washington Square and Provincetown Players long before the Theatre Guild, in 1928, took on two of his most experimental plays, *Marco Millions* and *Strange Interlude.* But other discoveries, like Susan Glaspell, Djuna Barnes, Wallace Stevens, Edna St. Vincent Millay, Zona Gale, and Edmund Wilson, went on to pursue more lucrative forms of writing. The real staples of the American stage were Chekhov, Maeterlinck, Musset, Ibsen, G. B. Shaw, Wilde, and Strindberg, and for a long time so remained even for the semicommercial theater that the Theatre Guild came to represent in the next three decades.

The Theatre Guild's high concept of the dramatic arts has been much extolled, as it should be, and it is not my intent here to minimize its reputation as possibly the single major influence in the creation of a theatergoing American public. But it is essential to an understanding of the course that American drama took—and the obstacles that faced the new playwright—to take note that in the first ten years of the Guild's existence (1919–29) it produced the work of only six American playwrights, one of which, *The Garrick Gaieties,* by Richard Rodgers and Lorenz Hart, was hardly to be defined as "drama." Other productions by Americans in that period were Elmer Rice's *The Adding Machine,* Sidney Howard's *They Knew What They Wanted,* S. N. Behrman's *The Second Man,* Du Bose and Dorothy Heyward's *Porgy,* and the aforementioned two plays by O'Neill. The next ten years had a little better showing—ten new plays by Americans, among them two (in 1939) by

William Saroyan. But more to the point than numbers is the fact that until the mid-1930s the American theater was dominated by European drama, or drama that was derivative of it.

Founded by three American playwrights, Philip Barry, Sidney Howard, and S. N. Behrman, and called a "guild" because it resembled the medieval trade guilds in its organization, the Theatre Guild held itself independent of Broadway commerce. Yet because it relied heavily on subscription audiences, it had to strike a balance between high standards of professionalism and the desire to spread the gospel to as wide an audience as possible.[4] Thus, even with its rising talents, the American theater was in a tough bind. To "Americanize" it, it was necessary to experiment, and experiment implied a return to the practice of the little theaters with their narrow interests and restricted theatrical possibilities. The unalterable fact was that in a large, non-homogeneous society, tastes and interests were inevitably diverse. Taking a cue from the motion picture industry, which had succeeded in aligning certain tastes and interests on an entertainment level, the stage turned to Broadway musicals, and for a long time the most "American" sounds and words came not from serious playwrights but from writers of musical comedy such as Cole Porter, George Gershwin, Irving Berlin, and Rodgers and Hammerstein.

Oddly enough, it was in a time of economic stress, during the worst period of the Depression when "escape" had high priority for Americans, that American sounds began to adhere to artistic dramatic forms. Through a national burden mutually experienced had come a new self-awareness and the realization that social changes must create a new reality, remote from old styles and old ideas. Though immediately apparent, the transformation was not clear-cut—if only because the individual talent (to rephrase T. S. Eliot) had no tradition from which to gain perspective and not enough support (financial and moral) to blaze new paths overnight.

There was another matter, too, one generally acknowledged. For all the dramatic nature of our history—the nation's birth in revolution, its Promethean reach for the elusive dream—American society lacked a basic component of the dramatic imagination: it lacked a self-contained, self-centered culture fed on myth and folk experience. If drama is, as Hegel put it, "the product of an already essentially cultured condition of national life," it is not surprising that in America the medium was not taken seriously for a long time. Moreover, to a society still in the making, with little or no rigid barriers for the individual to surmount, the Aristotelian concept of conflict and tragic finality had an alien ring. Oriented by a frontier psychology that favored the pragmatic act over the abstract ideal or ultimate intention, American dramatic art invariably fumbled in its initial drive to inwardness and the larger implications of human action. The career of Eugene O'Neill is a case in point: he is a vivid example of a serious American playwright who found his inspiration outside the pale of American experience, mainly sparked by the work of European masters like Ibsen, Strindberg, and the German expressionists. It was only in his later works that O'Neill began to speak as an American seeking to breathe authentic life into a still indistinct image.[5]

The influence of Broadway and the commercial theater aside, there were other problems as well. The Theatre Guild's bright hope of establishing a theater dedicated to "good drama on a permanent basis" that would ultimately draw "American authors of capacity" was hamstrung by financial considerations not easy to surmount.[6] In his book on the first ten years of the Guild, Walter Prichard Eaton lays much of the blame for the slow growth of an *American* theater on the fact that the Guild (its best supporter) was pledged to subscribers to produce "finished entertainment." It had, in fact, turned up some American work that was more than that—Elmer Rice's quasi-philosophical expressionist play, *The Adding Machine,* the earnest psychological dramas of Sidney Howard, and, as early as in 1925, a play about a miners' strike in West Virginia, *Processional* by John Howard Lawson. (Lawson would later write proletarian dramas.) And capping its efforts on behalf of artistic American work, it had backed the most ambitious of O'Neill's plays to date, *Strange Interlude.*[7]

But the radical conversion, the "Americanization" of the theater, would come about through an *indirect* influence, through the Guild's support of a new wave in acting and directing. Unwittingly, it was Harold Clurman's Group Theatre that would turn the trick. "Unwittingly," because the Group Theatre's original purpose was not to emphasize American works but simply to create a wider-based people's theater. Clurman still had one foot in the Theatre Guild when in 1931 he founded, with the help of Cheryl Crawford and Lee Strasberg (two other Guild members) the company that advanced a "collective spirit in America for the first time." It was in its efforts for this impassioned cause that the Group Theatre was able to furnish the soil for a new symbiotic relationship between playwright and audience. Magically, it seemed, they had at last found each other.

A metamorphosis now took place in the image of the dramatist from the well-bred, well-read "literary" writers (most of whom had gone to Harvard or Yale) to that of the people's writer, a tenant at best of what Virginia Woolf would call "the leaning tower," from which the writer gained a new perspective.[8] Having a wider experience of the life around him, the new playwright was no longer uneasy about finding an audience capable of measuring up to his elevated standards. In a period of economic levelling off, the dramatist had a wider range of subjects at his command and thus the opportunity to shift the tide from the esoteric to the radical passions.

Essentially involved, at first, with developing new techniques of theater production, the Group Theatre did much to advance the idea of drama as a socially motivated art. In the course of its nine years of existence (1931–40), its efforts spilled over into protest and even propaganda drama.

In his detailed survey of the Group Theatre years, *The Fervent Years,* Clurman recalls that he initially envisioned the company as "a celebratory theatre," one that would emphasize "the perfectibility of man, or at least, the inevitability of the struggle against evil."[9] But to the world outside, it gained a *political* dimension as well. In a talk to librarians, Waldo Frank, the writer, proclaimed,

The reason why I believe in the Group is because I am primarily interested in creating a new world. . . . [T]here must be a new society, a new humanity in the moral and spiritual as well as the economic sense.

And he went on to define the "new humanity" in lofty terms:

a group of conscious people . . . organized to work toward the creating of a new world, . . . an alliance of the men of mind, of vision, the artists, with the People, consciously working toward this creative end.[10]

Having moved (like Edmund Wilson and many other writers of the day) in the direction of the new politics, Frank was awaiting—for a time at least—the achievement of the Marxist prophecy, and was quick to see the theater as a potential tool.

With no explicit political position, the Group Theatre retained as its relatively modest aim—to quote one of its brightest lights, the actor-director Robert Lewis—"to save the American theatre, and, incidentally, change the world."[11] In its earliest and most prolific "find"—Clifford Odets—its expectations loomed large.

Odets—a high-school dropout from the Bronx and a young actor turned playwright—typified the new dramatist. Skilled in theatrical technique and endowed with an impassioned social consciousness, he not only proved an instant box-office success, but through a succession of stirring protest plays created a new Zeitgeist that lifted the heavy gloom so long projected by the O'Neill theater. In the course of one year, 1935, Odets would provide the noncommercial stage with five plays (some more successful than others) and three additional ones by 1940. Though not comparable, artistically, to O'Neill's work, plays like *Waiting for Lefty, Awake and Sing,* and *Golden Boy* would project an image of contemporary America so consistently vivid as to make O'Neill seem foreign and even dated in comparison.

The accolades Odets came to receive from prestigious critics like Joseph Wood Krutch and Stark Young have to this day sustained his reputation as a major radical playwright. Yet it had not escaped Ms. McCarthy's sharp eye—as early as 1938—that these dramas of strikes, unemployment, and the decline of the middle class were flawed by "the narrowness of his invention, the monotony of his subject matter."[12] Literal in detail and circumscribed by the economic realities of the day, they seemed to simplify the truth with their tacked-on political rhetoric. Indeed, a lyric romanticism hangs over Odets characters. In *Paradise Lost,* for instance, the step-by-step destruction of his middle-class family by "the system" does not prepare us for the resounding optimism of his hero at the end of the play: "I tell you the whole world is for men to possess. The world is beautiful. . . . [M]en will sing at their work, men will love." The words convey both more and less than the unreal expectations of the revolutionary who can envisage the end of "class war" and the dawn of "brotherhood" in the very midst of social chaos and degradation.[13]

Pathos in itself cannot give dramatic dimension to character; and in Odets' case, an implied determinism played havoc with a humanistic affirmation that seemed to mock rather than support the Marxist rationale. If nonetheless he was able to enter into a close, reciprocal relationship with his audience, it was because he virtually put his audience on the stage. The words his characters spoke were common, easy to understand, but they had passion and filled the theater with their intensity. His symbolism was threadbare, his metaphors and allusions hardly subtle, but who needed them? In the mid-1930s it was easy enough to relate to the injustices that plagued lower-class Americans in particular, and, admittedly, Odets had the gift of setting before our eyes both the exploiters and the exploited in our midst.

What is still left to explain about Odets is how against all odds he was able to secure a place in the American theater that even at this distance seems well deserved. In an era that was run over with banal theater fare that passed for serious protest drama, he was able to sidetrack the deadening impact of "collectivity" and pluck out of an alien ideology what was particular to the nation's temper, revealing what America had not yet clearly perceived about itself. Having skirted the naturalist's trap, Odets had remained open to experience, able to hear in the common speech of the day the echoes and overtones of mythic America, with its unappeasable drives and expectations, its grandiose Emersonian faith in individual destiny. In dreams aborted and delusions exposed, he had found a potent source of drama for the American theater.

In his personal life, as in his work, Odets would prove an imperfect Marxist. His defection to Hollywood and its easy lucre have been cited as evidence that he sold out to the "bourgeois" creed of self over society. But we also know that by 1940 he had abandoned his earlier exalted notions of the "collective" theater as the only real theater.[14] In the year of his last play with the Theatre Group (*Night Music*), he wrote

> Communism needs to be Americanized before it will have any effect in America. My personal feeling about social change is this. I have no opinion as a private citizen. But in the world of the theatre, in relation to my plays and audiences for them, leftism as understood by the Communists is impossible.[15]

Nor did the playwright hide his need to reach a wider audience:

> I once thought it would be enough to play in a small cellar, but I soon saw that those who would come to the cellar were not the ones in need of what I could say.[16]

The dramatist's attitude toward the collective theater was changing with the times. What had once been liberating in its radical thrust to bring social relevance to a flagging, eclectic theater now became confining for the playwright with a more wide-ranging view. Lee Strasberg himself in the Theatre Group's later years would own to its steady encroachment on the dramatist's territory:

> As long as the Group was not in existence, the people are concerned only with their hopes and their dreams, but once the Group becomes organized then certain contradictions appear.

It ends, he points out, with "a disproportion between what each individual demands for his own development and what the Group activity demands for each individual."[17] If the final product was more perfectly turned out because of the combined effort of experts, there was always the risk that in the process the independent voice of the writer would grow dim, his intended ambiguity or irony muffled by a blatant ideology in which he only half believed.

On the positive side of the ledger, there is no denying the ingenuity, energy, dedication, and, best of all, humanity that the radical theater inspired. The great profusion of theater groups, from the much heralded government-sponsored Federal Theatre (which mirabile dictu produced T. S. Eliot's *Murder in the Cathedral* in 1934) to the less distinguished Theatre Union, Theatre Action, the Workers Theatre, and many agitprop groups of short duration, speak for themselves. Their lure resided as much in the great actors, directors, and stage designers as in the dramas themselves. If they were loud and crude in their satire, simplistic in their ideas of human behavior, and totally unschooled in the aesthetic sense, they nonetheless succeeded in making drama a very special thing for those who had had no experience of the theater until then.

Paradoxical as it may seem, in bringing the theater to the masses, the radical theater of the 1930s accentuated the high seriousness of the dramatic arts; by favoring those who spoke in the political accents of the day, it encouraged national concerns of immediate moment. Ideas and ideals struck home. There was, moreover, no question of its being an "alternative" theater—the concept of off Broadway had not yet emerged—attempting, rather, to be a part of the mainstream of serious drama to be considered alongside the perennial Ibsen, Shaw, and Chekhov, the Shakespearean repertoire, and the classics and literary drama based on contemporary novels, such as *The Good Earth*, *Ethan Frome*, and *Of Mice and Men*.

With regard to its own productions, the radical theater's one concession to popularity was a theatrical thrust that ultimately played havoc with critical evaluation. In an era of great performers and eye-catching staging, the secret of good theater was no longer a secret. No one knew this better than Harold Clurman, who held that "the significance of a play inheres in all its parts, that is, in its acting, setting, sound and movement—the production—and not exclusively in the writer's work."[18] More extravagant still was his belief that the combined creativity that goes into a "production" should equal that of the dramatist. There is a lesson both for critics of the drama and their readers in a further observation he makes, which I venture to quote at some length because of its importance to latter-day critics of Saroyan's plays. In his support of the "ensemble" method, Clurman writes,

> The theatre speaks through its mouth, its limbs, its apparel, its physical posture and structure—of which are tangible forms of its heart and mind. These are related to the audience which gives it birth, hence the society of its day. Very little of what we see, hear and feel in the theatre is altogether accidental or entirely inconsiderable in any epoch, *even when it is intellectually poor or shallow as literature.*[19]

I have italicized the last phrase because it inadvertently gives us the clue to the dissatisfaction we feel in reading most drama criticism in retrospect; Clurman's statement supports our sense of the unreliability of much dramatic criticism based solely on the initial performance of a work.

The art of the theater has often been referred to as an "impure art" because of its dependence on audience support. What Clurman observed as a further aspect of its "impurity" was its resistance to general criteria of literary criticism. For more than *literature* is necessarily involved in the complex of the arts that go into a dramatic performance. The drama critic's job is not only arduous and challenging, it is often specious, being based on ephemera that reflect an audience's transitory tastes and interests. This leads one to conclude that it is not enough to examine the era from which a dramatist emerges; one needs also to examine the critics who were there to receive him.

It was a motley crew that greeted Saroyan in 1939 when his first play, *My Heart's in the Highlands,* was produced, first by the Theatre Group and subsequently by the Theatre Guild. Dramatic literature in America can boast of no real historians who have dealt with the subject in a broad and encompassing way. On the theory of the drama, one is hard pressed to think of any one outside of Edgar Allan Poe, who in *The American Drama,* said it all so cogently and briefly, when he protested that there was a paucity of "spirituality" in the American theater. In our time, critics like Eric Bentley, Martin Esslin, or Robert Brustein have eschewed the historical approach, dealing often with personal passions and concerns, and an encyclopedic critic like John Gassner was too hidebound by reviews in the press to give us a complete and dependable overview. A critic like Joseph Wood Krutch, on the other hand, was a man of letters with more than one string to his bow and in the theater it was the journalist that had the upper hand.

As an all-round man of the theater who examined plays in their

original scripts (as indeed he had done with Saroyan's play), Clurman had had an advantage over most drama critics who worked
under the limitations of journalism while being asked to make judgments on the basis of a *performed* text alone. You could have been
a young genius in the theater in the 1930s and 1940s and never
have made it to the top for the following reasons: (1) You had no
political leanings, (2) Your work was not particularly "theatrical,"
or (3) You were solely dependent on the daily newspaper critic
who had working-man's hours, often limited experience, and the
pressure of a next-day deadline. Of these three reasons, the last
was probably most fatal. Outside the daily newspapers, there was
a somewhat higher level of critical competence. I have mentioned
Mary McCarthy's often perceptive work for *Partisan Review;* and
there were a few other still remembered names who appeared regularly in weekly and monthly publications. But even these critics
were not without individual bias (sometimes ideological), which in
retrospect is much more evident than it must have been in their
own day.

John Mason Brown and Joseph Wood Krutch, who wrote for
The Saturday Review of Literature and *The Nation* respectively,
were thoughtful and open-minded, but Brown himself characterized the unrewarding life of a drama critic as that of "a happy leper
on an island no Father Damien will visit." The poor wretch, he
went on, had to

> rationalize reaction, interest his readers, suggest quality, recapture
> mood and atmosphere, comment on the theatre in terms of the theatre,
> no less than of life, be true to what he is personally while being imper-
> sonal with those upon whose work he presumes to pass judgment—
> and do all these things under pressure of time.[20]

Krutch's problem was different: a literary historian, he was too
readily given to encapsulating a work within a genre or tradition.
In taking a long view, his eyes failed to alight on those small depar-
tures from the norm that announce a writer's originality. Even
when his praise was overblown—as when writing about Odets—
he seemed to miss the particular genius of the playwright, and
failed to suggest the full force of his passions.

Equally prominent was the erudite playwright-critic Stark
Young, who leaned toward the classics and literary foreign plays
of the last century. This long-time editor of *The New Republic*
would readily verify his opinion from a printed text, but if on
occasion he showed enthusiasm for a new American play, he was

less inclined to expend his critical acumen on it. In none of his extensive commentaries on O'Neill do we find him contending with the playwright's special relation to American life.

Finally, one cannot exempt from the list of fallible drama critics the two most important voices of the 30s and 40s: the sprightly cosmopolite George Jean Nathan of *Smart Set* and and *American Mercury* fame, and *The New York Times'* pillar of authority, Brooks Atkinson. Eminently skilled and frequently moved to enthusiasm (to the infinite benefit of one new playwright, William Saroyan), they were not without their blind spots and unexamined opinions. Foolhardy as it may seem to poke chinks into their armor, one is compelled to do so if only to undo the damage to playwrights who may have slipped through their fingers, or who, when caught, remained locked thereafter within incomplete reports or misleading judgments. For the probability of redressing the balance at some future time is all too slim. To this day, there is no practice of historical reappraisal in American drama criticism, and still no permanent theater repertory of the sort that keeps European dramatists alive long after they have died.

One thinks of the curious fate of Maxwell Anderson, a poet manqué and rare American tragedian, whose quarrel was not with the public but with a few influential critics who failed to acknowledge what was permanent in his work. As far as I can tell no one has yet bothered to controvert the unduly harsh things that were said about his plays when he turned from the conventions of the realistic theater to write drama in blank verse in the early 1930s. Like O'Neill before him, he aspired to the tragic mode (which the philosophy of Marx was making obsolete), while holding that the exalted emotions could only be expressed in poetry. At a time when mere physical survival was the major preoccupation, it took courage to turn to *meta*physical concerns. Indeed, even O'Neill, who had made high tragedy his exclusive province in the twenties, would virtually abandon it in the next decade. Armed with high moral purpose, Anderson seemed to be reverting to an earlier American faith in the individual's capacity for self-transcendence.

Though Anderson had tasted acclaim with his social comedies (*What Price Glory?* and *Both Your Houses*), this uncommonly cultivated dramatist was becoming increasingly uncomfortable with the radical theater and the banality it engendered in the name of "modernity." In an essay, "Poetry in the Theatre," he would later complain that the stage was "dominated by those who wish to offer something immediate about our political, social and economic life." Though himself a socially conscious man, he saw the stage as "a cathedral," and the American theater as "the one really living American art" capable of reflecting the "racial dream."

It is incumbent on the dramatist to be a poet, and incumbent on the poet to be a prophet, dreamer and interpreter of the racial dream. . . . [W]hat we become depends on what we dream and desire.[21]

Having begun his experiment in the poetic theater with two historical plays set in Elizabethan England, *Elizabeth the Queen* and *Mary of Scotland,* Anderson had had no trouble adapting Elizabethan verse conventions to his two subsequent plays, dealing with American history: *Night over Taos* and *Valley Forge.* His purpose in using history was not, like Eliot's, to capture an aura of irony. It was, rather, to provide a dimension that would make possible "the language of emotion" and the use of broad themes of loyalty and conscience. But in 1935 he ventured (against his better judgment) to write a verse play on a contemporary subject. Going back to the Sacco-Vanzetti story he had used in coauthoring *Gods of Lightning,* he now attempted to consider, in *Winterset,* the far-reaching ethical implications of the case. Anderson had done it again—the play became a hit and won the Pulitzer Prize. But critical acclaim was not unanimous. While Stark Young jeered maliciously at its attempts at "Shakespearian" verse,[22] and Joseph Wood Krutch beat his head against the wall trying to explain why Anderson succeeded where O'Neill "failed,"[24] Edmund Wilson laid down the fiat: "Blank verse has no longer any relation to the tempo and tongue of our lives." Declaring that Anderson's play was "the most striking example of obsolescence of verse technique," he further protested that "instead of getting deeper into reality as he progresses in his artistic career, [Anderson] is carried by his blank verse farther away."[25]

But "getting deeper into reality" was just what Anderson and a few others like him were after: realism in the theater had to be overhauled before reality could be found again. While Anderson would remain essentially a voice of the didactic thirties (hence his popularity), he helped in no small way to advance the radical conversion. By allowing the light and dark to mingle in Elizabethan fashion, he restored a measure of ambiguity and complexity in the dramatic encounters of self and society. What captivated audiences and newspaper critics of his day was his power to transform reality by the magic of his words and an impassioned recognition that drama ultimately emerges from the individual's soul. The shining, lyric moments of *Winterset* are few, but the fact they existed at all was a sign that new possibilities were opening up for the American stage. If Anderson himself did not sufficiently advance the poetic theater, his work was paving the way for the language of emotion, and it was that concept that would eventually break the back of the Realistic theater everywhere.

The idea of a poetic theater did not end with Anderson. It would go through many mutations on the American stage. In the same year as *Winterset,* the poet Archibald MacLeish wrote an agitprop verse play, *Panic*—about a national crisis on Wall Street—that ran for three nights on Broadway. Though he would write only three more verse plays (all exclusively for radio) MacLeish became an ardent advocate of poetic drama. In pointedly political terms, he argued, in an article titled "The Hope of Poetry in the Theatre" that the time was now ripe because a "new community of interest" was making possible an understanding between audience and poet. He identified that "common experience" as "social injustice"—so far recognized only by the political Left. He warned that

> as long as that common experience was so limited, those who do not share it must continue to take their theatre in a rotting house and miss altogether the delight and excitement of the building of a new.[25]

But as the decade came to a close, the "common experience" underwent a sea change, as did the nature of the poetic theater. As the utopian aspects of the revolution in Russia grew dim, even the political Left in America would begin to question the validity of social realism. In 1939, with the signing of the Nazi-Soviet Non-Aggression Pact, the concept of "social justice" had been stretched to accommodate humanity at large, most particularly the multifarious victims of political oppression in Europe who were making the headlines. The light and dark of human behavior, no better understood than before, now became invariably ambiguous, undefined. One might venture to become a "political" dramatist again—though now the tag would be antifascists, not Leftist—or one might try to look beyond politics and see the poetic, universal truths invisible to the naked eye.

The arena of a developing American theater was ripe for a new kind of playwright. Saroyan was moving in these Broadway years from discursive dialogue to dramatic dialogue. He was to produce four major plays: *My Heart's in the Highlands, The Time of Your Life, The Beautiful People*, and *Love's Old Sweet Song.*

My Heart's in the Highlands and its Satellites

At the end of the decade, two new playwrights in America took the second course, and the poetic theater experienced still another mutation. In 1938 the Pulitzer Prize-winning novelist Thornton Wilder gave Broadway its first non-naturalistic hit in his first produced play, *Our Town*. Using no verse at all, and dealing with ordinary scenes of American life, he cast a poetic eye on the totality of man's earthly experience and evoked a feeling of eternal harmony with the universe. A year later, William Saroyan, a writer who had made his mark in fiction, unexpectedly captivated both audiences and critics with two unconventional plays. Also devoid of verse and not totally unrealistic, *My Heart's in the Highlands* and *The Time of Your Life* breathed poetry into everyday scenes and speech, displaying that the Saroyan flair for the theater matched the flair he had shown some five years before with the short story.

No two writers could have been more unlike in terms of background and personality than Wilder and Saroyan, yet they had certain things in common, most obviously a sense of having arrived at a crossroad in the American theater. Wilder's dramatic reputation rests solely on three plays (the other two being *The Skin of Our Teeth* and *The Matchmaker*, which was made into a musical, *Hello, Dolly*). He had come to the theater as an established novelist, with a critical following for his works of literary and historical inspiration. This cosmopolite who had sat at the feet of Gertrude Stein in the Paris of the 1920s, absorbing her new ideas for *Everybody's Autobiography*, had had the further advantage of personal acquaintance with Edmund Wilson, the prestigious reviewer of *The New Republic*. But if the slim Wilder repertory was quick in finding its literary litany and and subsequent acceptance into the critical canon, it would remain even less examined over the years than the plays of Clifford Odets. Saroyan's dramatic work, considerably larger in bulk than Wilder's, would be examined least of all, for reasons that should become clear as I discuss his plays.

Like Wilder, Saroyan was extravagantly acclaimed, but with a good-humored indulgence for his lack of wordliness and literary cachet; at thirty-one, he was welcomed as the white-haired boy whose theatrical future was heralded as much by himself as by others. Though his active career in the theater, actually, did not extend beyond the 1940s, his commitment to the dramatic form never waned. He continued writing plays until close to his death in 1981 and left behind a huge batch of unproduced and largely experimental plays.

But a more pertinent parallel between the two dramatists would be revealed in the distinctly native qualities they projected. A year after Wilder's success in turning the tide of the radical theater by *celebrating* instead of *criticizing* American life, Saroyan was announcing his aspiration to become an *American* playwright who would reveal the real America to Americans. As he would soon write, in tones of bravura, in a preface to his printed play, *My Heart's in the Highlands*,

> It is surely impertinent for me to believe that the greater and truer American theatre shall begin its life after the appearance and influence of this play, but God forgive me, that is what I believe.[26]

As immediately perceived, *Our Town* is a more American play than *My Heart's in the Highlands*; Wilder's cozy, homey atmosphere of a New England small town is more easily recognizable than Saroyan's run-down rural home of an immigrant family about to be dispossessed. But Wilder's philosophical tone is curiously stoic and only distantly affirmative. In this panoramic play, the poetry that surfaces is centered on the knowledge that death is the equalizer, that wondrous as life actually is, only in death can its values and beauty be apprehended. (Wilder's second play, *The Skin of Our Teeth*, went a step further into abstraction to consider not America alone but the eternal pilgrimage of the human race; and in its composition, he reverted to European sources, most especially Pirandello and the protosurrealist Alfred Jarry.)

Nourished as he was on the Reality principle, Saroyan would find it hard to be so abstract. "In the time of your life, live so that in that good time there shall be no ugliness in death for yourself or for any life your life touches," he would counter in his second play, quoting from the Credo. Steeped in an Emersonian faith in the individual's capacity to control his destiny, Saroyan found the theater especially congenial to his view of life: in the arena of the theater the spectacle itself would affirm that life *while lived* is what matters.

* * *

If I have gone on at some length on the American theater and its special florescence in the 1930s, it is because I believe with Eliot that no artist has his complete meaning alone. Only when we place Saroyan's dramatic work within the framework of an evolving

American drama can we perceive its more than passing value. For the measure of his importance as a playwright lies beyond the often uncommonly pleasurable theatrical experience his work affords; he was clearly a pivotal figure—more than any other of his day— in bringing about a major imaginative and technical shift in the American theater of the post-World War II years. In his unusual ability to combine the commonplace world with the poet's "language of emotion," Saroyan glided straight into that open-ended "people's theater" that the proletarian playwrights had struggled to achieve and failed for lack of sufficient art. His own struggles would lie elsewhere.

That celebrated "daring young man" from the West with the guileless, foreign-looking face, brashly berating his critics and making headlines with pronouncements that he would "revolutionize" the American theater was an unsettling presence in the hub of the theater elite; and as he swung from high seriousness to spoofing self-adulation, he became endlessly exploitable. Eager to be noticed, he was fair game for personality hunters looking for copy to fill their daily columns; one playwright even wrote a nasty parody of him as a "Saroyanesque" character. Indeed, in the decade that he remained close to the Broadway scene—where he was both lavishly praised and cruelly ridiculed—it was the rare newspaper writer who treated him halfway seriously as an artist.

One such exception was the *New York Times* reporter and interviewer Robert Van Gelder,[27] who had an uncommon empathy for new writers.[28] In a full-page interview in the *New York Times Book Review*, Van Gelder managed to get beneath the artificial veneer of "the great Saroyan" by skillfully keeping pace with the writer's quick switch from one topic to the next. Far from striking an arrogant pose, Saroyan seems "extremely friendly, one of those rare people who have managed to get along without seemingly erecting any barriers against others."

> Black-haired, about medium height, with a jutting nose that is not so large as the nose of Cyrano de Bergerac . . . there is a suggestion of considerable vitality beneath a nervous manner that is just surface.

What stands out is his "courtesy . . . grown directly out of an extraordinary sensitivity, an inescapable consciousness of the reactions of those about him." Perceptively, Van Gelder also captures the underlying tone of earnestness when he questions Saroyan about his sudden fame as "the golden boy of the theatre":

It's just that the door was opened to me. My first show was put on and the people liked it. Naturally I'm turning out more. . . . it is part of my general plan. I'm still writing short stories and I'll go on from this to novels. . . . But right now the theatre is wide open. No one's making full use of its possibilities.

Van Gelder does not miss the writer's overriding belief in his own gifts; he makes it plausible by suggesting its source. Though Saroyan confesses he is reading Strindberg and Molière under the guidance of George Jean Nathan, he readily assents when asked if he is a "natural." This is something he has known, he explains, since the age of eighteen, when he tried to follow the pulp-story pattern, and failing, decided he would have to write in his own way.

When asked about his gambling, he responds in all seriousness that he goes to the racetrack not so much to gamble as to

listen to the talk and watch the people—it is a fine place to loaf. And these idlers, too, are part of the American scene. . . . Don't get me wrong, I don't hang around a bookie joint in the name of art. But art comes into it, it comes into every department of life.

An example of his "extraordinary sensitivity" comes at the end of the interview. As the two men walk through the Theatre Guild's waiting room on the way out, Saroyan is suddenly "shy" before a roomful of unemployed actors. In an instant, he is eagerly expounding a scheme to lift these down-and-out artists out of their plight. But as he speaks he is so moved he is "unwilling to meet again the hopeful, expectant looks of these people he was powerless to help."

Perhaps because his own passage into the theater world had been relatively easy, Saroyan could feel sympathy for those less fortunate than himself. A series of fortuitous circumstances had led to the production of his first dramatic effort (one not originally even written for the stage) and its subsequent unexpected success. A letter in 1935 from Brooks Atkinson inquiring about a rumor that he was writing a play had prompted Saroyan to write a short, evocative piece, "Subway Circus," about the fantasies of riders in a subway car. But the work did not have the approval of the editors who had joined Saroyan in publishing *Three Times Three*, and he had shelved it. When in the following year he was tapped again, this time for a collection of sixteen one-act plays being edited by William Kozleulo, Saroyan plucked from his bag of pieces "The Man With the Heart in the Highlands" (already printed in *Three Times Three* as well as in an avant-garde magazine in Paris) and recast that fragile sketch of poetry and poverty into a one-act play. But it was ultimately Harold Clurman's direct invitation to Saroyan to write a play for the Group Theatre that led to a true resurrection of that story into the longer work he titled, *My Heart's in the Highlands.*

In point of fact (as Saroyan was himself to admit), whatever fortuitous elements led to his "break" in the theater, it was an inevitability fated by his own nature that provided its realization. As he was soon to boast in articles and prefaces to his plays, his first attempt at publication had been at the age of thirteen with a play, "a tragedy about a junkman."[28] As a newsboy, and later a messenger, he had never been far from "whatever theatre my home town Fresno, California could provide"—movies, vaudeville, stock company, circus—he would sneak into any house that held a spectacle. But more than all these, what he loved was "the world theatre": "I saw drama in everything because there was drama in everything—because there was drama in myself," as he put it.[29] At age fourteen, he had tried to imitate Oscar Wilde but realized in time that he could not learn from the author of *Lady Windemere's Fan.* As he put it,

> My world was a world of plain poor people, broken down houses, casualness, good health, poverty and uproarious laughter, rather than world of complex and wealthy people, magnificent houses, cultivated ease, . . . [and] discreet laughter.[30]

The theater, he knew, would be something quite different for him. As he had remarked to Van Gelder, he had seen its door "wide open" and felt compelled to enter and make "full use of it." Psychologically and artistically, too, it had been the right moment for him. In the heady rush of fame since the publication of his first book, some of the wide-eyed innocence had begun to wear off. The complexities of adult relationship, both professional and personal, had left their mark, deflecting him from his earlier clear-cut path to love for the whole world. The unguarded optimist with his penchant for proselytizing, had had his day, and no one realized this better than Saroyan.

In the volume of short stories from this period, *My Name is Aram,* the rhetoric is minimal; never before has he so consistently and skillfully maneuvered youthful innocence into the melding of dream and reality. Indeed, what redeemed this sentiment-soaked "memoir" of childhood, making it popular in a time of duress (it was published the year before Pearl Harbor), was its large doses of humor, which often disguised, or underplayed, its undercurrents of pathos and irony. Sentiment might go by the board, but humor was safe and would remain viable even in a world about to venture on its own destruction.

But more than his unique brand of humor, it was Saroyan's particular amalgam of poetic fantasy and realism that would shock the drama critics to attention. Beginning with *My Heart's in the Highlands,* it was clear that what this playwright wanted to do was nothing less than make theater history.

A transitional work that curiously draws its strength from its seeming ineptness as drama, *My Heart's in the Highlands,* as already mentioned, belongs to an earlier time, the core of the play having had its origin in a story written in 1935 and published both in his collection, *Three Times Three* and in Paris in an avant-garde magazine, *The Booster.* The magazine's experimental nature, with its emphasis on "the poet's world," had drawn Saroyan to its pages. What is interesting to observe in the light of the play it would become is that while story and play remained substantially the same in subject matter, their difference is marked by the distance Saroyan has traveled artistically between 1935 and 1938. In *My Heart's in the Highlands* he is more skilled in the use of his metaphoric powers; his poetic principle has acquired a broader base, which allows him to move from the simple fable form to a more subtle mythic structure. For the first time the authorial voice does not block the cutting edge of metaphysics.

Turning back to the story, the first thing we note is the absence of an ending that draws a parallel between the personal displacement brought on by World War I and the social displacement of the Depression years. In the dramatic version, we are no longer in the isolated "poet's world" echoed by the title of Robert Burns's romantic poem. It is still the eve of the war in Fresno, California, and the cast of characters is virtually the same: the poet, his son (who is nine, having aged by three years), a non-English-speaking grandmother, and an itinerant old man who makes beautiful music on a bugle. But whereas the story was narrated by the boy in a high-spirited style that seems solely intent on showing the artist's proud hopelessness, the play breaks through the sealed-in realm of the fable to take a longer, harder look at the human condition.

Without sacrificing the logic of emotion, the play adds social resonance by showing how man's need for beauty is held back by the realities of survival. To make a realistic surface convincing within a mythic structure is no easy task at best (even for the writer of children's fairy tales), but to complicate matters, Saroyan makes repeated demands on his audience to shift its focus from one to the other.

In the story, a lively but lonely boy of six, Johnny, tells of his meeting with an old man by the name of MacGregor "on his way to the old people's home, playing a solo on a bugle." The garrulous old man announces that while his heart is in the highlands, he is dying of thirst and would the boy bring him a glass of water. Bemused by his speech, Johnny is slow in responding. Whereupon Johnny's father appears roaring "like a lion that has awakened from evil dreams," and scolds the boy for his lack of manners. Johnny asks why his father can't bring the glass of water himself since "You ain't doing nothing." "Ain't doing nothing?" the father shouts, "Why Johnny you know God damn well I'm getting a new poem arranged in my mind."

The tone of the story is light, understated, and matter-of-fact. Like all fables, it supplies no references (except in passing) to past events. Nor does it indicate character motivation beyond the obvious. The poetry seeps through by indirection—through the boy's perceptive eye, which seizes on small but significant details, like the fact that his father sits at the table "with his head in his hands, dreaming," or that the old man "drank a whole pitcher full in one long swig." For a long time nothing is said to indicate that the family is on the verge of starvation. We know only when Johnny is sent by his father to coax the neighborhood grocer to give him food on credit. The tone is humorous, for the trick is to keep a semicomic balance.

On hearing the old man play, the neighbors appear, one by one, and are so entranced that each contributes something from his own meager larder to hear more. When finally the old bugler plays "My Heart's in the Highlands," Johnny observes that "each good neighbor and friends wept and returned to his home." His own family "feasted and drank and [were] merry." The food is avidly catalogued, "an egg, a sausage, a dozen green onions," etc. When the old man asks to stay with them "some days," Johnny's father replies, "My house is your house," and indeed in the language of fairy tales, the old man stays "seventeen days and seventeen nights," until a man from the old people's home comes to take him away.

There the old man's odyssey in the story ends. But the semi-comedy of life resumes. This time the grocer gives the boy only birdseed and maple syrup. In a quick ambiguous ending, the grandmother begins to sing "like a canary," while Johnny's father complains, "How the hell can I write great poetry on bird seed?"

Written on the eve of an appendicitis operation that Saroyan claims nearly killed him, this fragile tale of poverty deftly used humor and irony to disguise a benign protest directed at no one in particular. Saroyan himself called it "goofy and tragic, and comic and classic," adding, in an introductory note to the story,

> I was very glad I hadn't died. . . . If it's all the same to you I'd like to stay in this world until they figure out a way to give everybody enough to be able to be easy-going about everything. I'd like to stay in this world until they figure out some way to let everybody be a millionaire.

I quote this rather glib statement on the problem of staying alive in 1935 (when this was written) to show how vastly it differs in tone from the wistful dedication he wrote to the printed version of the play:

> To the pure in heart.
> To the poet in the world.
> To the lowly and the great, whose lives are poetry.
> To the child grown old, and the child of childhood.
> To the heart in the highlands.

In the theater where the eye is our guide, pathos and irony cannot be hidden behind the humorist's glib facade. The feelings of the poet must now find objective correlatives in the words and actions of diverse characters as they try to accommodate to the real world. But the real world is never abandoned even as we view the spectacle of life impinging on the ultimate fable of man. What makes Saroyan's method elusive in this play is that the technique evolves straight out of its theme—the displacement of reality when strong attachments are made to inner worlds. The double vision that until now Saroyan has used to combine human poignance with philosophical largeness fuses here into a metaphysical statement.

From the moment that the curtain rises on "an old white, broken-down frame house with a front porch, on San Benito Avenue in Fresno . . . [with] no other houses nearby, only desolation of bleak land and red sky," we are caught up in the plight of an impoverished American family. The voices we hear are not those of backwoods people mired in hopelessness. Rather, we are in the presence of gusty exuberance, an easygoing humanity, fraternity, and concern. Poverty has not demoralized the young poet, who continues to compose at a feverish pitch. Nor is the motherless Johnny a no-good delinquent. When the curtain goes up, he is visibly "dynamic and acrobatic" (to quote the stage directions) as well as "deep in thought of a high order." While standing on his head, the boy hears "the most amazing music in the world," leaps to his feet and runs to an old man with a bugle, "amazed, delighted and bewildered." The bugler likewise is not what he appears to be. No ordinary beggar or outlaw, he is a fugitive from an old people's home, a self-styled artist and Shakespearean actor who has never really left his highland dream.

No overtones of Odets or Steinbeck here. This poverty-stricken family (which includes an immigrant grandmother) has somehow remained spiritually whole. Though all that's left for them to eat at the moment is popcorn, they do not turn away the thirsty and weary old man but, rather, listen enthralled to the "golden-throated" music he is playing. Though he has nothing but water to offer the old man, the poet-father (Ben Alexander) is the soul of hospitality; his resourcefulness in getting Johnny to wheedle food from the grocer and the boy's precocious powers of persuasion create such a genial atmosphere that even the immoveable grocer ends up admiring the starving poet, visibly moved by his gift of a rejected poem. Life's enchantment, it appears, cannot be erased— so long as the bugler has his music and the poet his poetry.

Is this, then, sheer fantasy? The romantic idyll of another day? Even today it appears so to some, and indeed in its initial presentation the Theatre Group's innovative director, Robert Lewis, pulled out all the stops one has come to associate with the Saroyan mystique.[31] Yet on closer observation, the play is antithetical in many respects to romantic fantasy. Its language, in the first place, is simple and down-to-earth, with no traces of the self-conscious poeticism of Wilder or the lyric heights of Anderson. Moreover, aside from the play's title, the poetic impulse in Saroyan has little to do with imagery and symbol. The metaphoric transformations he achieves are the product, chiefly, of a mythic imagination in which the eternal human experiences, freshly felt, create "the illusion of the real" (to use MacLeish's phrase for what he identified as the principle business of poetry.[32]

Mostly it is the gravity at the core of the play, always poignantly edged with humor, that lifts it out of the genre of fantasy and "pure theater." Saroyan's humanism, we are reminded, was from the first infused with a sharp awareness of the human spirit's vulnerability in a materialistic world. From his own Armenian family background, he had learned about dreams lost and regained and lost again. The Depression years of his youth taught him about dreamers of another sort. Indeed, embedded in the humor and pathos of this little play is a kind of *Pilgrim's Progress* whose lodestar and guide is the New World's elusive dream.

Without resorting to polemics, *My Heart's in the Highlands* attempts to persuade us that the needs of the soul can defeat—or hold at bay—the material needs of life. Poetry and and music cannot substitute for bread—but they sometimes almost do. As the old bugler puts it, "Bread, My God, how savagely it quarrels with the heart." Still, no one in this play really "quarrels" over *why* one should do without. "There will always be poets in the world," the idealistic Ben says defiantly when *The Atlantic Monthly* rejects his poems and he must face the loss of his home with all its belongings. For, unlike MacGregor, whose ideal dies with him, the poet's dream extends into the life of his son: "We are the same person," he tells the bugler, "he is the best of my youth." To the degree that these dreamers hold on to their expectations, they can retain their human dignity. Their drama—like that of all seekers—emanates from within.

Because he has remained an "alien" in the New World, and is now old and ill, MacGregor's death is tragic and inevitably verges on melodrama. But his death scene is saved from pathos because it is juxtaposed in the play with young Johnny's sense of loss, along with his awakening to the crassness of the world. At almost the same moment that the bugler collapses, uttering poignant lines from *King Lear*—a play about another old man betrayed by his dreams—the grieving Johnny stoops to pick up the coins that the girl of his dreams has offered him in return for the gift of himself. In our parting view of the boy (who might be Saroyan or the "new American") we glimpse the mediator between lost dreams and practical visions. As before, when he had bargained for their food, Johnny stands ready with his agile mind to take on the forces he must confront. "I'm not mentioning any names, Pa," he gives vent to an outburst of feelings that have been mounting, "but something is wrong somewhere."

As frequently happens in the Saroyan theater, it is the least visible and articulate character who carries the burden of the deeper layer of meaning. Here it lies with the Armenian grandmother. The silent presence of this immigrant woman allows Saroyan his final subtlety. Through her he broaches the part that the culture plays in the making of the dreams and illusions we carry around with us. The stoicism with which she accepts dispossession—from one more home—speaks of her people's tragic historic past. Her ancient knowledge stands in eloquent contrast to the stubborn individualism of the humanist artist and the quixotic self-reliance of young Johnny as they make their way into the unknown.

That *My Heart's in the Highlands* was not recognized as a landmark in the American theater of 1939 was as much due to the fact of its faulty presentation as to the insipid reviews it generally received. Saroyan himself in his introduction called it a "classic," explaining that "A classic is simply a first work, the beginning of a tradition, an entry into a fresh realm of human experience, understanding and expression." Though the play may be "relatively a trifle," he continued, "I also know of no one else who hopes for more for the American theatre than myself, and plans to do something about fulfilling these hopes personally."

Saroyan's faith in himself was so pronounced and easy to mistake for conceit that no one noticed the boyish wonder that went with it, with perhaps the single exception of the play's director, Robert Lewis. On the eve of the playwright's entry into the theater world, this scarcely visible undercurrent was not to be missed. Lewis conveys it when he writes in *Slings and Arrows* how Saroyan

> seemed to be theatrically ingenuous, walking around the stage after dress rehearsals like a bemused child, touching the props, the scenery,

and how he suddenly exclaimed, "I just realized my initials are the same as Shakespeare's!"

Yet fame itself was not all he cared about. After the play had premiered on 13 April, Saroyan's high spirits had visibly dampened. The report that Harold Clurman gives of this disappointment is insufficient. In complaining that the Theatre Group's production had emphasized the play's "fable" quality over its "virile realism,"[33] Saroyan was not simply referring to the stage setting, which admittedly was not "true to life." Symbolic touches, like the placement in the middle of the stage of an enormous, stylized evergreen tree, were quite out of line with Saroyan's instruction for a backdrop showing "the desolation of a bleak and red sky." What he had hoped to establish and found wanting was the suggestion that fantasy and realism could coexist: "the meaning of the play," he wrote in his introduction, "is the meaning of reality itself."

The "new reality" was not to be simply imitation (though at that moment he would go no further to explain). Clearly, Saroyan is after something closer to the concept of "mimesis," the word Erich Auerbach has used in describing the two levels of consciousness Virginia Woolf was able to convey in her novel, *To the Lighthouse*.[34] In many of his short stories, Saroyan in his own way had combined the poetic principle and the realistic principle, as I have earlier pointed out. But he was still new at translating this skill onto the stage, and there are times when he goes off keel and allows his autobiographical impulse to take over. (One thinks, for instance, of the characters of the newsboy in the opening section of the play, and later, of the postman; both add colorful touches but do not add anything of substance to the form or meaning of the play.) And there were other signs of technical insecurity that helped lead the critics away from him.

But in all fairness to Saroyan, the initial response to *My Heart's in the Highlands* was so weighted with irrelevancies that it might as well have been an essay that was being reviewed. In reading the group of reviews Saroyan has appended to the printed play ("for scholars and for the record"), one cannot but note how often belittlement combined with bewilderment. The inevitable remarks that emphasized Saroyan's origin, such as "the flashing young Armenian," "the antic Armenian," or "the unbridled Armenian," often verged on insult and injury.[35] Searching for a "coherent" meaning in the play, most of the critics thought him either mad or pretending to be a surrealist. One called the play "a crackpot comedy," another "a whimsical poem." A major critic, Edmund Gagey, compared it to "a medieval miracle play."[36] All agreed that it was unintelligible, though a few were so taken with its surface charm that it didn't seem to matter that it had nothing to say.

The drama critic of the *New York Post,* John Mason Brown, saw the play's formlessness as "intentional" and guessed that it was "an allegory of sociological significance." He thought the play had "widened the theatre's horizons," but like all the rest he didn't explain why.[37] For Brooks Atkinson, who had the power to make and break playwrights, the play was ultimately "enchanting"—and that was the word that stuck most. No need to look for inner meaning in this "bit of virtuoso scribbling," he wrote, it was enough that "he had created lovable, wandering characters and given an impression of joy, hospitality, loyalty and sadness."[38] Throughout Saroyan's theatrical career, Atkinson would repeat virtually the same inflated adjectives to describe Saroyan's work, evading a more serious assessment that would place him in the mainstream of American drama. Even his high praise, in the balance, seems only condescendingly genial.

But in that fateful year of 1939 even the misjudgments of the critics would scarcely penetrate Saroyan's overpowering sense of euphoria. Rather, they would become grist for his mill, allowing him to sharpen his own ideas about the theater's potential and his aspirations as a playwright.

For the first time in his life his voice counted: there was magic in the very sound of his name. Hearing his words endlessly and haphazardly quoted would awaken the lure to power that must lie in the depth of every soul. Never mind that it was not dignified to say it, he would have to make it known that he was "the greatest writer in the world." To say it was simply to acknowledge a deep reality of his own without which he could not lay his large claim on the future.

The fact was that for the second time in five years, at the age of thirty-one, he had walked straight into an elite segment of the literary world—this time overnight—and had promptly been accepted by the writers, critics, and all the theatrical folk who made the Great White Way a magical ribbon of light. He must have felt blessed not to find himself in the shoes of those countless young Johnnys setting out with no support or destination on the proverbial "open road." Indeed, within a year, Saroyan's life would be radically transformed and he himself would undergo the kind of metamorphosis that abounds in all his writings. His discovery of a new form would make it possible for him to release a fount of potentially dramatic experience that had lain dormant and now begged to be set before an expectant new audience.

Spoken on stage, his words would become an education in self-revelation. The image that emerged would no longer be of himself alone, but of a freshly minted American (West Coast frontier version), who paradoxically appeared more ancient and legendary than what the rest of the country was passing off as "American." Saroyan would revel in the advantage he felt he possessed for making this mundane and barely visible prototype into a "phenomenon"—revealing to him a truth that other writers had so far missed or ignored. No one, it seemed, had noticed those special endemic qualities of the species and the extravagant, unfeasible dreams out of which they evolved. Since the mold was largely contained in himself, he would not have far to go in his search.

Though Saroyan would find it easy to explain his affinity to the theater, its real importance to him would elude him for a while. With its easy access to symbols, the dramatic form could be manipulated to reach deeper layers of meaning than he had been able to achieve through the colorful action of his stories or his sinuous, discursive narrative style. It would finally compel him to recognize and contend with the new power he had sensed in himself to transform and reinvent what he remembered and experienced. He had always been alert to the panorama of the American scene, but he had yet to evaluate the spectacle and measure its substance. His critical bent in the short story had largely depended on an ironic tone, best achieved in the oblique style of the fable (as in the story version of *My Heart's in the Highlands*). But there were times when it flowed against the grain of his special brand of humor. In Saroyan's theater of poetic experience, where shifting moods were easier to achieve, his humor would not detract from the underlying irony but only enhance and give it poigance.

Having virtually exhausted the world of his eccentric uncles and cousins, Saroyan was ready to tackle a broader canvas of American life in a medium that was receptive to spectacle and diversity. Because the best skill at this command was that special amalgam of sly and teasing Old World humor combined with a spirited bonhomie somehow wrested from an ambitious boy's life of hard knocks, he would help tear down the gloom and doom that hung over the commercial theater. In the tense period before World War II he would have no trouble finding a response to his call for "fun" on the stage.

In a volume of sixteen short plays, which he called "variations" on ballet, opera, circus, vaudeville, carnival, sideshow—some of them suggesting spin-off from the *The Time of Your Life*—he soberly described what he meant by "fun":

> The theatre—all theatre—should be fun from beginning to end, inside, out, backstage and front, but it isn't fun for the people who turn to it for one or another of the reasons that all of us turn to art of one sort or another. By fun I do not mean trivialness. Real fun is capable of being trivial and nothing human has greater dignity or more importance than fun, or livingness, I mean ordinary, everyday, natural fun.

After some deliberation, he had called this grab bag of pieces for the stage from the years 1939–41, *Razzle-Dazzle* because that

> strange American word always made me smile and see all kinds of furious and comic American activity, like girls at the front of patriotic parades twinkling shining sticks and prancing around in joyous delirium.

Razzle-Dazzle had, indeed, suggested what he had found wanting in the American theater—the element of "play."

> [A]ll kinds of ridiculous and yet beautiful efficiency; people doing things smartly for no reason in the world; showing off; having fun; raising hell.

In its totality, in fact, the book carries the prepackaged stamp of the freewheeling, Saroyanesque style that (with the author's own help) has stuck in the public's mind.

In his desire to foster an American theater dealing with American subjects, he would coast on easy waters for some time, not only because this was something that came naturally to him but because the times were demanding an intensification of the national image. Not surprisingly, Saroyan would fall into the general drift, though remaining cautious against the false ring of political propaganda. However expansive his vision, there would be no toadying in his approach, no condescension. Unlike Wilder, he would not distance himself long enough for us to forget that this land and this people constituted the substrata of his personal faith.

Though not immediately perceptible, the second play in *Razzle-Dazzle* makes this clear. Called a "ballet play," and written for Eugene Loring of the Ballet Theatre, *The Great American Goof*[39] reflects simultaneously on mythic American and the Saroyan creed. Indeed, the Goof (a slang word for a well-meaning fool) comes through as a stereotype of the author's stance. He is characterized as "the white hope of the human race, . . . a nameless young man delighted to be alive, curious about all things, eager to understand, full of affection." The short play consists of his search for something to dedicate his life to. His refrain "I want to resign" stands for his disillusionment along the way as he meets one obstacle after another, most prominently an unsmiling, athletic woman who appears to want only to "wrestle" with him. A character called Dummy, described as "tradition and the ordinary," tries to steer him to some authentic pursuit. Without success. Only through trial and error, moving in turn from love to poetry, to a five-century plan, to music, to philosophy and religion, does the Goof arrive finally at his true vocation: to change the world, "beginning from the very beginning—the beginning of breathing to the end of it." Now at last the woman smiles, and seeing her thus transformed, the Goof declares his love: "You wait and see. It may take six or seven thousand years, but I'll change it [the world]."

In the Goof's erratic behavior, his repeated declaration that he will resign, one is reminded of the pantomime figures of Pierrot and Columbine. But the Goof's caprice does not extend to reaching for the moon; there is no masquerade or buffoonery. And this Columbine is too blunt and self-involved to be a flirt or goad her man to do impossible deeds. Saroyan is clearly not writing a salon piece. Designating the character of the woman as "the bright potential," he is suggesting "the bright potential in all things which in the

world is never visible to men." No reader of Saroyan's stories will
miss in the young man's resistance to "wrestling" with the woman,
Saroyan's affirmation of romantic love. Against the sullen, athletic
woman who practices casual sex (or "wrestling") he places the
smiling woman (Dante's Beatrice?) whose love will finally redeem
his life.

But what is new here is that the romantic touch becomes at the
same time the touch of irony that Saroyan injects into the ballet.
The clue turns up in the preface when he explains how he had
come to write this work. An invitation from Loring had triggered
his remembrance of an extraordinary performance he had witnessed by Leonide Massine at London's Covent Garden on his
first trip abroad in 1935. He had always admired great dancers like
Pavlova and Nijinsky, having perceived (even through drawings)
their "achievement or improvement of inner grace." It had made
him envious, knowing how hard a writer must try for the same
achievement in himself and, through his art, in others. It was this
aspect of ballet that had led him to write *The Great American Goof.*

The Goof's greatness consists for Saroyan in his unending quest
to fulfill himself; restless, unsatisfied, he is avid for new experience,
loath to remain (like the Dummy) within preordained bounds. Un-
afraid to make a fool of himself, he can be heroic, but his single-
mindedness makes him fair game for exploitation. Determined to
remain his own man, the Goof renounces the accumulated wisdom
of the past in order to begin at the beginning, "to change the world."
But in his "greatness," the Goof is inevitably hollow; the woman
he idealizes is "a bright potential" he is unequipped to deal with.
His faith is based on a false premise: the reality of the world.

The foregoing is one of many interpretations that can be made
of this work based on a mere reading of it. It is, after all, a new
form. This ballet *with words* needs the guidance of both one's eyes
and one's ears. Many of the commentaries Saroyan provides for
his work have a way of distracting us from the matter at hand. But
persistence in this case is rewarding.

"A ballet or ballet play," he begins, "is an oversimplification of
one or another of several aspects of the experience of living." After
a few more reasonable remarks, he suddenly lets loose a barrage
of hyperbolic notions, conceits, and witty turns of phrase (benignly
Twainesque) on the nonexistence of reality and the world:

nobody other than myself seems to understand that the world is not
real. That in reality there is no such thing as the world. There is, of
course, but I mean for all practical purposes. When I say practical I

mean poetic and wonderful. The world which everyone other than myself seems to have identified and accepted as the World is in reality a
figment in a nightmare of an idiot. No one could possibly create anything more surrealistic and unbelievable than the world which everyone
believes is real and is trying very hard to inhabit. The job of art, I say,
is to make a world which can be inhabited.

In that final sentence on art Saroyan upholds his basic tenet that
we are the substance of our dreams, our creations.

What the ballet says is that you need six or seven thousand years to
get the world out of the idiot nightmare it's in now.

Which is not exactly the same as Saroyan's contention that

Probably the most any man can ever save . . . or has the right to save
is himself, which ultimately is very little. No wonder nobody bothers
about it any more.

That final caustic note is not to be missed. It turns the little play
around, making a pathetic if not an absurd kind of hero out of
the Goof.

Plays should not have to be explained, even indirectly as Saroyan
does here. Yet the instinct to do so makes sense because this is
not a real play but a work dependent on the language of the performing arts, most often on music and on dance. Saroyan appears
to recognize an essential aspect of his writing for the first time. In
one of the Shavian-style prefaces in *Razzle-Dazzle,* in which he
explains why he has always wanted to write an opera and has
finally done so with *Opera, Opera,* he announces:

I am a writer who is a composer. You will see music in all my writing—
the form and quality of music is in all of it. The very nature of life
enduring is to me musical—the whole universe a great musical
creation.

He goes on to say that he sees behavior as music: "There is no
day in the life of any man in the world which is not opera, no
human state which is not a solo of singing." He has felt closer in
spirit to a certain composer, Sibelius, than to any writer:

There is an absence of purity in writers and the works they make, but if
a composer is great you know he cannot be anything but pure, too. . . .
[M]usic pretends nothing, and is everything or anything.

And he amplifies still further why there is music in his writing:

> the truth of art is the truth of emotion, not intellect. Emotion and intellect are essentially or eventually inseparable, and the quality of one depends on the quality of the other.

Creation is "an act of living, not thinking," he asserts, and thinking is certainly not the special and separate thing we make of it.

The essay ends with a charming and appropriate image:

> The nonsense that comes from me as I seek to sing is the nonsense of things themselves, and the false notes which occur in my work come from wanting most of all good things and not quite being able to get them.

His predicament as a writer reminds him of the little Armenian boy prodigy at a church party who attacked a virtuoso violin work only to find himself suddenly overwhelmed by the music's *emotional* level. The boy had stopped short, burst into a wide grin and lifting up his instrument had tried balancing it over his head— "something truly exciting to him, or at any rate not altogether over his head." He confesses: "That's what sometimes happens to me."

This is Saroyan's indirect way of telling us he is not an Aristotelian dramatist, one whose meaning is to be found through words. What a reader infers is Saroyan's self-propelled motion toward an evolving dramatic form (in line with Antonin Artaud's) where meaning is no longer dependent on pure speech. As he continues experimenting with short plays, it becomes clear to him that the "reality" he seeks is emotional, whether it leads to a poetic truth or to a comedic vision of life.

Among the many invitations that created opportunities for such experiments (soon after *My Heart's in the Highlands* was presented) was one from Vincent Minelli, who asked that Saroyan write an all-colored musical review. *Elmer and Lily* was inspired by his visit with Minelli to Harlem's famous Apollo Theater, where Saroyan sensed "all kinds of American freshness, innocence and unrest—various kinds of seeking, various kinds of effort, hope and dreaming." Accompanied by two producers interested in the venture, he had sat in the theater for hours, fascinated by the dancing, the enormous energy, and especially the laughter. He had wanted not to "reproduce" these things, but "to bring forth the insides of these things. . . . [W]e wanted the material of the show itself to laugh that way—all the way through. Burst out laughing for no reason."

Saroyan's reach, in this instance, exceeded his grasp, and while he did not exactly land in the shoes of the would-be boy virtuoso, he hardly succeeded in making *Elmer and Lily* the American fable he intended it to be.

In the corner of a city street, a pathetically inadequate salesman, Elmer, is trying to sell a mechanical toy, advertised as "society's favorite." As he repeatedly fails to make the Moonbeam Dancer work, he heckles himself in a long monologue that reveals his insecurity and his desperate will to succeed. As symbolically viewed by Saroyan, "a variety of things happen in the small space of the world [Elmer] is trying to occupy, but he is so eager to stop being a failure and so absorbed in the problems involved that he is only faintly aware of them." Just as we are becoming acquainted with his dreams and aspirations (which mainly involve the unattainable Lily) our attention is shifted to typical scenes of American life and character that lend themselves to satire. Saroyan lapses into a teasing mockery: A sign in a college lecture hall announces a New School of All Kinds of Miscellaneous Research; the professor's lecture (given in full) is on "Good Health, Its Cause and Cure." Other easy targets of humor are the Marxist radicals with their quick-fix reforms, the hocus-pocus of the medical profession (involving the psychologists), and the gadget-mindedness of modern man, with his concomitant faith in statistics. But most of all it is the hype of public relations (so alien to Elmer) that best suits Saroyan's method of spoofing. Although the play ends with Elmer's sudden, accidental success, the irony hangs midair, and the finale in which everyone joins in dancing and singing leaves a muddled impression of what seemed intended. Pathos in this instance has been heavily superimposed on a feeble kind of mocking humor.

This was the era of radio, and Saroyan now fortuitously turned to a form that was congenial to him as a short-story writer and essayist manqué. His radio poem, *A Special Announcement,* is one of the more successful experimental pieces in *Razzle-Dazzle,* and the initial work in which he shows a growing responsiveness to the approaching war. It is an expression, too, of the writer's dissatisfaction with the uses to which radio has been put. Like newspapers and motion pictures, this latest medium, he complains, "has cancelled whatever integrity has been brought into being by the printed word of the poet." In his little play he would show what radio can do in terms of art.

The opportunity had come his way when *Story* magazine suggested that he convert two of his stories into radio plays for its own radio series. After giving it some thought, Saroyan had responded that "radio requires a special and separate attack," and thus offered to write something new. Two current radio plays by the poet Archibald MacLeish—*The Fall of the City* (1937) and *Air Raid* (1938)—had demonstrated the possibility of combining poetic expression with public topics (in this instance the coming disasters of war), and in characteristic fashion Saroyan had instantly assimilated the lesson, adding a new twist of his own. Though *A Special Announcement,* like the MacLeish plays, deals with the cruelty and futility of modern warfare, it ultimately veers in another direction. Their approach is alike in that they both utilize the voice-over as the unifying scheme, but they achieve different results: MacLeish's omniscient radio announcer has the detached, ironic tone of a prophetic god as he describes step by step the fall of a city; while Saroyan's narrator tries simply to forewarn and interpret the generally invisible danger signals with an impassioned concern. As against the elevated rhetoric and literary metaphors of MacLeish, Saroyan lapses into commonplace word images with which all can identify.

In a series of questions put to the listener, the narrator suddenly brings home the long-term results of a war in Europe:

> How would it be to be a soldier?
> How would it feel to die before you had a chance?
> Would it help? Would Europe be better?
> Would Brahms become everybody's favorite?
> Would people tell the truth?

And again the narrator puts into perspective the listener's future in the kind of world that is being created.

> What is the connection between cigarettes
> And the interruption for the special announcement?
> With so many things still to be concluded,
> Is there ever going to be time enough?
> You always meant to write a poem.
> You thought you might like to play the piano.
> If the worst came to worst,
> You might have said something.

A brief dialogue between two characters, Proud and the Humble, becomes an exposure of war as simple murder:

> Ten minutes ago in Europe a man was killed . . .
> His name was not Hitler, but should have been,

His title not Reichsfuehrer.
He weighed one hundred and sixty pounds.
Had one head. Two arms, two legs,
Two eyes . . .
If he lived, he would have finished
The table he was making for his wife . . .
His name was Kurt.
His murderer was a man
A good deal like *himself.*

There's irony in the way the play registers the waste of lives, the pathos of deaths unrecorded, but the bitterness and despair in the final analysis are held at bay through the narrator's empathy, his own bewilderment:

The living who die will be overlooked.
And the living who live will be overlooked.
There will never be time enough to know
Who was one and who was the other . . .
At your radio, in the hall, in the parlor,
In the kitchen for a drink of water,
In the world, in the street,
Will there be truth? . . .
Will anybody die because it is time to die . . .
Will anybody have time to live
And write his name on a passport,
Or at the bottom of a poem?

Unlike MacLeish, who has tried to awaken terror in the listener's heart while describing a mythic/real fall of a city and the populace in an air raid, Saroyan merely wants to remind the listener that war would be antithetical to all that he holds most dear in life, indeed of life itself.

In a second radio play of this period, written for the CBS Free Company Broadcasts, Saroyan seized the opportunity to use radio rhetoric for what he called "my propaganda . . . the same propaganda that is in all my work. Namely, to reveal the essential goodness and humble greatness of people."[40]

Leaving the berating of enemy nations to others, he prefers to eulogize what he finds to admire in his own country. He writes in his eloquent preface,

I have no greater affection for the British in general than for the Germans and Italians and Japanese in general, and I despise none of them in general. I despise only the specific which is evil in *all* of them. The

confusing of goodness and evil by politics I cannot allow to confuse
me, however enormously it may succeed in confusing everybody else
in the world.

While he feels honored to be an American ("I do not believe that
anyone loves this land and its people more than I do."), his first
allegiance is to "truth itself, without regard for politics."

> The inferior, the second-rate, the corrupt, the brutal, the evil are my
> enemies in myself, in my family, in my neighbors, and in all the peoples
> of the world; and the good in them, the generous, the noble, the decent,
> the honest, the gracious and the faithful are my allies.

Choosing at random a single block in the city, the young commentator (or writer) turns his attention to some ordinary individuals with private hopes and aspirations. There's the young artist
who leaves his door open for neighbors to come and examine his
paintings, explaining to one of them

> I believe there is more good in things than anybody ever bothers to
> see, and so I keep looking for it all the time, and when I find it, I try
> to keep it in a painting, so other people can see it, too. After they see
> it in a painting, well they see it everywhere else, too. That's what
> painting's for.

Earlier the young man had pointed out,

> After a while, as you learn more and more about painting, you start to
> paint what's *inside* of things and always coming out—light comes out
> of most things, especially people. . . . [W]ell, I sort of concentrate on
> that light.

There is mawkishness in the totality of the little play, but because
of an unalloyed earnestness, the pronouncements are genuine and
compelling, and never more so than when the realist in Saroyan
takes over. Speaking again for the artist, Saroyan writes,

> I've looked a long time and it's gotten so that I can see right through
> people who look as if they're bad. They're not bad—they're having
> trouble—they're up against something—things have been going
> wrong—they've lost faith.

Saroyan's liberal humanism mingles personal faith with an artistic
credo that will mark his future work in the theater.

Another work in *Razzle-Dazzle* worthy of attention at this distance is, of course, *Hello, Out There,* a one-act play frequently performed to this day. But because it was written in 1941 and marks a certain advance in Saroyan's work in the theater, it will be dealt with later in relation to the two major works at that time.

Still another play from this volume is worth some notice because it is very much a part of the transitional period when Saroyan has not yet succeeded in letting go of the intruding self. *The Hungerers* is again more distinguished for the ideas in its preface than the somewhat disjointed one-act play itself. Unlike Shaw, from whom he has learned a trick or two, Saroyan has no sociological intent; he merely wants to let the reader know what he has left out of the play so he can concentrate on its spirit rather than its letter, in other words, its poetic essence. Once again he broaches the poetry of poverty. Like the bugler and the poet in *My Heart's in the Highlands,* "the hungerers" in this play hunger for something more than bread: "To be truly alive in spite of poverty is to defeat poverty." "The hunger of these hungerers," Saroyan declares, "is not for bread alone, though that hunger is beautiful enough. It is a hunger for immortality." To which Saroyan adds,

> The simple immortality which comes about when human beings rid themselves of all world-imposed absurdities and know the foolishness of pride. Which comes about when they truly see the objects of the world, including one another, and they stand alive calmly and humbly. When they know love. When they know there can be no death if there is love.

Then, without transition, Saroyan goes on to expound his ideas of "form." "Nothing exists without form." It is because living forms are imperfect and aspire to wholeness and perfection that art exists:

> Art always has a better chance of having whole and unbroken form than the living have, but the only reason art seeks to achieve this unbroken form is to encourage its achievement in the living. Art is for the living, whether they come in contact with art or not. It's theirs. Any form I achieve in art is form I have achieved already in myself.

Form in and of itself is meaningless to him. It "should not exist apart from a specific person. It should not be something agreed upon at the outset." To be truly good writers, he believes, "we must make form out of ourselves." Whenever in the future the critics bring up the absence of form in his plays, Saroyan will hark back to the view he has so deliberately stated here.

As for the little play, it is more subdued than *My Heart's in the Highlands*. Here again is the artist, again the homelessness, and again the power of love. But in *The Hungerers*, (closer to the fable), the scepter of Death is personified—as a friendly little man! The young writer who dies happy in the the arms of the girl he loves makes no reference to eternity; a certain undaunted acceptance has replaced the old daring of the idealist on the trapeze. He dies content that he has "written some of the greatest unpublished stuff in the world."

The irony of that statement is not to be missed. Saroyan's brand of realism will not permit him to give death more than its due. In Wilder's *Our Town*, Death redeems by giving life its completion; in Saroyan's play, it is the aspiration—the will to capture the shining moments, the poetry—that redeems what Death leaves incomplete. What is tragic is the loss of the potential, the perfection that might have been achieved but for starvation or war.

The concept of the human potential would become the substance of Saroyan's writing for the theater. At the very beginning, while ruminating on *The Time of Your Life* in May 1939, he was writing to George Jean Nathan about titles he was considering for the play that had come to him like a bolt of lightening. *Pacific Elegy* was not really to his liking, and he explained why:

> Elegy means, I believe, something in the nature of a hymn for the dead. The nobly dead . . . whereas the play is closer, I believe, to a hymn to the dying who are undying, a hymn to the deathlessness of the living.[41]

To the challenge of the Depression has now been added the horrors of an impending world war, and it is a more sober and somber Saroyan who contemplates the future. Three months later, on his return from Europe, he writes to Nathan about "the present hysteria," which he finds "absolutely unreal, but with the incredible reality of the murderously real."[42]

> I have a fine understanding of the whole mess, but can't explain it readily. The obvious thing, though, is People don't count. Millions of them don't count.

Because civilized man is quick to turn his back on it all, he writes, "world-destiny is conditioned or manufactured by the diseased nerves of clinical cases. . . . I am not opposed to people dying sooner or later. . . . All I believe is that they should be personally involved in their own private destiny."

There are many faces to the Saroyan of 1939–40. The legend begins to mount in the six-month period between his premier play and the production of *The Time of Your Life*. Of the man and his life, it is reported that in San Francisco he lives in an old wooden house with his mother and sister and works in an unheated room with the radio running and floor littered with magazines and manuscripts. It is said that his mother is his best critic but Saroyan has to translate his stories into Armenian before she can give an opinion.

Another persona emerges in New York, where he is hailed by none other than *Life* magazine as "the Great Saroyan—Fresno's elfish Armenian boy." Both humble and brash, he is the egalitarian who prefers eating at automats from coin-slot machines; he is often caught talking to bootblacks and their clients. He is his own best fan and has a low tolerance for drama critics, even those who praise him. He bets on horses, likes to drink, and is never bored with girls. Because his second play is written in less than a week, legend has it that he never rewrites. In the words of a contemporary young critic, Alfred Kazin, he wants to appear "a tower of strength . . . his own man all day long." It was Nathan in the end who would implode the legend with his oft-quoted article that began, "Is Saroyan Crazy?"

However he appears, he is in truth deeply immersed in all sorts of writing even on the eve of the out-of-town trial run of *The Time of Your Life*. On 2 October he writes to Nathan that he had done a lot of work on the play and is going to write a long preface consisting of half dozen different essays on the theater. His essay on "The Coming Reality" is to appear in *Theatre Arts Monthly*. He is finishing his third play, *Something About a Soldier* (with which he hopes to interest the Lunts), and has begun talking with his agent about still another play, *Love's Old Sweet Song*. "I'm aware," he writes, "that I've probably worked too much lately, and ought to take a rest and let fresh material and ideas arrive." He ends, "I'm as happy as the devil about everything, largely the consequence of your encouragement, and have never worked as much as I have these past six months or so."

The theater, in short, has become his home. How intensely he has begun to live in it is can be gleaned from the last page of *Razzle-Dazzle* where he notes,

This is the other side of the book, the page before the last page, the moment before the lights of the theatre go up and everybody comes out of the trance of art, shakes his head, and goes home to continue the art or artlessness of his own life. It is all over now . . . but for the opening of the eyes to the nearby real and the shutting of them to the nearer real—the opening of them to the actual world of accident, and the shutting of them to the super-actual world of art.

For Saroyan it was in drama that life and art seemed finally to merge.

6

A New Dramatic Vision:
The Time of Your Life

Living is an art. It's not book-keeping. It takes a lot of rehearsing for a man to get to be himself.
— Saroyan, *The Time of Your Life*

"A book," wrote Marcel Proust—in an essay demolishing the "system" of the renown nineteenth-century French critic, Charles-Augustin Sainte-Beuve—"is the product of a different self from the self we manifest in our habits, in our social life, in our vices." Although it was part of William Saroyan's essential creed (in a variant of the Whitmanesque tradition) to meld himself with his art, the artificiality of life outside the close bounds of the footlights came to hinder this process, ultimately calling forth a more profound search into the self that Proust identified with the artist's "innermost self."[1]

No true and useful discussion of Saroyan's major plays, it seems to me, is possible without a preamble of this sort. For it is by now incontrovertible that from the beginning of his Broadway years, Saroyan's superficial, self-proclaimed image interposed itself between the plays and their interpretation, often veering the critics away from the play's true intent and originality of vision. Given his gift of articulation, his explosive energy, his sense of dedication, and his fierce belief in himself, Saroyan had glided effortlessly into media celebrity. And because it appeared that all things came easily to him, it was hard to take him seriously on his own artistic terms. No matter how diligently he set forth his ideas about the drama and his high ambitions for the American theater, it was the simplistic aspects of his public self, summed up in the word *Saroyanesque*, that impressed itself on people's minds.

That word—*Saroyanesque*—has gathered many variants over

208

"The Time of Your Life." Photo by Vandamm. Billy Rose Theatre Collection. Courtesy of The New York Public Library for the Performing Arts, Lenox and Tilden Foundations.

the years, but it initially emerged as a sermonizing kind of rhetoric whose chief message was a supreme optimism about the essential goodness of people and the ultimate triumph of good over evil. Almost in fairy-tale fashion, it affirmed that life was a miracle and no man the superior or inferior of any other: it was Whitman's Democratic Vista reincarnate—and lots more fun. But where once, during the Great Depression, it had been welcomed as a useful stance, by 1939 the charm had gone flat. Under the gathering clouds of World War II, the shining bright message elicited condescension if not mockery. For a while it was just a small band of critics who saw beneath the façade (and then not too clearly) that Saroyan had sufficiently moved away from the simple fairy tale to confront changing circumstances.

It is easy enough for us at this distance to excuse the myopia of Saroyan's early critics. But the eager young playwright who had made such a meteoric transition from narrative prose to dramatic form and been so productive as well (turning out seven plays, four of them full-length, in five years), the experience must have been sobering, to say the least. It must have hurt to see his deepest notes skimmed over, his irony confused with humor, his humor mistaken for sentimentality. He wasted no time in setting the record straight for the critics, singly or en masse, and in an expansive moment conceded diplomatically that "A writer needs criticism almost more than he needs an audience."[2] Controversy was better than total indifference. But there were other aspects of the Broadway scene that would prove more lastingly troublesome to Saroyan.

His disillusionment set in early in the game. If he swallowed the irrelevant comments about his work, he could barely cope with the arbitrariness and fickleness of those who held the future of a playwright in the palm of their hands. An innocent in many respects, he was not so naive that he could miss the spiral of deception that surrounded the preparations for his second play—from Harold Clurman's out-of-hand rejection of the script (which he would later regret) to the Theatre Guild's misrepresentation of it in its original New Haven run, down to the greedy pocketing of half the play's proceeds by his eager agent/producer, Eddie Dowling. "Bankers, lawyers, dentists, and agents," he would write some years later, "I deplore them all, but they *do* keep the game going, no doubt about that." At the moment he was determined to salvage the play. He decided to become its director, transforming it "from a sure flop into a kind of hit, even in terms of money."[3]

Saroyan's belief that he was writing "a new kind of play," one that "demands a new kind of theatrical method and style,"[4] would compel him to direct and produce his own works, with his own money. And because the bond between himself and his new literary art was rapidly gaining ground, he dreamed for a while of starting his own theater. Like his publishing venture, it did in fact materialize, but like it, too, it was short-lived.

Much has been written about *The Time of Your Life,* though little that has gone to the heart of the matter. After *The Human Comedy* and *The Daring Young Man on the Flying Trapeze,* Saroyan's second full-length play is his best known work and the one by which he is best represented in the American theater. His renown was at once secured when it was awarded the Pulitzer Prize in 1940 and his notoriety clinched when he turned it down on the ground that he did not believe art should be sanctioned by commerce. (In the same year, the play also won the New York Drama Critics Circle Award.) It has had two distinguished Broadway revivals, one in 1955 and the other in 1969; it has been widely produced in other parts of the country, made into a successful movie in 1948 with James Cagney in the lead, and televised at least twice since 1958.[5] More than any other of his works it has been the subject to study in academic journals and holds a prominent place in Ph.D. dissertations, where speculation over the hidden role of its leading character has ranged from that of the Artist to the Capitalist to Jesus Christ. With its sardonically edged title, it introduced a new comic vision wholly native in its inspiration, to the American stage.

Even at its most earnest, Saroyan's work had never been devoid of the comic strain. If at times it seemed incidental, cropping up unexpectedly between paragraphs of lyric prose, it generally had no trouble merging with what came through as sheer poetry. In his stories of schoolboy battles with authority and prejudice, humor had served as a weapon against despair, turning private hurt into gently ironic laughter with a universal tinge. When later he learned the art of transforming memory—as in *My Name is Aram*—humor became a part of his essential vision, shaping all he saw and felt in a language that was his very own. Since comedy by definition deals with people as members of the larger society and seeks to encompass the world in all its variety, Saroyan's native inclinations would serve him well; and his unceasing fascination with the panorama of the American scene would further guarantee him easy passage into the comic theater.

In a larger sense, too, the comic vision was philosophically right for Saroyan. The comedian's ready acceptance of human flaws and his faith in poetic justice spoke directly to Saroyan's unshakable love for mankind and his unwillingness to believe in "hope-lessness." But there was a difference in effect between his use of the old humor and the new, and it was here that he sometimes faltered. Saroyan would never be able to suppress the messianic conscience that stamped his work from the beginning. However benign his overview, it never obscured his ultimate purpose: to improve society by first improving the individual. In the theater, where an author is less visible than in plain prose, the trick was to let the "message" surface *without* destroying the spectacle he wished to create on stage. In *The Time of Your Life,* as in so many of his subsequent plays, Saroyan would grapple with these prob-lems. But it could not have troubled him much: when success in its conventional terms eluded him, there was always the possibility that his new form of dramatic tension would lead to a reexamina-tion of "success" itself.

His choice of a title is in itself significant. On the face of it, there is nothing original in Saroyan's turning to the book of Ecclesiastes for inspiration. He had already done so for a short story, "The Living and the Dead," as had a slew of writers before him and since: Hemingway, most conspicuously in 1926, with *The Sun Also Rises* and Lillian Hellman, in the same year as Saroyan's play, with *The Little Foxes.* The Biblical preacher's devastating refrain (unorthodox for his day) that "all is vanity and vexation of spirit. . . . There is no remembrance," had been especially fitting for the "wasteland" mood of the 1920s and seemed on the mark again in the wake of World War II.[6] But to Saroyan what came through beyond the revelations of life's vanity and the absence of a caring God was the curiously contradictory affirmation of life's beauty and pleasures. If "the dead know not anything" and the will of God remains forever unknown, the Biblical voice had concluded, the only way for man to ward off despair was to enjoy his life:

> Man hath no better thing under the sun than to eat, and drink, and to be merry . . . *and make his soul enjoy good in his labour (which is) from the hand of God.*[7]

I have emphasized the last part of this statement because it is in the implication of something other than hedonistic enjoyment that Saroyan's imagination takes wing.

The old preacher's appetite for creature pleasures is both poetic and Epicurean: "Truly the light *is* sweet," he says, "and a pleasant thing it is for the eyes to behold the sun."[8] The words speak to the earthy core of Saroyan. But when the biblical voice goes on to evoke old age—that final round of nature when the senses flag and a feeling of void returns—Saroyan parts company with the common interpretation of Ecclesiastes and alights on a less explicit message it contains: the nature of our enjoyment and what we do with it.

> In the time of your life, live—so that in that good time there shall be no ugliness or death for yourself or for another life your life touches.[9]

Saroyan has moved some distance away from the hedonist's self-centeredness, which creates its own dead end in surfeit and disillusionment. Each line of his own creed is a plea to take our pleasure in "labour" (or acts) that come from "the hand of God" (or grace)—and so to deprive no one of his share of life's bounty.

The credo Saroyan would have the play represent is based on awareness of others. "Remember that every man is a variation of yourself," he reminds us, and he goes on from that egalitarian stance to affirm our dependence on one another: "No man's guilt is not yours, nor any man's innocence a thing apart." There are many "seasons" in a man's life, the world-weary biblical voice reminds us ("there's a time to love and a time to hate"), but the only season Saroyan recognizes is the constant present when acts of grace are made possible by "the clear eye and the kindly heart."

Beyond this awareness, there is also a mission: "Seek goodness everywhere," Saroyan's creed pleads, "and when it is found, bring it out of its hiding-place and let it be free and unashamed." The ancient commandments had asked only that we look into our own souls. Saroyan asks that we also look into the souls of others—to discover "that which shines is beyond corruption" in all things. Instead of the usual prescription to "Change the World," he asks simply that we "live—

> so that in that wondrous time you shall not add to the misery and sorrow of the world, but shall smile to the infinite delight and mystery of it.

Printed as an epigraph to the play, the "Credo" is better left unread from the stage. As a prologue to the play's action it would diminish the playgoer's sense of "discovery" (which must differ for every one). A play so rich in sights and sounds that tries to speak to the variousness of life would suffer from the restraints of a summary however eloquently expressed. Writing the play in a short span of time, at a moment in his life when opportunity and promise loomed large, Saroyan would momentarily waver between the indelible darker impressions of his youth (befitting a tragic view) and the more positive images that were becoming the transforming agents of his comic vision. Indeed, as the drama unfolds, with all the ambiguities and shifting realities that life imposes, the "Credo" (like all credoes) begins to seem hortatory and simplistic.

Though the shadow of the impending war hovers over the entire play, it is the commotions of life, not of death, that charge the atmosphere. Every character—or almost every one—is out to declare his presence in the world. And with so much energy on the loose throughout the five acts, it is hard to think of it as the "doomsday play" Walter Kerr imagined he was seeing in the 1969 Broadway revival. Kerr was not, however, far off the mark when he firmly denied that *The Time of Your Life* was the "incorruptibly sunny" play that he (and so many others) remembered it as being.[10]

The fact is that nearly always, and particularly at this time in his career, Saroyan resists such extremes of mood. From his new vantage point as a playwright with a comic vision, he cannot praise the dead at the expense of the living—"vanity of vanities" notwithstanding. He can no longer see himself as the tried-by-fire idealist, the young man filled with despair at the sight of a crying child's face framed in a windowpane. Struck by the absurdity of life, he had reflected, "If a child who is innocent cannot see good in the world, then certainly there must be little good in it." That outcry had seemed right in "The Living and the Dead," his flawed but stirring short story from the mid-1930s that was to prefigure *The Time of Your Life* in details of plot and setting. Despite its touches of comedy, the story had been solemn and elegiac, coming as it did from the Saroyan who had not yet been released from the tragic sense.

Now on the eve of World War II, in the face of the historic moment's hopelessness, Saroyan's response hinged less on his quintessential faith than a new, canny perception of America.

It was as if on the crest of his success, he was experiencing a heightened sense of his Americanness. "*I* was the art, *I* was the whole business," he had declared with pride. He had never made a secret of his love affair with America or his desire to make what was special about it known to the world. But now he also saw himself as part of its myth—that alluring Adamic myth, enhanced by the immigrant experience—which he revered to the point of awe, though now without an acute awareness of its endemic flaws. He had been moved to draw a parallel between the dogged fortitude of his Armenian ancestors and the staunch faith that propelled the American Dream, knowing all along that the optimism of Americans had nothing defensive about it, being simply the consequence of belief in their "inalienable right" to "life, liberty, and the pursuit of happiness."[11] This double dose of yea-saying did not always affect Saroyan's work in the expected way. There were times, as his writing grew in sophistication and his vision gained a critical edge, when his luminous humanism would contend with the demands of his art. Measuring one kind of affirmation against another, he saw unlimited variety in the captives of the dream, and from his enlarged perspective was persuaded that the best, indeed the *only* truth was the truth revealed by art.

The Time of Your Life is his perception of an emblematic America caught in a moment of truth for the nation and the test which its character must suddenly meet. The dreamers in the San Francisco "honky-tonk bar," where the main action is laid, are not typecast after Sean O'Casey's boozy Irish dreamers who talk themselves out of reality. Nor in their high spirits do they have much in common with those "lost" souls of O'Neill's *The Iceman Cometh* (still unwritten in 1939). The habitués of Nick's Pacific Street Saloon, Restaurant, and Entertainment Palace area dreamers by nature, trying to shake off the "dreamed"—expected—images society has imposed on them. It is a play of contradictions, like America itself, and it makes no apologies for it.

"Almost pure vaudeville," Mary McCarthy had called the play in her 1939 review, "almost every incident and character can be translated back into one of the old-time acts." And indeed each of the characters in *The Time of Your Life* begins by doing his "act" in a quickly recognizable fashion. There's the quasi-cynical bartender, the lonely prostitute, the young gambler, the lover, the cowboy, the failed comedian, the cop, the villain, the irrepressible barfly. Life has fixed them into molds—but this being America—with not too much finality. Saroyan has put them on stage not simply to exhume obsolete tradition, as McCarthy would have it, but rather to let us see them apart from their stereotyped aspects, and in the process to reveal their relation to the culture that has shaped them.[12]

Although none of the characters is drawn in depth (this being a collective portrait), one of them, Joe, stands out as pivotal to all the action, such as it is. Identified by Saroyan as *"a young loafer with money and a good heart,"* he remains fixed at a table throughout the play, sipping champagne—*"always calm, always quiet, always thinking."* (Saroyan is generous with stage directions.) We don't know why he is in this saloon, but can see by his expensive

clothes and choice of drink that he is well-to-do. A boyish appearance and sense of fun mask an underlying seriousness.

Much of the play's fascination derives from the spectator's
speculations about Joe as man and symbol. Is he simply—in Mc-
Carthy's words—an "indolent alcoholic"? Is he a "good man," in
spite of his way of life? From the first his words and actions reveal
him as a humanist and do-gooder with a sentimental streak. He
appears to be fumbling at a role—as if attempting to emulate the
new hero of the day, the polio-ridden, charismatic friend of the
"common man" who made benevolence his chief source of power
in the mid-1930s. As the play unfolds, Joe's persistent retreat from
aggression becomes another reminder of America in the age of
Roosevelt, before the President's "I hate war" pronouncement became history.

The play begins in a low key, with a comic sequence of mythic
overtones. After the newsboy has deposited his wares and an old
Arab *(an Eastern philosopher and harmonica player)* has uttered
his summary of the headlines, "No foundation. All the way down
the line," Willie, *the marble-game maniac,* makes his entrance,
calls for his beer, and puts his nickel in the slot machine. Saroyan's
stage directions read,

> Willie vs. Destiny. His skill and daring vs. the cunning and trickery of
> the novelty industry of America, and the whole challenging world. He
> is the last of the American pioneers.

This "last challenger, the young man with nothing to do in the
world" contends with the mysteries of the machine, while the phonograph plays "The Missouri Waltz." When the music stops, Joe
suddenly comes out of his reverie, calling loudly for Tom, "his
admirer, disciple, errand boy, stooge and friend," as he is identified.
This young recipient of Joe's philanthropic urge is "a great big man
of thirty or so" who "seems as if by all rights he should still be a
boy." In the brief dialogue that ensues, Joe's tone is scolding and
paternalistic, while Tom's is in turn meek, reverential, and slightly
alarmed: Joe is a "boss" he would never offend.

Joe's questions to Tom are both pointed and speciously motivated for a man so lackadaisical in his stance: "Who saved your
life?" he asks, and he persists in making Tom remember "the whole
story" of his charity and caring while Tom was down and out. But
the sharp reprimand—"I want you to be around when I need
you"—is followed by a more casual tone of speech as he sends
Tom off on a quirky new errand. He's to go to the Emporium, "up

to the fourth floor . . . to the toy department and buy a couple dollars' worth" of little toys he can place on the table.

It is clear that Tom has never tried to understand the nature of Joe's desires or demands; but there's a small note of rebellion in his complaint that reminds us of Johnny confronting his father in *My Heart's in the Highlands:* "I'm the guy that gets embarrassed. You just sit in this place and make me do all the dirty work." Making things still more uncomfortable for Tom, Joe asks him to replay "The Missouri Waltz" and sit and listen to it with him. It is while they are listening that Joe's concern for Tom becomes apparent. He watches him squirm with discomfort and confusion as the waltz is "played dreamily and softly, . . . with a theme of weeping in the horns repeated a number of times." Suddenly Tom is "carried away by the melancholy story of grief and nostalgia of the song." Joe seems not to be listening. He continues observing Tom.

Up to this point, Saroyan is writing with the dual vision of his sad/funny stories. With the entrance of Kitty Duval on the scene, however, the play takes on a life of its own. Described as "a young woman with memories," Kitty walks slowly to the bar and utters the word, "Beer." Giving no description of her attire, Saroyan introduces her to us, in the text, from within:

Her reality and rhythm [were] a perfect accompaniment to the sorrowful American music, which is her music, as it is Tom's. Which the world drove out of her, putting in its place brokenness and all manner of spiritually crippled forms.

Saroyan departs still further from the stereotype to tell us "she seems to understand this, and is angry." She is angry both with herself and the world, and "full of pity and contempt for its tragic, unbelievable, confounded people."

She is a small powerful girl, with that kind of delicate and rugged beauty which no circumstance of evil or ugly reality can destroy.

Whoever is to create Kitty Duval on stage will have to make the audience feel that "she is somebody."

If this portrait is idealized, its components fit like the pieces of a jigsaw puzzle into the childish romanticism that Tom projects. "He becomes dead to everything in the world but her":

He stands like a lump, fascinated and undone by his almost religious adoration of her.

With a sense of urgency, he suddenly asks Joe if he can bet on a horse: "I got to have money." But Joe points to the street, reminding him of his errands, and Tom is off.

There is a marked skill and deftness in the expository scene that follows. As Saroyan introduces us to Kitty, he deepens, at the same time, his portrait of Joe. It is swift and brief: To Joe's question, uttered with "great compassion," "What's the dream?" Kitty replies, startled, "What?" Joe persists, "holding the dream for her": "What's the dream now?" Kitty, who has moved closer, is still bewildered: "What dream?" The contact at last established, Joe can exclaim, "What dream! the dream you're dreaming."

From this simple exchange, a new Joe emerges: where earlier we had seen an effete, socially conscious meddler, we now perceive a gentle, concerned person, not afraid of making a fool of himself. But the mask will not soon be discarded. When the bartender interrupts the dialogue to ask what he would do with the watermelon he has ordered Tom to bring him, Joe shifts gears to give a flippant answer:

> I'd put it on the table. I'd look at it. Then I'd eat it. What do you think I'd do with it, sell it for a profit?

This gives the bartender the wedge to ask him what the audience has long been eager to know:

> How should I know what you'd do with anything? What I'd like to know is, where do you get your money from? What work do you do?

Reverting to his preoccupation of the moment, looking at Kitty, Joe makes no reply, simply asking Nick to bring them a bottle of champagne. Kitty's suspicion is aroused: "What's the big idea? You can't push me around." But though she protests, she does not move away. "Gently but severely," Joe lays his cards on the table: He is not there to judge her.

> It's not in my nature to be unkind to another human being. I have only contempt for wit. Otherwise I might say something obvious, therefore cruel, and perhaps untrue.

Kitty upholds her own rights when she retorts, "You be careful what you think of me." Joe, who is not looking at her, declares unselfconsciously: "I have only the noblest thoughts for both your person, and your spirit."

Nick, who is operating on a different level of consciousness, suddenly stops to ask what they're talking about, and Kitty is again on the defensive. She resents being tagged by the bartender as "a two-dollar whore," and protests that she was, in fact, in burlesque. Now the dream proliferates:

> I played the burlesque circuit from coast to coast. I've had flowers sent to me by European royalty. I've had dinner with young men of wealth and social position.

And when she's told by Nick that she's dreaming, she adds,

> Kitty Duval. That was my name. Life-size photographs of me in costume in front of burlesque theatres all over the country.

Unlike Nick, Joe encourages the image she holds of herself and offers to call her by her "stage name," saying, "I believe you."

Nick remains unconvinced, and still puzzled by Joe's motivations: "Why don't you have champagne at the St. Francis," he asks, adding pointedly, "Why don't you drink with a lady?" As Kitty's ire reaches its peak, she calls Nick "a dentist." Nick, all the while, keeps nagging Joe as "a guy who doesn't belong here," and tells Kitty, "He's crazy or something." But Joe is unperturbed. "Nick. I think you're going to be all right in a couple of centuries," he says, implying it will take that long a time to raise his consciousness. He then lifts his glass "to the spirit, Kitty Duval." To which Kitty, looking very gratefully at him, replies, "Thank you."

This is not like any barroom we've seen or read about before. The vibrant notes that have so far emanated from Nick's Pacific Street Saloon are a far cry from those we remember coming from "A Clean, Well-Lighted Place" of Hemingway's famous story (which Saroyan must have read in the mid-1930s). That brightly lit bar had stood ironically as a symbol of refuge; one of the older waiters could not bear to go home to face, alone, the night and the "Nada" of the world. Saroyan's old Arab, crouched in a corner of the bar with his harmonica and the refrain, "No foundation, all the way down the line," reflects no such metaphysical fear, only a weary, superior knowledge of life. But then, neither is Nick's saloon remotely like the one in "The Living and the Dead," where "the odor of the death of man, of man live, yet dead," moves the young idealist to identify himself with the common lot, in order, eventually, to save it.

It is not the social reality of the place itself that the emerging comic writer in Saroyan wants to convey in *The Time of Your Life*.

Impending war and poverty and hopelessness are closely woven in the fabric of that reality, but more than events and their ultimate impact, what concerns Saroyan is how the reality of the moment is being absorbed. And what he once translated into fable or fantasy, he now turns into an empathic critique. (The term would seem to be contradictory, but the separation between author and subject is not yet complete.) Saroyan sees himself as part of his America, if only a bit more sharp-eyed.

Kitty, it appears, is not the only dreamer to inhabit this saloon. Each in his own way, even Nick, has a bit of the McGregor "highlands" in him, if not so plainly visible at first. Nick, who professes indifference to music and calls Tchaikovsky "a dope" ("He let women drive him crazy"), confesses that he has been moved by Tchaikovsky's music:

> I stood behind that bar listening to the God damn stuff and cried like a baby. None but the lonely heart! He was a dope.

Having revealed more than he has wanted to, Nick turns to the *Racing Form* and dashes out to make a bet.

As Kitty resumes her dream about "champagne and everything that goes with it," other "dreamers" walk in, among them Dudley R. Boswick, a character made comic by the obvious variance between his aspirations and the limits of his capacity. Clearly Saroyan has no use for this "ordinary yet extraordinary young man in love." A supercilious young man with "a banal mind which has been only irritated by what it has been taught," he possesses a native drive, aiming for something "simple and basic: a woman." And so great is this force that it "elevates him from nothingness to greatness." Editorializing to the limit in his stage directions, Saroyan adds, "There is little innate or cultivated spirit in him, but there is no absence of innocent animal force." Throughout much of the play we see him at the telephone booth, relentlessly trying to reach his unreachable girlfriend.

Arriving next on the scene is Harry, another kind of loser: timid and awkward though he is, the same kind of "animal force" makes him *"determined to fit in somewhere."* Making his way to the bartender, he tries to persuade him that he's "a great comedian": "I can dance, do gags and stuff," he tells him with great enthusiasm. The audience's attention is not riveted three ways, with Kitty fantasizing about reading a poem stretched out on a big lawn under a tree: Harry showing off a dance routine to Nick, and Dudley on the phone, loudly demanding to talk to "Elsie Mandelspiegel," a nurse at the South Pacific Hospital. But in an instance we are pulled back into reality when a half-starved black boy wanders slowly into the saloon seeking work—"run errands, clean up, wash dishes, anything" nearly fainting as he pleads, "I don't want no charity."

Despite the play's undercurrents of pathos and frustration, it is hard to agree with Walter Kerr's dictum that "there isn't a shred of hope in *The Time of Your Life*." Nor can we accede when he adds, "Saroyan is sentimental about the likableness of people [and] equally sentimental about the doom they are headed for."[13] There is actually nothing particularly "likeable" about Willie, the pinball maniac, or the slow-witted Tom, or the priggish Dudley Bostwick; indeed, the autocratic side of Joe holds little appeal. But Saroyan is not so much asking us to *like* them as simply to *see* them, to take them out of their anonymity. Because they carry within themselves an image of their invincibility, they remain curiously remote from "the doom they are headed for."

Though Saroyan has both claimed and disclaimed "sentimentality" on different occasions, in this case, the "sentimentality" that Kerr and other critics see comes not from Saroyan himself (who remains clear-eyed about their self-deceptions in the long run), but from his characters or rather our perception of them. They are persons so commonly encountered in life that we scarcely take notice of them in terms of their individual plights. But it becomes another thing when we see them close up. We become (and I say this generally speaking) so surprised by their display of common feelings that any expression of them seems to us excessive or suspect.

It is Saroyan's awareness of the supreme faith that moves their lives and makes their world swing between pathos and comedy that enables him to hint a social connotation beyond any that McCarthy or Kerr can see. It is hard to speak of hopelessness or tragedy in the face of such amplitude of energy and expectation. In reading the play, we cannot but appreciate the skill with which Saroyan uses humor to cut through the sentimentalism that forces its way to the surface throughout.

It is not long before we begin to see that each piece of action is tinged with social meaning. There is more than a suggestion of the national mood of the day, for instance, in Harry's situation. This self-styled comedian is out of step with his audience in the crucial year of 1939 and must try to compensate by being cosmic. Thus, his monologue involves, as he puts it,

> The whole city. The whole world. People going by. They're going some-
> where. I don't know where, but they're going.

Being solemn by nature, he doesn't understand simple farce, however hard he tries. And so he turns to the topic of the day.
"WAAAAAAR." He tries initiating a soldier, but his heart isn't
in it:

> I didn't do anything to anybody. Why should *I* be a soldier?
> BOOOOOOOOOM. WAR! O.K. War. I retreat. I hate war. I move
> to Sacramento.

Getting no encouragement from Nick, he turns to Willie for
sympathy:

> Nobody's got a sense of humor any more. The world's dying for com-
> edy like never before, but nobody knows how to laugh.

As a man who wants to "make the world happy," Harry is an
anachronism. (One wonders if Saroyan was beginning to see himself in that predicament.)
    If Harry is frustrated in his urge to happiness, Dudley is even
more so in his pursuit of a date. Having declared his love to the
voice at the end of a "wrong number," he proceeds to make a date
with a total stranger. And when his ruse backfires, this untalented
young prig is shown for the fool he is.
    The genial laughter created by these two sequences makes it
easier for us to accept the sentiment-soaked episodes that follow.
Throughout the hurly-burly front stage, Kitty and Joe have been
drinking together silently. Now as Joe asks again, "What's the
dream?" Kitty makes her longest speech in the play, reaching into
a more remote time to the days when her name was Kornovsky
and she was one of several children living on a farm in Ohio. The
recital of her life evokes searing emotions in her:

> I dream of home, Christ, I always dream of home. I've no home. I've
> no place. But I always dream of all of us together again.

First they had lost Papa, then their home, moving on to Chicago.
There, one brother was killed, another ran away. Then Mama died.
"What's the dream? I dream of home," she ends in anguish.
    The ethereal-looking Julie Haydon, reading these lines in the
original production, convinced audiences that a woman of the
streets could know such feelings, but most of the critics found the

scene sentimental and untrue to life, especially because soon after finishing the speech, Kitty takes off with Tom (with Joe's blessings). Being now head-over-heels in love with Kitty, Tom tells her he's got five dollars, adding quickly, "but I love you." The scene is, of course, not meant to be taken too literally—the characters are too thinly sketched for that. What Saroyan would have us perceive through Kitty is that no dreamer sees life as irreversible, that romantic love is the source and miracle of metamorphosis (as he had so often shown in his short stories).

In Saroyan's day, the American theater still had to persuade the audience that ordinary people had the same capacity for tender feelings as those who were more advantaged. Though we have already glimpsed a gentler Nick behind the tough exterior, he would seem an unlikely person (like Kitty) to bare his soul. But Nick now takes center stage for just this reason. Having dispatched the black boy, Wesley, to the kitchen to be fed, he launches on a monologue that reveals his satisfaction in his new role as impresario. Delighted to see Wesley return from the kitchen and head for the piano, he muses,

> I run the lousiest dive in Frisco, and a guy arrives and makes me stock up with champagne. The whores come and holler at me that they're ladies. Talent comes in and begs me for a chance to show itself. Even society people come here once in a while. I don't know what for.

He decides, "Maybe they can't feel at home anywhere else." The saloon, in other words, is an arena of possibility American style, with the genial bartender mediating between their dreams and reality.

Saroyan expands his stage directions at this point, and it is significant that he twice uses the word *American* to convey the scene:

> The atmosphere is now one of warm, natural, American ease; every man innocent and good; each doing what he believes he should do, or what he must do. There is deep American naivete and faith in the behavior of each person. No one is competing with any one else. No one hates any one else. Every man is living and letting live.

There's "unmistakable smiling and humor. . . . From the world-imposed state of stress and fretfulness," the lingerers at the bar have arrived at "the more natural state of casualness and grace. Each person belongs to the environment, in his own person, as himself." This last statement in the stage directions is of particular significance since it does not conform to the usual view of the dreamer as an individual *outside* reality, but rather as someone creating reality from *within*. A crescendo has been building:

> Wesley is playing better than ever. Harry is hoofing better than ever. Nick is behind the bar shining glasses. Joe is smiling at the toy and studying it. Dudley, although troubled, is at least calm now and full of melancholy poise. Willie, at the marble-game, is happy. The Arab is deep in his memories, where he wants to be.

It is at this point that Blick enters and single-handedly transforms the scene. Designated simply as a "heel" among the cast of characters, he is given a much fuller characterization in Saroyan's stage directions:

> Blick is the sort of human being you dislike at sight. He is no different from anybody else physically . . . There is nothing obviously wrong with him, and yet you know that it is impossible, even by the most generous expansion of understanding, to accept him as a human being. He is the strong man without strength—strong only among the weakling who uses force on the weaker.

"A man reading a play," Saroyan had stated in an essay in *Razzle-Dazzle*,[11] "is a better man than a man seeing a play." Indeed, the importance that he gives his stage directions supports his view. They serve the playwright not only in establishing a mood but to point up aspects of a character that are prototypical and words of ordinary dialogue. Blick has to be more than a melodramatic character.

He is, in sum, the Nazi prototype. The ensuing dialogue between Blick and the bartender establishes Blick as a member of the vice squad who has been on Nick's track before. In response to his *mock-friendliness,* Nick asks, "What do you want?" Blick's voice rises as he bellows, "It's got to stop." The scene is charged with *"a strange fear and disharmony"* as everyone becomes mesmerized. Only Nick is determinedly rebellious: "There's no vice here," he retorts, and he ruffles up Blick by adding, "The only way to find out if a lady is a streetwalker is to walk the streets with her, go to bed and make sure." To Blick's threats that he will have the joint closed, he rejoins, "Do yourself a big favor and don't come back. I don't like your personality."

With Blick's departure, the hubbub resumes with the suddenness that it had halted. Joe, winding his toy, needles Nick, "Do you want to kill that man?" But Nick is already having second thoughts, wondering why he got so worked up: "He's nobody. He's a mouse." He suspects any one who doesn't want to sit down, drink, and "take things easy." "What's a punk like that want to go out and change the world for?" he asks Joe. But Joe, revealing new depth, takes the long view: "It's not him, Nick. It's everything." And though Nick goes on accusing Blick of hurting "little people," Joe will not judge him—even as earlier he had not wished to judge Kitty. "He may not be bad, deep down underneath." One hears in Joe's words the emerging American Liberal, dispassionate, tolerant, fair-minded—ambivalent.

Sharing the climate of the period, Nick and Joe are not far apart in their social philosophy. As proprietor of Nick's Pacific Saloon, Restaurant, and Entertainment Palace, Nick is ready to give anyone a chance to prove himself. For his part, Joe would supplement laissez-faire with philanthropy. Act One ends on a note rich in pathos, with Joe displaying the toy Tom has brought him. Watching it in motion, along with Nick, is Mary L., "an unhappy woman of quality and beauty" who has just walked in. To Nick, who asks about it, Joe explains,

> Nick, this is a toy. A contraption devised by the cunning of man to drive boredom, or grief, or anger out of children. A noble gadget. A gadget, I might say, infinitely nobler than any other I can think of at the moment.

As everyone gathers now to look, Nick makes "a very strange, funny and sorrowful sound."

"Delightful. Tragic, but delightful," says Joe, his mind suddenly far removed from the world.[14] Like McGregor's golden bugle, the music dispenses comfort and harmony to the young in heart. Suddenly, Nick recalls Kitty's angry designation of him as "a dentist." He wonders why: "I wouldn't hurt anybody, let alone a tooth," he tells Joe. As the black boy imitates the music box theme, and Harry dances like the figures on the music box, the lights dim as only the music lingers on.

Joe's role as a spectator in life, a man with no intimate relationships to distract him from his larger mission, is put to the test in the play's second act, which again begins on a light note. Though Joe has had a few too many drinks by now, he is still in control, and now conducts a frivolous banter with a woman at a nearby table, who is also a bit tight.

In trying to guess her name through the initials on her bag, Joe uncovers not only some facts about her—that her name is Mary and she's Irish—but also facts about his own background. We learn that he is Irish on both sides and he once met and fell in love with a girl named Mary in Mexico City. He had been in love, but the woman had married someone else. Asked if he still loves her, he says, "To tell the truth, I'm not sure." But he still thinks about "the kind of kids we would be likely to have." Then, characteristically, he embellishes his "dream children."

> My favorite was the third one. The first two were fine. Handsome and fine and intelligent, but the third one was different. Dumb and goofy-looking. I liked him a lot.

The woman feels free now to ask what he does. He replies, "Do? To tell the truth, nothing. I live all the time." The chitchat leads to his drinking (which he "likes as much as I like to breathe") and his deep-set motivation. He drinks because "I don't like to be gypped. Because I don't like to be dead most of the time and just a little alive every once in a while." After a pause he explains,

> If I don't drink, I become fascinated by unimportant things, like everybody else. I get busy. Do things. All kinds of little stupid things, for all kinds of little stupid reason. Proud, selfish, ordinary things. I've done them. Now I don't do anything. I live all the time. Then I go to sleep.

In other words, Joe's use of alcohol is not for the purpose of *evading* reality but for coming to firmer grips with it, thus becoming really alive.

He admits to Mary that he has no plans; "I just get up," and "smiling abstractly," "tries to come to a more "scientific" conclusion about his drinking:

> Every day has twenty-four hours. . . . Out of the twenty-four hours at least twenty-three and a half are—my God, I don't know why—dull, dead, boring, empty, and murderous. Minutes on the clock, no time of living. It doesn't make any difference who you are or what you do, twenty-three and a half hours on the twenty-four are spent waiting.

And to emphasize his point, he gestures, loudly,

> And the more you wait, the less there is to wait for.

The next stage, he informs his new apt student, is that

> The first thing you know all the years are dead, all the minutes are dead. You yourself are dead. There's nothing to wait for any more.

Nothing but minutes on the clock. No time of life. Nothing but minutes, and idiocy. Beautifully bright, intelligent idiocy.

That rare state of pure spiritual awareness is then lost, never to return. Thus the vicious cycle of his drinking.

To offset Mary's possible discomfort from so much self-revelation, Joe now questions her. She seems happily married, with two children. Why is she so sad? Mary's answer is that she was always sad and that after her marriage she was allowed to drink. Like Joe, she's not waiting for any one, she says, but then corrects herself and admits she's waiting for her husband: "He's a lawyer," she adds. Sight unseen, Joe offers his approval of him. Still goading him on, she now asks if he has responsibilities. Joe replies,

One and thousands. As a matter of fact, I feel responsible to everybody. At least to everybody I meet. I've been trying for three years to find out if it's possible to live what I think is a civilized life. I mean a life that can't hurt another life.

Joe has now come pretty close to revealing the uniqueness of his predicament. But once more he changes the mood, gallantly offering to dance with Mary. But when she accepts, he has to admit that he can't dance, never could. Having indirectly affirmed that he has fallen in love with her and will be "very unhappy if he doesn't see her again," Joe is almost panic-stricken when she gets up to leave. Mary, on her part, confesses she is pleased to know how he feels about her. We know as she leaves that once more he has renounced life.

Though visibly moved by his encounter, Joe readily reverts to his former role as observer of the human comedy. A newsboy now enters the saloon announcing his ambition to become "a great lyric tenor." To his amazement, Joe buys all eleven copies of the paper, reads only the headlines and promptly throws them away. "What's lyric about you?" Nick throws a wisecrack at the boy, but then shows his sympathy for talent by inviting him to demonstrate his ability. The song he chooses, "When Irish Eyes Are Smiling," especially pleases Joe, and even though the boy confesses to being Greek, not Irish, Joe declares his wholehearted approval. "Don't wait a year," he advises, contradicting Nick's decision to return in a year's time, "Come back with some papers a little later. You're a great singer." Thrilled to the core, the boy runs out, while Nick laughs and responds with words cleansed of wisecracks: "Joe, people are so wonderful. Every one of them is wonderful." Then, adding meaningfully, "A nation like this can't go wrong."

This brief episode was an afterthought, written presumably to give Saroyan's cousin, Ross Bagdassarian, a role in the play. The critics were quick to pounce on the hyperboles coming out of the mouths of the two men. Yet when we recognize that the sentimentality is meant to represent an emblematic American stance (especially suited to the patriotic climate of the day), our response shifts and we see that Saroyan's purpose is to give one more instance of Joe's spontaneous desire to encourage "goodness." To use the words of the Credo, Joe feels "no shame in being kindly and gentle." At the same time the audience gets to observe Nick's gradual unbending under Joe's influence.

Up to this point in the play, Joe has been able to combine—if not reconcile—his personal lifestyle and his ultimate philosophy. But as the play's action escalates, we begin to glimpse his uneasy slide down the path of self-doubt.

Two men come in talking. "An intelligent and well-read longshoreman," McCarthy, and his friend Krupp, "a water-front copy . . . a naive man, essentially good. After greeting them, Joe apparently eavesdrops, for he interjects now and then as they turn to him for confirmation with the word, "Right?" The conversation revolves around Krupp's dissatisfaction with his job, particularly as keeper of the peace on the waterfront. As a longshoreman, McCarthy is naturally sympathetic—Krupp's orders could lead to his being hit over the head with a club, "Right?" he asks Joe. Joe's response is a melancholy "I don't know." A bit later, after a wry noncommittal answer from Joe, McCarthy asks suspiciously, "Joe, are you with me or against me?"

Now Joe is prepared—as well as he can be. "I'm with everybody. One at a time," he says. To Krupp's challenge that McCarthy doesn't know what he's fighting for, the longshoreman blurts out, "For the rights of the inferior," looking to Joe, "Right?" The response from Joe is equivocal: "Something like that." Then, despite's Krupp's denial that McCarthy is "inferior," McCarthy blasts away,

> I'm a longshoreman. And an idealist. I'm a man with too much brawn to be an intellectual exclusively. I married a small, sensitive, cultured woman so that my kids would be sissies instead of suckers. A strong man with any sensibility has no choice in this world but to be a heel or a worker. I haven't the heart to be a heel, so I'm a worker.

McCarthy goes on to mouth the cultural myths about writers being the most important heels:

Right now on Telegraph Hill is some punk who is trying to be Shake-speare. Ten years from now he'll be a senator. Or a communist. . . . Writers are mischief makers. Right?

He turns to Joe, who once more evades a straight answer, perhaps because the truth escapes him: "Everything's right. Right and wrong," he replies.

McCarthy now turns to the old Arab who has been listening carefully and asks, "What do you think, Brother?" The old man answers with some deliberation:

No foundation. All the way down the line. What, what-not. Nothing. I go walk and look at the sky.

McCarthy and Krupp are puzzled, but Joe, who feels a metaphysi-cal affinity to the Arab, offers an interpretation:

That means this side, that side. Inhale, exhale, What: birth. What-not: death. . . . That man in his own way is a prophet. He is the one who, with the help of beer, is able to reach that state of deep understanding in which what and what-not, the reasonable and the unreasonable are one.

With a couple of more beers under his belt, McCarthy begins to reclaim his innate will to success. No longer seeing himself as "inferior," he grows loquacious: "I come from a long line of McCar-thys who never married or slept with anything but the most power-ful and quarrelsome flesh." He goes on,

The McCarthys are too great and too strong to be heroes. Only the weak and unsure perform the heroic. They've got to. The more heroes you have, the worse the history of the world becomes. Right?

McCarthy no sooner leaves the saloon than Joe insists that Nick bet everything he's got on the horse, McCarthy, in the last race. His reason? "McCarthy's name's McCarthy, isn't it/ It may be a risk, but it doesn't matter to Joe." It's McCarthy's breed of winners (man or horse) he'd like to bet on.

By the time Tom returns, Joe appears much more decisive. Tom reports that Kitty has gone to her room crying in remembrance of a past that is half-dream, half-reality. It's apparent that Tom loves her, and when Joe learns that he wants to marry her "because I don't like to think of Kitty out in the street," Joe now thinks quickly about making it possible. He sends Tom with a wad of money to go out and bet "on the nose of McCarthy." Tom runs out but quickly returns to say he got there too late; had he arrived in time, they would have won fifteen hundred dollars. Joe appears undismayed; he is hatching another scheme. He asks Tom to bring him a map of Europe and a revolver. "What are you going to do," Nick asks suspiciously, "Study the map and go shoot somebody?" Joe's answer is evasive: "I want to study it [meaning the revolver]. I'm interested in things." Then, in a moment of inspiration, as Tom is leaving, he orders the young man to take the toys on his table to Kitty, saying, "Toys stopped me from crying once." (That was when as a child he had lost his mother.)

Just as Nick asks Joe again what he will do with a revolver, "an old Indian fighter" stalks into the saloon, looking "as if he might have been Kit Carson." Standing at Joe's table, he announces, "Murphy's the name. Just an old trapper. Mind if I sit down?" Ordering a beer for him, Joe studies the man who has started a conversation by asking, "I don't suppose you ever fell in love with a midget weighing thirty-nine pounds?" In typical Western tall-tale fashion the trapper proceeds to give an account of his trials and tribulations as a cattle breeder some twenty years past, totally forgetting his story about the midget. Herding cattle on a bicycle also proves a good opener when he's offered another beer: "Easiest thing in the world. Rode no hands." Joe is soon in the grip of apocryphal Western tales involving several self-transformations. "Of course I believe you," Joe assures the old trapper, "Living is an art. It's not book-keeping. It takes a lot of rehearsing for a man to be himself." This Kit Carson is a literal demonstration of the self-made man at the core of the American myth.

When Tom returns with the book of maps and the revolver, Joe immediately inquires after Kitty. Tom reports that she has not stopped crying, despite the toys. Tom is having regrets about the money they just missed winning and asks Joe how much of it he would have given him if they had won. All of it if Kitty would marry him. "In this realm," he adds, "there's only one subject, and you're it. It's my duty to see that my subject is happy." As he now gets up from his chair with Tom's help to visit Kitty in her hotel room, the young man's gratitude is overflowing: "You're some kind of a guy," he looks up to Joe. "Don't be silly," Joe replies with some anger, more toward himself than toward Tom: "I'm trying to understand things. I'm trying to understand them."

Joe's lines at the end of Act Two, as quoted above, are telling in more than one respect: They reflect the growing confusion in Joe's mind as he seesaws between his ingrained idealism and the exigencies of life that are blatantly unfolding around him. They are also the first real hint one gets of the play's implicit social critique.

Joe happens to have many of the earmarks of the Saroyan character; indeed now and then he even sounds like the author. But as the play progresses, as the image of Joe develops in ways all his own, we cease to identify the author with his character. Saroyan is no longer faithful to the double vision of his short stories that allowed him to remain essentially one with his creation. His new dramatic vision enables him to stand aside and let his characters live according to the dictates of their nature and circumstances. If he is not totally dispassionate, it is because he can now see that his own "innocence" is part of the mythic America he is setting out to recreate.

Act Three is the play's lyric interlude. Its separate setting— Kitty's room at the New York Hotel—remains part of the main stage, which is now darkened, the figures immobilized and silent, except for Wesley's soft piano playing. It is the only time in the play when a set of characters is isolated and the scene serves— like a poignant motif in a symphony or an extended aria in an opera—to heighten and amplify the play's theme. Nothing momentous has happened. Tom and Joe are briefly involved in trying to restore Kitty's self-respect. Angry and hurt, she has been crying on her bed and gazing at a photo of herself at age seven, which she now passes on to the two men. The toy carousel Joe has brought to pacify her only revives memories of her aspiration as a young girl to become a great actress, of having a kind and handsome young doctor fall in love with her and rush her off to beautiful cities where he would dispense money to the poor and cure the ailing. No longer a mere observer, Joe is deeply moved and goads Tom to "go ahead, correct the errors of the world"; and for a moment Tom "becomes" Kitty's Prince Charming in her recollection of an unfulfilled dream. Now Tom himself is transformed, and when a drunken sailor barges into the room, he nearly knocks him out. Restraining Tom, Joe announces he will go find a car so they can all drive to the ocean "to watch the sun go down," have supper, and dance. Tom can't believe Joe's generosity: "You're going on an errand for me?" he asks. Joe replies simply: "That's right." But the stage directions add

He gestures toward Kitty, indicating that Tom shall talk to her, protect the innocence in her which is so much in danger when Tom isn't near, which Tom loves so deeply.

Meanwhile, Tom sets the carousel in motion, moving it toward Kitty, "as though the toy were his heart," the stage direction adds. Before the blackout, the saloon setting reasserts itself with the sound of Harry's dancing and Wesley's piano playing.

Without Joe, Tom, or Kitty, Act Four seems at first like nothing more than a barroom skit, with familiar characters coming and going, their talk intended to entertain rather than move the play forward or create suspense. Kit Carson's sudden appearance on the scene seems to have had no other purpose than to provide colorful dialogue. And although Nick can be overheard talking angrily over the phone about Blick's recent visit and threats, the general tenor of the banter around the place gives no hint of any pending crisis. In a brief cameo, we witness one more swing in mood for tough-talking Nick, who suddenly melts when his little girl walks into the place "with warm, beautiful pride" and calls out, "that's my father." Quickly and firmly ushering her out, he waxes tearfully sentimental about the child, and Carson, now in his cups, echoes the bartender's feelings as he remembers his own two children. His heart softened, Nick sends Carson (who is broke) to the kitchen to work and eat. With much of the same grace as the bugler, MacGregor, he accepts the offer gratefully, remarking as he leaves, "Anything at all. I know a good man when I see one."

The remainder of the act provides Saroyan with a counterpoint to the love motif we have heard earlier, in which dream has prevailed over reality. Now we see that reality can also crush the dream, or nearly so. Dudley, who until now has seemed a comic figure, hung over by his inability to contact his real love, is transformed suddenly into an earnest young man when he finally meets the elusive and overworked nurse, Elsie Mandelspiegel. Though described as "a beautiful, dark girl with sorrowful, wise, dreaming face," we soon realize that Elsie is no Kitty Duval. Her feet are firmly planted on the ground. When Dudley tells her tearfully that he cannot live without her, she has a ready reply at hand: "Don't you see love is impossible in this world?" Without a trace of cynicism, she goes on to explain,

> Love is for birds. They have wings to fly away on when it's time for flying. For tigers in the jungle because they don't know their end. We know our end.

She has no false expectations. The poor dying men she tends at the hospital at night have brought reality close to her. Drained of romantic feelings, she is resigned that "we can never know love or greatness." Without any feeling of embarrassment, she argues that they could go together "to a cheap hotel, and dream that the world is beautiful, and that living is full of love and greatness." But they can never escape "the debts and duties, and the cost of ridiculous things." However, when none of this alters Dudley's "blind faith" that things will work out, Elsie's resistance gives way. After all, she now reasons, there is so little time before "the new pathetic war" comes along, "before they dress you, stand you in line, hand you a gun, and have you kill and be killed." Gently she takes his hand and embracing shyly, they leave "as if they were a couple of young animals."

As the disenchanted young lovers depart, one of the street-walkers at the bar turns to Nick to vent her annoyance: "It's floozies like her that raise hell with our racket," she puts it plainly. Though the line gets a laugh from the audience, Nick is not amused. He is anxious to get the girls out before the cops arrive. Just as he's hustling them out, Krupp enters and they call out to him in challenge: "We were formerly models at Magnins." But Krupp's mind is elsewhere; he has come to let off steam again. He has had an illumination and he must tell Nick about it:

> It came to me while I was on my way to Pier 27. All of a sudden it hit me like a ton of bricks. We are in this wonderful world, full of wonderful things—here we are—all of us, and look at us. Just look at us. We're crazy. We're nuts.

Nick is in agreement, but he's learned to accept it. "Even so, we've got to go on living together," he waves at the people in his place. Krupp continues unburdening his hopelessness: "Why are we so lousy?" he asks again, his belief mounting: "This is a good world."

> It's wonderful to get up in the morning and go out for a little walk and smell the trees and see the streets and the kids going to school and the clouds in the sky. . . . So why do we make all the trouble?

He has momentarily captured the essence of "the American Dream," and knows that things are not right any more.

> We're crazy, that's why. We're no good any more. All corruption everywhere. The poor kids selling themselves. A couple of years ago they were in grammar school. Everybody trying to get a lot of money in a hurry.[15]

He has made up his mind to quit. "Let someone else keep law and order." Yet even though his words are emphatic, he wonders:

"What'll I do if I quit?" He has a wife and two sons. "Where's money going to be coming from?"

Nick is sympathetic and wise; some of the Old World experience of his ancestors has rubbed off: "That's one of the reasons we're all crazy," he remarks, "We don't know where it's going to be coming from." We're at the mercy of circumstance, he explains, taking what we have to take whether we like it or not. This is why we can't be who we really are.

But Krupp persists. What troubles him most is that he catches himself being mean, "hating people just because they're down and out, broke and hungry, sick and drunk." Vehemently he asserts: "I don't want any part of it."

The old Arab, who has been listening and moving closer to the speakers, now has his cue and once more utters his refrain: "No foundation. All the way down the line." He repeats it three times, as Krupp questions and then affirms what he has said. When asked what he does for a living, the Arab responds with little emotion:

Work. Work all my life. All my life work. From small boy to old man. In old country work. In new country work. [He enumerates all the cities and sites.] No beg. Work. For what? Nothing. [Speaking of his two sons whom he has not seen in twenty years.] Lost. Dead. Who knows? What. What-not. No foundation. All the way down the line.

"Nicest guy in the world," Nick remarks as the Arab turns away to play his harmonica. Krupp is in agreement but adds, "But crazy. Just like the rest of us. Stark raving mad." Everybody appears to be moved by the music coming from the Arab's corner. Wesley decides it is "deep, deep crying . . . a thousand years ago." Harry is inspired to invent a dance for it. To Krupp it brings a change of heart. He suddenly tells Nick to forget what he's said. "It gets me down once in a while." Then, assuming his public role again, he turns to Nick. "Keep the girls out of here," he shouts as he leaves. "Take it easy," is Nick's loud and friendly riposte. The music and dancing are at their height as the curtain falls.

Perhaps the hardest character for us to accept is Krupp—a police officer who appears totally "unconditioned" by his long confrontation with the life of crime. The loss of a sense of goodness would seem the natural thing, not the extraordinary. But in the era when the world's crime was so glaringly emphasized, Krupp's labor violence beat seemed comparatively mild.

When the curtain rises on the fifth and final act, things have come back to normal: Joe is sitting in his usual place, studying a book of maps and drinking; a dreamy-looking Tom is at the bar; and a bemused Kit Carson is watching the marble-game maniac struggling with the machine. The new element on the scene is an elegantly attired couple, the man in top hat, sitting at the table next to Joe's—their occasional comments on the happenings around them lending the effect of a Greek chorus. There is a momentary intrusion of loud Salvation Army singing coming from outside, followed by the reappearance of a drunkard who walks in announcing his conversion, though his words are barely intelligible.

Thinking out loud, Joe gets Tom's attention when he calls out the name of an obscure city in Czechoslovakia. A bewildered Tom rushes to his side and starts lavishly thanking Joe for treating him and Kitty to a drive along the ocean. Joe is full of praise of Kitty, whom he calls "one of the finest people in the world," adding extravagantly, "Those three hours were the most delightful, the most somber, and the most beautiful I have ever known." Now as Tom searches Joe's motive in being so generous Joe again becomes self-revealing:

> Why? I'm a student. I study all things. All. All. And when my study reveals something of beauty in a place or in a person where by all rights only ugliness or death should be revealed, then I know how full of goodness this life is. And that's a good thing to know. That's a truth I shall always seek to verify.

This is Saroyan's voice—the words of the credo; it is the side of Joe that makes him aware he is still alive. The society people at the next table are bemused by Joe's speech, and the man concludes, "He's either drunk, or naturally crazy."

Now Tom innocently asks what the audience has wanted to know all along: "Where does Joe get his money? "Three years now and I've never asked."

Though Joe's words in reply are uttered clearly and emphatically, they are also quixotic: "Don't be a fool, Tom," Joe says, as he looks at him "sorrowfully, a little irritated not so much with Tom as with the world and himself, his own superiority":

> Listen carefully. If anybody's got any money—to hoard or to throw away—you can be sure he stole it from other people. Not from the rich who can spare it, but from the poor people who can't. From their lives and from their dreams.

He admits to being no exception. He, too, stole and hurt people. He's glad he doesn't know who they are or where: "If I did, I'd feel worse than I do."

On the face of it this is Marxist talk, with lines that could have come straight out of a play by Clifford Odets. But Joe's diatribe doesn't stop there. There is another side to the picture: "I've got a Christian conscience in a world that's got no conscience at all," he says and this makes him feel superfluous and vulnerable. "The world's trying to get some sort of social conscience, but it's having a devil of a time trying to do that." By drawing a distinction between a *Christian* conscience and a *social* conscience, Joe is both defending his superiority over the impersonal "humanitarianism" of the reformer and acknowledging his defeat as an idealist. He regrets that he no longer works. "I don't make anything," he says pathetically. He lifts up the gun from the table and looks at it as he talks:

> Well, you can't enjoy living unless you work. Unless you do something. I don't do anything. I don't want to do anything any more. There isn't anything I can do that won't make me feel embarrassed. Because I can't do simple things. I haven't the patience. And I'm too smart. Money is the guiltiest thing in the world. It stinks.

Joe's anguish arises from regret for the loss of holiness in his work (such as the preacher speaks of in Ecclesiastes)—not from the absurdist's sense of futility. Money creates guilt in more than one way; a surfeit of pleasures has dulled Joe's enjoyment of his work, which ultimately equates with life. There is scarcely anything "existential" about his hero manqué. The "paralysis" from which he suffers is not metaphysical in origin but rather psychological, the "innermost self" having become detached from the center of his consciousness. When he says earlier to Mary L. that by doing nothing he "live[s] all the time," he is referring quixotically to his immobility, which by deferment of action creates an illusion of living within the bounds of repeated moments.

It is soon after his confession to Tom that he asks the young man to fetch him a book of maps and a gun. The impending war is no doubt behind this odd request, since Joe (as he says) is a "student" of life, but it could also be that the thought of suicide has crossed his mind—or only brushed it. For soon after, as if resisting the idea, he orders Tom to get rid of the revolver ("Give it to somebody who appears to be in need of [it]," he says). When Joe next brings up the subject, he turns to Kit Carson—with a new trend of thought. His spirits suddenly renewed, he send Tom off on another fool's errand. Lest he forget, Tom recites the long list of items Joe has requested on the spur of the moment:

O.K. Joe. I got it. *Life, Liberty, Time,* all kinds of gum they're selling, jelly beans, six panatela cigars, a dollar for a news-kid, a dollar for an old man, two dollars for the Salvation Army. *(Going)* Let the lower lights be burning, send a gleam across the wave.

The society lady thinks "he's absolutely insane," and her husband asks in exasperation, "Do you want to go back to where people aren't crazy?" But the woman is having fun and is reluctant to leave.

Meanwhile, Kit Carson has come over to Joe's table and is soon singing the Salvation Army song with him, "raising hell with the tune," as they sip champagne and discover they're both Presbyterian. When the society lady joins them in the singing, Kit begins to flirt with her. But Joe has not forgotten the gun and he now takes advantage of Kit's expertise.

Kit is in his element as he shows Joe how to load the revolver, all the time reviewing his career as a veteran six-shooter. For a moment the society couple is terrified at Kit's announcement that the gun is now "ready to kill." But carefully unloading it, Joe humorously aims it at a bottle on the bar, shouting, "Bang."

From the other end of the room, in counterpoint, comes Willie's loud voice directed at Nick: "Thought I couldn't do it, hey? Now, watch." In a crazy-quilt succession the machine lights go on and off, red and green, and a bell rings six times. As an American flag appears, Willie salutes: "Oh, boy, what a beautiful country." And as the music-box version of "America" rings out, everyone, including Joe, rises singing.

There is moot irony in the long monologue in which Willie sums up the American work ethic—something that could apply equally to marble machines or the stock market. Willie brags that it took him a while, "but I finally did it. It's scientific really." Though it isn't exactly what he wants to do, "I just don't like the idea of anything getting the best of me," he declares proudly.

Myself, I'm the kind of guy who makes up his mind to do something and then goes to work and does it. There's no other way a man can be a success at anything.

As his mood grows expansive Willie reveals that he is Assyrian. "We've got a civilization six or seven centuries old, I think," he brags. Then, in a tone of camaraderie, "saluting Joe and the world," he departs.

The noisy, heady euphoria has now rubbed off on everyone, and it mounts to a still more feverish pitch when Tom returns with the wads of gum and all Joe's other requests and deposits them at his table. In the best Mark Twain tradition a contest is now launched (between two men instead of children) to see who can chew more wads of gum at a time—Joe or Tom, with Kit Carson serving as referee. This parody serves as a sign that all is not hanging together as it once did. Alcohol has intensified the dissociation of the psyche into behavior that the cop and the society people can only see as "crazy." No one appears to be affixed to a single identity, least of all Joe, who remains curiously detached from his feelings, playing a silly game with Tom while discussing Tom's possible future with Kitty. In response to this mixture of levity and seriousness the old Arab once more reiterates, "No foundation," with Nick finishing his comment this time, "All the way down the line."

Strangely, Joe is almost sober when Kitty arrives, confused and self-doubting. She has agreed to marry Tom but does not feel she sis good enough for him A new aggressive Joe now dispels her insecurity, telling her about the job he has fixed up for Tom as a truck driver. Once more he reassures her: "Kitty Duval, you're one of the few truly innocent people I have ever known." Overcome with gratitude, Kitty replies, "I'm not sure about love any more, but I know I love you, and I know I love Tom." "I love you, too, Kitty Duval," Joe tells her and, with an enthusiasm we have not observed in him before, he wobbles out of the place to find Kitty a book of poems to read while she waits for Tom to return.

With both Joe and Nick away, it is Blick's moment to arrive on the scene, and it is not inappropriate that the first person to greet him is Harry, the failed comedian, who has been complaining of the humorless American. For that is the impression Blick gives as a stereotype-villain with no redeeming quality. Not very Saroyanesque, to be sure. But if we think back to Joe's initial impression of Blick ("It's not him, Nick. It's everything"), we can see Blick as a symbol, as part of a larger evil scarcely known to the people in the saloon. In diagnosing Blick, Joe had added, "He may not be bad, deep down inside." So blinding is Joe's faith in people that his confidence must ultimately backfire. In a play about dreamers and persons vulnerable to illusion there has got to be a con man out to defraud believers.

Blick is out to get Kitty, and with the self-righteousness of the inquisitor hurls a barrage of questions at her. She is no longer dressed like a streetwalker, but her presence in the barroom makes her suspicious. Standing up to Blick at first, Kitty tell him to "go to hell," but as fear overtakes her, she becomes speechless. With no clear-cut case against her, Blick can only get his way by degrading her and pushing around those who stand in his way. Physically and spiritually he is a destructive force, taking on the strong (Kit Carson) as well as the weak (Wesley) who come to Kitty's defense. Kitty now confesses tearfully what she had come to put behind her: "I'm a whore, you son of a bitch."

The society people object to Blick's "attitude," but when put on the defensive, they promptly walk out just as Blick's verbal attacks reach their peak. Because Kitty has said that she had danced in burlesque, Blick now asks her to start stripping. At that very moment Joe enters and, as if reincarnated, takes on the role of hero. Incisively he orders Kitty to step down from the stage, and then protectively takes her in his arms. Tom now appears and rushes at once to Wesley who is being beaten up by Blick. Overtaken with fury, Joe pulls Tom away and pushes him out with Kitty, instructing them to take off in Tom's new truck. Joe is now ready to take on Blick. Drawing the revolver out of his pocket, he pulls the trigger, saying, "I've always wanted to kill somebody, but never knew who it should be." But no shot is heard. Nick enters the fray, grabs the gun from Joe, and draws him aside: "What the hell do you think you're doing?" He is frightened for Joe, but Joe is filled with anger that Tom has brought him a faulty revolver. He collapses on his chair, "dead to the world." The brawl reaches its climax as Blick returns, breathless, from his clubbing of Wesley, and Nick, pouncing on him, grabs him by the collar. As Nick pushes him out, he threatens that he will murder him "slowly—with my hands" if he returns. He turns to Harry: "Go take care of the colored boy," he orders.

In the midst of all this commotion, Willie returns. Noticing nothing, he resumes his stand at the machine, which now refuses to honor his commands. The flag goes berserk, causing Willie to keep saluting endlessly. Distressed, he turns to Nick; "This machine is out of order," he complains. As two shots are heard in the distance, this scene of comic relief suddenly assumes a social connotation. A moment ago Willie had stood saluting the flag and declaring, "As far as I'm concerned, this is the only country in the world." Now, like the machine, "the country" (or their perception of it) is out of whack.

At this moment the newsboy runs in with his wares and makes his way to Joe but gets no response from him. He tries arousing him by getting the phonograph to play "The Missouri Waltz," but even then Joe does not budge. It is only when Nick returns with the news that Blick is dead and that even the cops aren't trying to find out who killed him that Joe looks up at last. He's happy to know that Blick is dead, but he is still worried that "the God damn gun wouldn't go off." Nick can't believe that Joe really wanted to kill "that guy," and he now offers to reward him with a bottle of champagne. But he is suspicious when Joe rises, takes his hat off the rack, and starts putting on his coat, with help from the newsboy. "What's the matter?" he asks. "Nothing. Nothing," Joe replies, waving away the champagne, "Thanks." Nick wants to know where he is going, reminds him "It's not even eleven yet." But Joe says simply, "I don't know. Nowhere." He is noncommittal when Nick asks he'll be coming back tomorrow. "I don't know. I don't think so," he replies. But a moment later, on seeing Kit Carson his tone changes as he pointedly inquires, "Somebody just shot a man. How are you feeling?" Kit's response is characteristically upbeat: "I never felt better in my life," he says, as he proceeds to reveal that he himself was Blick's killer. He tells it in the indirect manner of the tall story, ending with a cold-blooded, casual regret: "Had to throw the beautiful revolver in the Bay." An audience has gathered around the teller of tales. As he prepared to leave, Joe takes the revolver out of his pocket and hands it to Kit, *looking on him with great admiration and affection.* Then he loudly asks, with Kit's own inflection, "Kit, did I ever tell you about the time I fell in love with a midget weighing thirty-nine pounds?" Kit is amazed: "Now, son." As Joe walks to the street waving, all wave back "and the marble game goes into its beautiful American routine again," as the play ends.

The ambiguity of Joe's departure, his sudden change of heart as he apparently sides with the pragmatic American—Carson—is intended, not accidental. It is one more instance of Joe's contradictory self; within a larger framework, it represent America's contradictory, ambivalent self. (Had not President Roosevelt himself declared not too long before that he "hated" war, yet he would be leading the country into World War II in the months to come?) The need to act momentarily cancels the desire to *become.* Joe is the "student"—by extension, the writer (Saroyan himself) in search of the original American now suddenly caught between myth and reality. Because he had been acting according to his own lights, Joe was unable to fire the gun intended for Blick; yet in his rescue of Tom and Kitty we have proof that he has absorbed the credo in its essence. As to the future, Joe's recognition that "no man's guilt is not yours" makes it dubious that his "conversion" (or atonement) will be a permanent one.

"No foundation," the old Arab in the play had repeated pointedly. But the play's final resolution sidesteps such self-righteousness in favor of a more gently ironic verdict. The legend that has created the American is impervious to "foundation"; it resists permanence in its continual need to renew and invent afresh. Its virtue is also its nemesis—for given no chance of being absorbed, reality comes to meld with the illusory, creating a source of perpetual drama. Clearly, it was something beside the mere trappings of the form that attracted Saroyan to vaudeville; he saw in its episodic, disjointed variety and discontinuity the very core of American life. It was from this fount of the popular culture and major source of entertainment that Saroyan culled his blueprint for the American character, with its traces of touching, often noble heartbreak. At its moment of crisis he saw it embodied—as he wrote to George Jean Nathan—in "the dying who are undying," and drew it close to his own faith in "the deathlessness of the living."

Behind plot and character, there is a philosophical thrust in *The Time of Your Life* in the denial of human conditioning. In this play of contradictions, Saroyan shows how life tries to fix us into molds, but even as we play our assigned roles, the true self, the soul, keeps surfacing. Saroyan's spokesman, Joe, urges those around him to "despise evil and ungodliness, but not the men of ungodliness or evil."

7

The Broadway Years

I began to see! I didn't used to see. The street cars going by
had people in them suddenly. There had always been people in
street cars, but now they were beautiful people.
                                        —Saroyan, *The Beautiful People*

"This man Saroyan will be the death of us yet," was how Brooks
Atkinson began his review of Saroyan's third play to be produced
on Broadway within thirteen months. *Love's Old Sweet Song,*
called by the playwright "a theatrical entertainment," had opened
at the Plymouth Theatre on 2 May 1940 after a brief out-of-town
run the month before. What had puzzled the *Times*'s critic was
how with all its "beguiling improvisations"—and the towering presence of Walter Huston in the role of "an amiable charlatan"—
"nothing had been accomplished." In a patronizing way he had
used before with this playwright, he both acknowledged Saroyan's
"inventive" and "original" gifts and complained of the play's "platitudinous" message. "Sooner or later," his review concluded, "Saroyan will have to put his mind to work."[1] This was not unlike the
verdict he had reached about *The Time of Your Life.* After praising
Saroyan for (among other things) "his extraordinary gift for writing
about human beings," he had stated, "nothing much of significance
is accomplished in [the play]."[2] It was shortly thereafter, with the
fourth production of a Saroyan play, *The Beautiful People,* that Mr.
Atkinson would attach the word "mindless" to Saroyan's theater
in general. Because it was uttered by that venerable critic, the word
or its equivalent would be forever batted about in any discussion of
Saroyan's dramatic work. Needless to say, the playwright was
never shy about doing battle on this score and he held his own on
more than one occasion.

What Atkinson's sudden outburst reveals in retrospect is how
limited a grasp he had of Saroyan's theater. Though he had initially

recognized his talents, Saroyan would forever remain for him that "enchanting" and "good-humored" fellow who "charmed" us with his fables. But that he should try to deal with "ideas"? In a corrosive Sunday *Times* piece, titled "Saroyan at the Bat," he latched onto Saroyan's introductory pronouncements to the volume of his three plays and mincing no words, stated, "His mind is shallow and unsettled and he sounds off like a sophomore." Referring to him variously as "the ebullient Armenian," "the enthusiastic newsboy," and "Cosmic Bill," he declared that Saroyan was "at his worst in any discussion of ideas." The deepest cut came at the end:

> Out of his natural ebullience, hospitality, decency of outlook and impudence he can improvise charmingly on the theme of life and recover some of the lost innocence of the world. The great works in drama require greater capacities—like O'Neill's knowledge and depth of feeling and O'Casey's experience, mind and passion.

Saroyan's reply the very next Sunday in Atkinson's own column drew blood in its own archly circuitous way:

> Having no mind to speak of in the opinion of many, it is awkward for me to call upon whatever else has been doing my thinking for me, but at the same time, this is, I regret, necessary.

Then, matching Atkinson's bluntness,

> I hesitate to say this but I sincerely believe that whatever "mind" may be, Mr. Atkinson has a good deal less of it than I have.

Taking up each point of the critic's attack, he persuasively shows up his literal-mindness and even catches him in a superficial reading of the Bible. Finally, with that typical mixture of high-minded humility and bravado he had used in turning down the Pulitzer Prize five months earlier, he lands on a morally superior plane:

> One doesn't simply write plays, or short stories, or novels, or whatever it happens to be. One lives, one accepts living, one believes in it, one is honest with one's self and with others, and so on and so forth.[3]

In the remaining three years of Saroyan's affiliation with Broadway, he would have many more admirers than detractors, but it was the rare critic who would get beyond the surface of his work. Not that the guidance he offered them was of much help. One can only commiserate with the Broadway critic-on-the-run looking for clues amid a morass of disingenuous autobiographical asides that couch his thoughts. Even an attentive reader, with some background in Saroyan, grasps at straws to get to the heart of the matter.

And there were other obstacles. While no one doubted that Saroyan was going against the tide, the "tide" itself had grown indistinct with the introduction of new concepts. There was Surrealism and Freud; there was "the new reality" of the moderns giving birth to a rebellious, new metaphysics—none of it yet residing in the American theater but infiltrating the critic's language, if not his imagination, via literature and the arts. Many of Saroyan's short plays were called "surreal," as was *My Heart's in the Highlands,* and found wanting as such. One Freudian critic in the late 1940s, W. David Sievers, in a book titled *Freud on Broadway,* contended that "William Saroyan represents a compromise position between the demands of the practical theatre and the cry of André Breton for automatic writing."[4] His analysis of Saroyan in Freudian/ surreal terms proved a futile endeavor: there was little to be gained in having the playwright's fable overtones translated into "childish wish-fulfillment" and much to lose in turning "the preoccupation with food" in *My Heart's in the Highlands* into "oral regression."[5]

What would further complicate matters was that in a climate of war the theater was becoming less receptive to experimental work, inclining once again toward the "drama of ideas." The most successful innovator in the theater since Maxwell Anderson, Thornton Wilder was turning away from poetic fantasy: his 1938 play, *The Merchant of Yonkers* (later to become *The Matchmaker* and *Hello, Dolly*) was a conventional farce, and his 1942 hit, *The Skin of Our Teeth,* would camouflage its Pirandelloesque fantasy with a heavy varnish of parody and mordant irony. With the "tide" now absorbing such cerebral and impassioned playwrights as Lillian Hellman and Robert Sherwood, it would take nothing less than a cocky playwright to try returning to the theater "the element of play." Still, Saroyan had enough sense to know that it would be the height of folly to repeat in his third play these aspects of his work that identified him as a spinner of fairy tales. Thus his strategy was not unlike Wilder's. Though by his own estimation *Love's Old Sweet Song* was "a sort of sequel to *My Heart's in the Highlands,* it came off more like a genial spoof of it. Whatever the play's ultimate intent (and in this case Saroyan had taken the precaution to direct it himself), it was palpably a mix of romantic comedy and broad farce that all but mocked Johnny's plaint in the earlier play that "something is wrong somewhere." Writing to Nathan, he had explained that he was inspired by a recent visit to his home town, and while he knew that it was "not the great work I figure I'll be writing one of these years. . . . I believe it is a very good play of its kind."[6] But the verdict on Broadway far from matched his belief, and the play folded after five weeks.

Apart from Brooks Atkinson, *Love's Old Sweet Song* created problems for the critics who were looking for the familiar Saroyan trademarks and, not finding them, either blasted the play or lapsed into double-talk. A special case in point was *The New Republic*'s critic, Stark Young, who had once let the orthodoxies of dramaturgy go by the board to accommodate the new drama of Saroyan that "wants mood in the theatre to serve as the equivalent to melody in music."[7] But detecting "rambling technical defects" in the new play, he urged the playwright to write in "theatre terms." Confusing the issue, however, Young went on to acknowledge Saroyan's "relish for the theatre as such," adding, "At this stage of the game, it is a certain innocence in Mr. Saroyan as to what is hackneyed theater and what is not . . . That sometimes lends the play its charming and loveable qualities." A little later, in a reassessment of Saroyan's theater, he would call this same play "a fragment from a torn surrealistic valentine," and conclude, "It has all those slipshod slightly balmy qualities which those who do not admire Mr. Saroyan are fond of ascribing to his plays."

Clearly, Young's confusion lies in his unwillingness or inability to take Saroyan seriously as a playwright. For while he confesses that he enjoys Saroyan's plays, he will not accept the fact that he achieves his effects *outside* dramatic conventions. He does not so much as wonder whether there exists a strategy beyond the writer's "charm" that enables him to escape the usual limits of dramatic action. Young's slapdash view of Saroyan's work, together with his preeminence as a drama critic, would present a major stumbling block to the playwright's ultimate dramatic fortune.

It must also be pointed out (if I may stray here a bit longer) that among the critics in general, curiosity about Saroyan continued to center on his personality rather than on what he himself had hailed as "the new American theatre." In the reams of newsprint expended on him, there was scarcely a mention of his extensive early association with avant-garde writing. Despite continued references to his "surrealism," it did not occur to anyone to review his closeness to the new writing and to see its relation to his most "difficult" play until now. (It was a closeness he would retain to the end of his life). I have previously mentioned his affiliation with *The Booster* in Paris, as well as his impressionistic work, "The Slot Machine," which appeared in the magazine *transition*. It was because Saroyan thought of himself as a trailblazer that he had insisted (against the advice of his editor) on including "experimental stuff" in his second book, *Inhale and Exhale*. Freedom of form and composition had been among his initial aims as a writer, and indeed it was through the encouragement of another little magazine, *Story*, that he had developed his original concept of the short story.

But to be an experimentalist in the theater of the 1940s was quite another matter—as Saroyan would discover soon enough. Ideology was back in a new guise, thickly entwined this time with aesthetics and a new metaphysics that bore a distinctive foreign stamp. In Europe, innovators in the theater were not satisfied merely to extend the borders of the imagination or, deranging the senses, to plumb an interior reality. They sought at the same time a special rhetoric to express the new Zeitgeist on the Continent on the eve of World War II.

For a very long time the new philosophies of Existentialism, Marxism and Neo-Nihilism would reverberate loud and clear in the modern European theater. But the innovations of a Sartre, Camus, Brecht, Ionesco, or Beckett would—not surprisingly— cross the ocean with some difficulty. With their essential antagonism toward the "bourgeoisie," these literary writers would perforce alienate the main staple of theater audiences (i.e., the middle class) in America. As objects of contempt and ridicule in the works of a Brecht or Ionesco, this large segment of society was deemed unequal to comprehending the modernist's vision. Looking back, it seems ironic that even as the world waged war for more than half a decade to protect the freedom of the individual, the new philosopher/artist was veering away from the individual to formulate a composite and somewhat remote portrait of Humankind. And because modern life had grown so fragmented, the center, they foretold, would no longer "hold." To recognize life's absurdity would henceforth become the height of sophistication. You could decide to *wait* and become a believer of sorts—as Beckett's theater would demonstrate a bit later. But the life envisioned for modern man in a play like *Waiting for Godot* was just as bleak and cheerless as if he had stopped believing altogether.

Given this set of circumstances, it is not hard to see why Saroyan would flounder at first in his urge to be free in the theater. Although he fell in line with the avant-garde in his rebellion against the "well-made play" and the banalities of the conventional theater, he would resist turning his back on the homespun "normalcy" of his own middle class. He would revel in chastising its materialism and poking fun at its pomposities, but his brand of humanism would not allow him to lessen his expectations of the "common man" or dilute by an iota his respect for the "ordinary" joys and struggles he experienced. Some of his faith would diminish with time, but he would be religious, as a poet is religious, valuing the particular moment alongside the eternal realities.

In *Love's Old Sweet Song* the rage to be "innovative" is almost overpowering. More secure now in his comic vision and no longer needing to coast on his past fame, Saroyan is ready to prove he is a more worldly chap that some have supposed. Turning once again to the tinsel-surfaced world of vaudeville, he mingles parody with paradox as he fastens on a fine point about love. He approaches the theme obliquely in his introduction to the play: "All kinds of love . . . are regard of self," he writes. "Doing good things is the ultimate selfishness."[9] It was this statement that had led Atkinson to call Saroyan an egoist, one apparently unacquainted with "a love that is a union and represents a surrender of self." But Saroyan had insisted: "It so happens that I know all about it and believe it is the ultimate selfishness. Only unrealistic thinking could change it from selfishness to heroism."

Where Emerson long ago had observed: "Beauty is its own excuse for being," Saroyan was now adding, So is Love. Like beauty, love seeks no reward beyond the pleasure it brings the lover. If this sounds perverse and a bit Nietzschean, it may be because what often passes for love lacks the element of self-fulfillment. In a society that identifies love with ethical conduct, connecting it with good works, philanthropy or social service, it is hard to see it in its pure form before it gets confused with altruism.

With an eye that is "simultaneously naive and sophisticated" (as he puts it), Saroyan focuses here on two kinds of love: romantic love, as spawned and perpetuated by Hollywood, and a universally acclaimed "humanitarianism" that manifests itself as social consciousness. By juxtaposing the two he creates an atmosphere of incongruity that readily melds the comic and, for that matter, "the naive and the sophisticated." The playwright is learning that with crafty handling foolishness and laughter (so easy to identify with "everyman") can often be more effective catalysts than a sermon or a credo. So Saroyan piles on the foolishness and laughter with a vengeance throughout the three acts.

First to appear on stage, in a setting that features an "old-fashioned house" in a small town in California, is a romantic lady who appears to be in her early forties. Smelling and then cutting some roses in the yard, she starts singing a nostalgic song about "the years, the years, they come and go." She sits on a rocking chair on the porch with a love-story magazine in her hands. She is the "Ann Hamilton" who is being paged by a postal telegram boy who then promptly introduces himself as "Georgie Americanos," adding for anyone's interest that he is the son of a wrestler from Smyrna, that he is a "radical" and reads philosophy. The telegram he insists on reading aloud has been sent by "Barnaby Gaul," who says he loves Ann and is on his way to woo her.

This telegram we soon learn is a fake—a hoax played on Georgie by a fellow messenger boy. But the truth remains undisclosed to the susceptible lady, who vaguely remembers the unknown suitor as a passerby of some twenty-seven years ago. At the mention of the world "love" she is catapulted out of her small world. When presently an imposing, red-haired, middle-aged gentleman arrives (played in the original cast by Walter Huston), he is introduced by Georgie as "Barnaby Gaul." He is, of course, no such person but (as we learn later) a carnival huckster who happens to be singing the very song ("Love's Old Sweet Song") that Ann remembers the stranger whistling in the dim past.

Though taken aback at first, "Barnaby Gaul" is in no time ensnared into accepting his fated role. A mutual need for "romance" draws the strangers together, and in the ensuing dialogue they mourn the absence of love in their lives. Ann voices her regret for the lost years. The intensity is operatic:

The years moved away . . . the roses bloomed and faded . . . the song died . . . the children I wanted were never born.

And Barnaby Gaul explains how love evaded him:

There were wars . . . there were famines . . . disasters at sea . . . and wherever a man stood his heart was not there.

In the hands of a present-day writer the scene would be full of innuendoes about the sex drives of the middle-aged. But for Saroyan, the sentimentality and pathos only affirm the inviolability of the romantic dimension. If an old truth seems laughable now, it is only because society chooses to see it in that light. To make his point, Saroyan abruptly clips the lyric mood, turning what might have been a Jeannette MacDonald/Nelson Eddy duet into gently ironical commentary. The two sentimental songs composed by Paul Bowles for the end of their scene—"The Years" and "Of All the Things I Love"—are poignant in essence but become less than romantic when viewed in the context of an ulterior comedy of errors.

Then, in the middle of Act One, the play makes a quick transition into outright parody. Sweeping aside all signs of romantic comedy, it ventures boldly into a travesty of the widely subscribed to model of contemporary realism—the Okies of *Grapes of Wrath* fame. All fourteen members of the Yearling family turn up on Ann Hamilton's lawn announcing that they have come to "rest a spell"—that is, until the birth of the latest offspring in three months. They are followed by a newspaper reporter (Oliver) who is trying to write a novel about them, and a lady *Life* magazine photographer (Elsa), both of whom are troubled by the absence of gloom and doom on the scene: these are obviously not classic Steinbeck characters.

Even though, like the Joads, the Yearlings claim to have traveled in an old Ford from their home state of Oklahoma, they are not about to cave in. Ranging in age from four to nineteen, the children are a rowdy bunch as they scurry around the house, pillaging and devouring everything in sight. The violence gets so out of hand that before the curtain comes down on Act One, Barnaby Gaul flees for his life, with the lovelorn Ann in pursuit.

The wild and wacky exploits on stage are accompanied by a sprightly banter. The experience of writing radio one-acters and ballet plays has helped Saroyan gain close rapport with the mass mind, and in the scenes involving the aggressive Yearlings, he displays an unsuspecting facility with popular quips and barbs. When Oliver warns Cabot Yearling that they are violating private property, adding, "Of course, after the revolution," Cabot retorts, "You stay away from us, with your God-damn propaganda. We voted for Roosevelt." And when Cabot tells Georgie that they are "Migratory workers," the boy snaps back, "Well, why don't you work? Or migrate?" The verbal absurdity reaches its peak when a young man selling subscriptions to *Time* magazine takes center stage to recite—like the litany of saints—a long list of names on the magazine's masthead, while the Yearlings listen entranced.

Behind all the horseplay is Saroyan's attempt to turn the much-exploited Depression syndrome around. Oliver objects that he cannot write his novel about these disposed farmers because they lack the noble traits he has been made to expect of them; having personally suffered violence from one of the Yearling children, he is readier to think of this crew as "white trash." Yet, how explain Cabot Yearling's ability to size up his situation?

The contradiction is not wholly unreasonable in view of Saroyan's belief that the character of man is neither steady nor predictable. Or, as Elsa puts it, "You write as you want the world to write in the first place, and forget all these little complications."[10] When she then goes on to lecture Oliver—"If you want the world to be better, be better yourself"—Oliver drops the whole matter, orders her to shut up, and tells her he loves her. As he wards off one of the pesky children standing in his path, he shouts at the whole crew, while holding on to Elsa,

> To hell with the people in the house. Let God take care of them, the same as ever. To hell with art! To hell with propaganda! . . . I love you, so shut up and let's try to live.

It is impossible to miss in this "live and let live" outburst a desperate sense of betrayal in a much touted "humanitarianism." It is expressed by Cabot himself when he is badgered by Oliver's endless questionings. As this unwilling "victim" puts it,

> It's . . . like never being able to lie down and sleep in the afternoon, without somebody waking up a body to ask if we know how to read or not, or if we want better working conditions.

Cabot even denies being "unfortunate," as Oliver would have it. "Unfortunate? I've got my driver's license," he corrects him. To which his wife adds: "We don't want nothing from nobody—hardly . . . We aim to shift for ourselves, the same as ever."

Beyond the attempt to correct Steinbeck's theatrical sentimentality in the handling of character is Saroyan's need to disabuse his audience of certain commonly held beliefs: that Americans instinctively honor private property; that the press is responsible in its search for the truth—and that the illusion-dispatching huckster is a less useful member of society than the fact-dispatching reporter.

In one scene the two are set side by side, with Barnaby Gaul comparing his trade to that of the magazine salesman who has just sold a subscription to *Time* to the illiterate Cabot. Denying the salesman's charge that he is all "nonsense," Barnaby retorts,

> You are nonsense. I only dwell in a world of nonsense. I have neither degree nor diploma, and yet it is not you who goes with tidings of hope. I heal the wounds of people. I instruct them in courage and fortitude, not you.

Mostly, he says, "I destroy death in the living."

Barnaby's sympathies are with the homeless. Though he is half in love with the woman whose house has been invaded, he tells the interlopers,

> I know this house is yours, no less than hers. . . . [T]here is nowhere for you to go. I go where I please, but when there is homelessness, I am not separated from any part of life.

"Here in this front yard," he declares with a great display of bravado, "I must wage with others the war in Europe, even." Not unlike the wealthy young loafer Joe, he has the humanitarian instinct and has come to the conclusion that if he can "cure" nothing, he can at least "do no harm." "With these bottles [of patent medicine] I carry to the people that which they need most. Faith." When the salesman scoffs that he does not need medicine but only wants back the dollar he took from him, the huckster replies, "You would reject Jesus, I believe."

The rest of Act Two reads like a trivialization of the melodramatic events at the close of *The Grapes of Wrath*. In a silly competition between Cabot and his son to repose on the mother's lap, the father is clubbed by the boy with a baseball bat and is presumably killed. With no forewarning, two of the girls are carried off by a talent scout who comes by and offers the mother an advance on their future earnings! Equally at random, a farmer arrives looking for workers to employ, and he is followed on the scene by a sheriff who comes to arrest the trespassers. To everyone's bafflement, the son suddenly announces he has murdered his father. To cap it all, before the curtain falls, Barnaby returns to find the house on fire—fortuitously in time to save the little girl who has been caught inside.

The final act returns us to an equilibrium in life à la Saroyan. In an oriental setting, Georgie Americanos's family plays host to the lovers. Georgie has steered Ann to his home where she is greeted by Pericles and his son Stylianos, one very silent and philosophical (grieving over his lost home in Smyrna), the other a gruff and strong wrestler who believes "the whole world is a man's home." They assure everyone that "everything's going to be satisfactory."

Seeing Georgie again on the premises of Ann's house has reminded Barnaby that Ann has been abandoned. He tries justifying his decision to depart on the grounds that he is a "traveler" at heart, but presently comes around to the realization that he is "a fraud" in more than one sense, denouncing his claim to be a traveler "in search of oneself." Then, as if in contradiction to his self-censure, he instinctively runs to save the child in the burning house.

But before Ann and Barnaby (whose real name turns out to be Jim Greatheart) can fall into each other's arms, the Americanos family must certify that the self-castigating huckster is worthy of Ann. "I gonna teach you manners," Stylianos tells Barnaby as he spins the large man around "in a full-nelson." Soon Barnaby is conceding that he is indeed in love with Ann. Despite his idiosyncratic ways with playing cards and patent medicines, the Greeks decide he is a "philosopher" and a "Christian." Even before the Yearlings reappear to testify that Barnaby's "5-Star Multi-Purpose Indian Remedy" has saved Cabot's life, Ann returns and promptly falls into Barnaby's arms. She is not a bit concerned to learn her house has burned down, and is all too eager to adopt the child Barnaby has saved when the child shows preference for the lovers over her own family.

In the final scene in which the Greeks' hospitality matches the Armenians' in *My Heart's in the Highlands,* Barnaby lines up the Yearling children ("each child a genius") for the singing of a ballad, announcing,

> Beyond this platform and across the street is the world. What will happen to each child as it wanders into the world only God knows, but now each child is a genius.

Georgie is saluted as the postal telegram messenger who carries the only message worth carrying—Love. But Saroyan's newest self-image is reflected in Barnaby's parting words describing himself:

> I like people, but I don't like the disgrace they've fallen into. The only way I know how to do anything about it is to set up my suitcase in the streets, get behind it, and talk to them.

8

And Beyond:
Saroyan's Later Writings

ALL along, Saroyan was listening to a different drummer. And he explained it thus: "Any form achieved in art is form I have achieved already in myself. Form in art should not exist apart from a specific person. It should not be agreed upon at the outset." His originality and strength lie in his being a singularly American writer, almost equally at home in four genres: short story, novel, essay, and drama.

The effects of certain personal experiences—success, the Army, marriage, Hollywood—create elements of conflict within Saroyan that enhance conceptions dealing with drama and fiction. The contradictions involve the reasonable man versus the man of faith, traditional versus open-ended experience, and the ethnic outsider versus the individualist American. These ambivalences established through brief references to simultaneous non-dramatic works, such as *The Human Comedy, The Adventures of Wesley Jackson* (with its accompanying diary), *Rock Wagram,* and *The Laughing Matter.*

My Heart's in the Highlands, first published in 1938, was, as we have seen, an early story translated into a play. It demonstrates the inner reorientation from the dual vision, which began with the self's ability to fragment itself to the dramatic vision. This form freed Saroyan from the limitations caused by unvarying self-confrontation in the subjective narrative form of his earlier stories. The drama would allow for more subtle criticism of society, perception of a broader panorama. Aiming for a larger audience, he would be able to say what he had to say.

As in the case of *My Heart's in the Highlands, The Human Comedy* is a conversion, this time from a film scenario in 1943 to novel form suggesting the ambition to deal with interrelationships.

Although he used the title made famous by Balzac, he did not admire Balzac, and his own meaning was distinctly different. For Saroyan's universe does not mirror as does Balzac's man's inhu-

253

manity to man, but contains the possibility of the reverse. The artist must show the way. The work carries a constant message of hope in the human race. In his faltering attempt to drop the first-person singular, he injects himself into a variety of characters. As a result, one hears intermittently his own voice in Ulysses, in Homer, in the mother, in Miss Hicks. We know they are disguises for Saroyan because none of them talk in the vernacular expected of their character identification and setting. The charge of sentimentality that critics made is understandable. There are too many sermons in the novel. But there are individual scenes that convey luminously his belief in the natural goodness of the humble and the lowly. And it was appropriate to its time. As Howard R. Floan puts it in his biography of Saroyan, "It was Saroyan's contribution to the national effort at a time when the question of morale was crucial."[1]

This was Saroyan's first attempt to deal with interrelationships rather than the conflicts within a single personality. He was also attempting to delve into the inner worlds of his characters *in relation* to the outer, the while they searched for self-identity and their particular truths.

In *The Adventures of Wesley Jackson,* published in 1946, Saroyan moves from the effects of the war on the home front to the war itself as it affected the combat soldier. Always intent on finding some good even in the worst of evils, he is weighing the gains against the losses of the war. As he is highly critical of the army, it was deemed courageous of him to have published it so soon after the war. The ineffectiveness of the novel stems initially from the fact that Saroyan cannot fully identify with Wesley, and when he wants to be ironic, he fails because the reader cannot accept his premise that *all* wars are unnecessary. He begins by placing a distance between Wesley and himself. Though Wesley is San Francisco born, his father is from London, his mother from Dublin, and he has been under the influence of a Protestant clergyman who has encouraged his writing ability. But in the end Wesley assumes the Saroyan spirit; he tells his father, "if you really meant for me to be an improvement on you, then I think I've got to find out how to get free from the machine and how to become human."[2] The foolish ending of the novel is obviously a spoof, reminiscent of *Tristram Shandy,* and of an American patriotic fetish. As a realistic novel, the world of characters remains too vague; when he uses double vision—his and presumably that of the other—his characters become abstractions. But there are some good satirical moments in the accompanying thirty-four-day diary, which is a critique of the waste of army methods.

In the 1950s he veers sharply from the original sources of his inspiration: the world of the earthy, innocent, first-generation American. The war has taken its toll of disillusionment with the Establishment. The new "form" he achieves in himself becomes that of the realist, interested in viewing man as a social being. But the realist is too often overshadowed by the incurable romantic and the fabulist, and except for some bright and luminous moments, the novels find him generally out of his element. Yet such works as *Rock Wagram* (1951) and *The Laughing Matter* (1953) are interesting for what they reveal of the distance Saroyan has traveled from the young romantic, rhetorically dreaming of a better world.

Rock Wagram in my view is by far the most ambitious of the novels. It involves for the first time the dual tugs of the human being versus the writer with a mission. A critic of the time, Charles Poore, aptly characterized the novel as "a portrait of the middle-aged man on a sighing trapeze." The mood is dark, suggesting that Saroyan is at a turning point in his own life. To accommodate the narrative style, he employs the inner monologue somewhat in the manner of Eugene O'Neill. But unlike O'Neill, he does not limit himself to achieving the authentic truth of his character; he is more interested in situating through this particular character the larger truth which eludes him in life. Sterling North wrote, "The novel is Biblical in more ways than its poetry. Almost alone among modern writers, Saroyan understands the Golden Rule and the Sermon on the Mount." What I personally find troublesome most about the novel is its tediousness in the way Saroyan repeats endlessly the same note of lamentation. But the importance of the novel lies beyond its actual accomplishment as a novel. It is Saroyan's attempt, through failure if necessary, to arrive at what he perceives as "inner growth." Part of the struggle evident in this work is Saroyan's effort to glean the meaning of his split Armenian/American view of life; the ethnic dimension is explored from a different perspective.

The Laughing Matter (1953) represents a totally new approach to the novel. On the surface it looks like an O'Neill or Dreiser tragedy. Yet, while it deals with realistic material in a situation in which a failed marriage leads to the literal destruction of human life, it is antirealistic in treatment, with a cast of characters designated as "the man, the girl, the boy, the woman," as though they were merely archetypical figures.

Even though he explores here the second generation dilemma

of living in two worlds, the Old World ethnic flavor is gone and instead a note of rancor creeps in. While he can still draw forth small epiphanies, the longer form of the novel gives away his essential lack of introspection; the modernist's fluoroscopic eye eludes him as he probes a more cosmic vision.

After this, Saroyan abruptly stopped writing novels. There was no reason given by him why he did this, but one might compare the pattern with a similar career decision on the part of his contemporaries, Carson McCullers, who also wrote non-realistic novels in the 1940s and who also reached the end of her novelistic career in the 1950s. Was the era responsible? The kind of stark realism that followed World War II was not compatible with Saroyan's vision; instead he went back to the theater with efforts to project poetic perception in the framework of realistic surroundings in the manner that was to be made famous by Beckett and Genet.

Retreating from the novel form, and rejecting at the same time the notion of another try on Broadway, he used the allegorical-poetic strand he had tried out with *The Beautiful People.* That play had a Broadway production only because Saroyan himself subsidized it. 1941 had been too early to interest the theater-going public in antinaturalistic theater. In the mid-1950s this theater—which was in fact a foil for philosophical meditation—would come into its own in what was to be called "the theater of the absurd." Concurrently with *The Beautiful People,* Saroyan had written two other works that were more openly allegorical, *Sweeney in the Trees* and *Across the Board on Tomorrow Morning* (which appeared in book form along with *The Beautiful People*). These works became the springboard for still further experimentation. The three subsequent plays mark the peak of Saroyan's achievement in the theater of poetic experience. Each of them along with artistic innovations in structuring antirealistic theater show the development of his philosophical concerns.

Jim Dandy or Fat Man in a Famine, written in 1947, is a play that takes place in a transparent eggshell. It picks up Saroyan's fascination with the American Dream from where he has left off in *The Time of Your Life.* He moves beyond America to the universal level. The search for Eden, for new horizons, is part of man's native heritage if only man could realize its nature. This is Saroyan's most complicated play in terms of production, but it has the movement and variety he calls "play" in abundance. It needs an imaginative director to turn it into a many dimensional spectacle. Here Saroyan has grown solemn, though the humor is still evident, sometimes in a grim way. He succeeds best in his comic stance because in a swiftly changing modern world errors are made in innocence.

The humor the play generates brings people closer together as they laugh at themselves. A major theme of the play is the conversion of Fishkin, the cynic, who is given to saying, "Drop dead." His last words are "I came here any man, to act my part, to create my role, to be whomsoever I should choose to be."[3] There is a scene of the sharing of bread that has mystical overtones and a suggestion of what the ultimate liberation of man means when Jim Dandy hands over his throne to a black man, calling out "To His Majesty, Man!" Despite a surface aura of irrationality and the repeated suggestions of truths invisible to the eye, Saroyan is not a *metaphysical* writer; it is not ontological problems that concern him in the last instance; his confusions are in the nature of man and not organized into a philosophical system. He is concerned to point out that what *appears* unreal is the result of the human condition pictured to be in absurd disarray only if limits are set on the incomprehensible workings of the soul.

Don't Go Away Mad, which appeared in 1949, is a play about a group of terminally ill men in a hospital waiting to die. It predates Beckett's *Waiting for Godot* by four years and has never been acknowledged as a precursor of that famous "waiting" play. For once Saroyan is humble in the realization that he has not achieved what he had hoped, lacking in the skill rather than in the truth of what he wanted to say. "Sickness ain't going to make a monkey out of me," one of the character says. The entire play is an affirmation of man's dogged will to "abide, hang around." But in Saroyan, and not as in Beckett, the waiting for the ultimate fate to arrive is done in dignity, with humor and shared concern, in the constant affirmation that man's spirit will prevail.

Nine years elapsed before the next play, *The Cave Dwellers,* in 1958. The setting of this play is an abandoned theater in ruins and the site establishes immediately the allegorical dimension— for according to Saroyan the theater is "the last arena in which all is always possible." The characters are given a fairy-tale dimension by being called King, Queen, Duke—nicknames they use because of the roles they have previously played in the the theater. The secret of "theater" is that it is a place where one *performs* rather than where one is *performed upon,* which is the situation of those who just live blindly in the world. There is also an implied political allegory in the conflict between group security and individual freedom. The individual who is really free has to be ever ready to take risks, and counts on love and kindness to help endure such freedom and to resist the limits placed on us by fear. As Saroyan writes in the introduction, "In the caves of the government and the church . . . all has long since stopped being possible, in favor of a pattern of formal repetition, which some of us find only amusing and monotonous, by turns." And the last lines of the King as he and his troupe are forced out of their shelter, with nowhere to go is, "Farewell, then—womb, cave, hiding place, home, church, world, theatre—a fond and loving farewell. Farewell and welcome!" The play is a hymn to the unconditioned self, to the possibilities open to the soul in its endless search. In its satirical attack on automatic human routine it has a kinship with Ionesco, but the obstinate option for an existing *soul* is the other side of the coin lacking in his clever Romanian nihilist contemporary.

Although most of Saroyan's publications in the last two decades of his life were to be autobiographical, he never ceased writing plays as well. I saw and read many of them in manuscript. They were never made available for production because, as he put it in 1969, "the situation in that area is so bad . . . that for almost thirty years I haven't even offered my plays to the bankers, businessmen, public relations specialists, real estate experts and tax avoidance geniuses who run Broadway."[4]

The poetic, fabulistic, and often surreal elements of his style turn many of his shorter plays into morality plays. Unraveled spontaneously from the imagination and from emotion, they lead us into realms of being rather than to real-life situations. The worldly writer of the novels, concerned with contemporary life, returns here to the inner world of the artist. Such plays as *Sweeney in the Trees, Hello, Out There,* and *The Cave Dwellers* embody what Northrop Frye calls "a third order of experience . . . that poetry urges us to have," where life as it is and life as transformed by the imagination meet. In his last years, Saroyan recognized the limitations imposed by the modern world on the writer who would achieve this "third order of experience."[5]

Although the reader of Saroyan's short stories has ample opportunity to glean from them the personality and life patterns of Saroyan with the rather obvious transitions from fact to fiction, later in his life Saroyan felt the need to write more explicitly about himself, in diary, letter, and autobiography. The Proustian mode of recapturing time passed is replaced by the dream of the passage of the centuries whirling in him and destroying the notion of time so that he is released from his momentary imprisonment as a cipher in a time called the Depression.

The inevitable forum for him now becomes autobiography, which will mirror what he has absorbed in the progress of his art. Impervious to the prevailing idiom of black humor or nihilistic despair, he wrote autobiographical works that almost expressively reaffirm his belief in the human race, having moved along from the old romantic way to the hard-won wisdom that flows from life experiences.

In his first venture as an autobiographer, *The Bicycle Rider in Beverly Hills* (1952), he may have seemed like Proust to be engaged in the recapturing of past time, but the effort is vastly different in intent; he wants the memories to "help make known how I became who I am." The implication is that there is an element that is constant in him, even though he admits that there is a variance between who he may be and who he wants to be. Proust's idea that we outgrow the various selves in us as we move on would destroy the very concept of autobiography for Saroyan, who believes in an essential selfhood, one that we get to understand better and better as time moves on. For Saroyan the past does not need to be "recaptured" through solidification in art. For Saroyan the past is constantly alive in the present as he recycles his memories in his writings. What his autobiographical writings have as their aim is to propel the continuous journey of living and growing, recording events as he goes along but keeping them in current file.

The Bicycle Rider in Beverly Hills, written at about the same time as *Rock Wagram*, is a straightforward diary that has many of the elements of that novel. He is recording thoughts, remembrances, revelations, situating them in the context of their moment of origin: "A man is his memories, but he is also the things he forgot. I want to think about the things I have forgotten. I want to have a go at them because I have an idea they will help make known how I became who I am." A little later on he writes, "Who a man is must always be a theory and it must always be a tentative one. A soul is an illusive thing. It ought never to be anything else. . . . The subject of this book is not so much myself, now and sometime ago, as it is the action of the human soul, to which there is no start or stop."

The turning points in his life are contained in five chapters entitled "The Phonograph," "The Typewriter," "The Fire," "The Family," and "The Streets." They deal with the influence on his life of his dead father, his resistance to education at Emerson High School, the development of humor out of necessity, his ambivalent feelings toward the Armenians in his milieu, his resistance to systematized religion, and his own concept of love and of God. Also discussed are the legitimate needs of the physical body and Saroyan's love of simple pleasures—what he called the Armenian in him—as against the discipline of work, and his discovery that "to write is not the same as to tell stories," that "to be a writer is to be in the streets. The people in the streets are the book." Bicycle riding is a metaphor for rhythm, pace, speed, and effectiveness. He realized that "the world was my home and I was glad to be in it," and at the same time he had a growing awareness that one had to get rid of "the debris, the dirt of the world" that was everywhere: "I felt it was important for the world to be a decent place. I felt that nobody could grow in spirit unless he knew what he was doing, and I didn't think anybody could concentrate on what he was doing, or find out what he *wanted* to do, until he had cleaned up around him. The dirt would annoy and distract him." That is why Saroyan decided to become a writer. "The job was never to be finished." The ending of the book is especially effective in explaining his response to life as he emerged from the orphanage, and his thoughts on the freedom, kindness he pursued as he emerged as an artist striving for "the integration of man, and the achievement of form and meaning *in his action*" (italics mine).

Here Comes, There Goes You Know Who was written in 1961, a few years after *The Cave Dwellers,* his last major dramatic production. At this time the autobiography takes a less direct approach. The book is like a confessional (St. Augustinian in its repeated suggestion that he is being matched): "I am famous, it is true, but not the way you might imagine I mean. I am famous the way you are: as myself to myself, and to the witness, another word for God, most likely, and the one I prefer."

At this point in his life he is in self-exile, in his Paris apartment, estranged from himself, his family, his fellowmen, his country, his world, his time, his culture, and God. For the first time he admits failure as a man, but he is hanging in. "I have made a fiasco of my life, but I have had the right material to work with. The metaphysical stance: (What do we think we are, and what do we think we're doing?)" The knowledge that his art has separated him from his life occurs to him: "There is something between death and myself that is very close, closer than anything else, but I hate the idea of losing the sun"; but this fear does not stop him from returning to his beginnings: stories of the orphanage, the grapes, the school, the first date, the job, and the gambler. He sees himself as "the free prisoner," a prisoner because to be born is to be captured, free because he has chosen to be an artist. The audience he is writing for now always is "the concealed race behind the 'obsolete race' of today," and "If we are sick, something isn't . . . Nothing matters and nothing needs to matter, but if we are to make it, it is to be made, and *we* are to do it." "I ain't going. I've got taxes to pay, and pieces to pick up" (i.e., from his own life).

In one of the best of these autobiographical fragments (which he continued to publish at the rate of almost one book a year) *Not Dying* (1963), Saroyan at age sixty-five had come to the full limit of himself, translated his art into his life. It contains "the essential Saroyan" slogan: "It isn't the book that matters, it's the writer." From this point on the autobiographical fragments become almost crotchety affirmations that he is still at the helm, still very much alive, perpetuating the movement, the continuity that has been created and that each of us plays a part in revolving toward some unknown goal. Saroyan has become aware of the fusing of the artist and the man, a metamorphosis that he allows us to behold. Having temporarily abandoned "the performance," he welcomes the return of the natural man in him. The writer can wait, he wants to live his life before he goes on. He reiterates his sense of failure (before God), saying that he has failed to see All, as he had hoped—but then he wonders if God sees all too: an example of the art of the essay in Chapter 17 of *Not Dying* demonstrates his metaphoric discourse: thistles along the railroad track that he once tried to fully observe. "Everything that I have ever written has been a prayer."

Rarely does any autobiography of any period reveal the man consistently in terms that are pertinent to his work; in our time, with the growing separation of the writer from his art, this has become virtually impossible. We see how, in Saroyan's case, writing and living have become synonymous; by way of the trivial, the ephemeral, the fatuous, and the true, all jumbled together (as they are in real life), he presumes to lead the reader into his inner world, the only world that matters to the artist. Though at that point interest in the future is somewhat diminished, he still retains the poet's gift for transforming the past into the present moment. Repeatedly clutching at the *mortal* moment, he abandons the dream (which is the world of his imagination) for a reality that has absorbed the dream. In Saroyan's "autobiographies," the fact and the fiction merge as he becomes his own truest convert.

There is a double vision in his autobiographical approach. He uses the first person to convey the simple joys of his life, but the third person when he wants to leave himself out and generalize. He also expresses his dissatisfaction with autobiographies by other writers. "I think that if a man has ability or even only the compulsion to broaden the area of himself which he hopes eventually to make whole, he had better broaden it." Most importantly, he gives his real reason for the continuous autobiography. He began this book "so that the writing of it would take the place of dying, of my own literal death, which I had been fearing for some time near. And I kept writing as if the writer had long since disappeared from among the living." He uses the metaphor of the bullfight to explain how even a bull dies when "spiritual health" fails it. "I knew the arrogant loneliness of the writer at work. . . . [I]f I was mad, I was also free to heal the madness." The book is dedicated to "the psychologist in the sky."

Another form of biographical material consists of Saroyan's views about his own writing and those of others. These consist of *After Thirty Years,* a preface to a new edition of the *Daring Young Man on the Flying Trapeze* (1962), *I Used to Believe I Had Forever* (1968), and *Days of Life and Death and Escape to the Moon* (1970). The substance of his outlook comes in the observation that life and art are not separate, that "the very thing I was after as a writer was to be in my writing precisely who I was in my life."[6] Throughout these texts are scattered his thoughts on the short story, on the American position on the literary scene, on the source of his optimism and style, on the creative vision, on critics, on the use of the fable in writing, and on the meaning of freedom.

In his last five books, Saroyan virtually weaned himself away from the autobiographical form, concentrating more and more on anecdotes about his meetings with a variety of persons in his life-long adventure. These were often chance meetings, and they possess the quality of his early stories; he sought his inspiration where he could find it at the moment. The meetings are also meditations on human relationships and their meaning to the writer. He concludes that universality can be achieved only by looking inward and outward at the same time, trying to understand man's relation to the universe. He plays a double game of keeping in touch with the outside world as well as monitoring the inner fluctuation of his essential commitment to the nurturing of the individual.

In *Letters from 74 Rue Taitbout* (1969), *Places Where I Have Done Time* (1972), and *Sons Come and Go, Mothers Hang In Forever* (1976), Saroyan offers a plethora of letters he has written to his father, to Freud, Jung, and Adler, to the mega-rich Armenian Gulbenkian, to the Armenian poet Charentz, to anybody. He evokes places with which he identifies such as Fresno, Paris, London—all in random fashion. In the third volume, he refers to people who have been important to his career. Here the tone is often acerbic, as he sees himself in terms of the world to which he only relates partially. He concludes that he is happy to have been "a fool," a word he equates with "artist."

In *Chance Meetings* (1978) he ponders the value of chance encounters. Because they have no starting and stopping points, they take according to him the quality of art in their spontaneity. "Geniuses are those who cannot be, or do not *want* to be, delivered from the feeling of being ridiculously involved in one colossal mistake." They try to improve on life. "Well, of course, this *trying* is all we really have, the rest is even less than this, the rest is really nothing when the tallying is done, the rest is ash, dust."[7]

Finally, *Obituaries* is in 1979 his last word on his contemporaries; it is also a last word on his belief in man's capacity to be more than he appears to be. He exhorts the reader not to die, "there's plenty of time." He affirms that it has all been worthwhile. He reviews the ambitions of his life. His first goal had been to rise above the particular circumstances of his birth and environment, and to have an impact on his family and friends; his second aim to find the right wife to bear his children, and as ultimate goal to explore the limits of his capacity as a writer. As he says,

to become stronger in all dimensions of humanity than I was by birth and early circumstances and environment, to make myself known to the world, to exert an influence first on myself, then on the members of my family, or more properly the family of my father and mother, and then on my friends and acquaintances, and then on the rest of the human race, and of course an influence that was deeply desired by everybody, nothing to be imposed upon anybody. After that my purpose was to attract the woman who was to be the mother of my children, to relive my own earliest moments, days, seasons, and years, in and through them and after that to continue loving in mind and spirit to the limits that might be permitted to me . . . in writing. . . . It's worth it, it's a fierce fight and you lose every day and you need time to try again in the morning, but yes, it is worth it, and this is why.

The struggle itself is a source of joy. "There is no movement after something has died, and it is action alone that permits anything—and out of anything it is always possible to make something, or even something else, and in anything it is possible to find whatever is needed for the continuing of everything, for the dance of life, for the deep waltz of the soul in all things."[8]

The more I read and reread William Saroyan's works, the more I become convinced that at its core it contains an artistic and philosophical meaning far more complex and viable than is generally conceded. Saroyan's unabashed attempt to uncover goodness and "a world that can be inhabited" has been labeled "innocent" and "naive." Yet a writer as sophisticated as Vladimir Nabokov has described the creative mind in terms that could be applied to Saroyan and his characteristic response to life: "This capacity to wonder at trifles . . . these asides of the spirit, these footnotes to the volume of life, are the highest form of consciousness, and it is in this childishly speculative state of the mind, so different from common sense and its logic, that we know the world to be good.[9]

The checkered pattern of Saroyan's life is reflected in the dark and light of his writings. So high was the ever renewed surge of optimism that he did not even believe in the terminal character of the cancer that put an end to his vibrant life. The belief of the young that they are exempt from death survived in Saroyan into old age: "I thought they would make an exception for me," he muttered on his deathbed.

Notes

CHAPTER 1. THE TIME, THE PLACE, THE MAN

1. James Agee and Walter Evans, *Let Us Now Praise Famous Men,* 1941, 14.

2. Sir James Jeans, the English astronomer and physicist (in such works as *The Universe Around Us* and *The Mysterious Universe*), an American physicist, Robert Andrews Millikan (in such works as *Science and the New Civilization and Time, Matter and Value*) were instrumental in bringing to the general consciousness in the 1930s the so-called "new physics," with its emphasis on the quantum theory and the theory of relativity.

3. John Dewey's enormous influence on the progressive education movement spread to other areas of American life, among them philosophy, psychology, and the arts. Such works as *The Quest for Certainty, Art as Experience,* and *A Common Faith* were widely reviewed and discussed.

Having worked with working-class immigrants in Chicago, Harry Stack Sullivan, the American psychiatrist, sought to ally psychiatry with social science. Though widely quoted in the thirties, his major work, *Interpersonal Theory of Psychiatry* was not published until 1953.

4. Jay Martin, *Nathanael West: The Art of His Life* (New York: Farrar, Straus & Giroux, 1970), 188–189. Writing of West's 1933 novel, *Miss Lonelyhearts,* Martin notes that West "has hit upon a subject essential to the imagination of the thirties. Loneliness and personal alienation, he showed, were as pervasive in that era as economic disaster." Based on that novel, Irving Berlin and Moss Hart wrote a revue that same year called *As Thousands Cheer,* Martin continues, "West's *Miss Lonelyhearts* was part of the daily news, integral to the imagination of the time. Hart and Berlin wrote the news report on the suffering of the lonely crowd. West penetrated to its archetype."

5. Quoted in Daniel Aaron, *Writers on the Left* (New York: Oxford University Press, 1977), 109.

6. By the end of the decade, a hard-headed consciousness would change all this. The movies would grow up and become part of a strong undercurrent of national self-awareness that had been building in various other cultural areas.

7. Alexis de Toqueville, *Democracy in America* (New York: Washington Square Press, 1968), xiii.

8. Malcolm Cowley, *Exile's Return: A Literary Odyssey of the 1920s* (New York: Viking, 1951), 286–287.

9. Malcolm Cowley, *Think Back on Us: A Contemporary Chronicle of the 1930s* (Carbondale: Southern Illinois University Press, 1967), 387.

10. Irving Babbitt, *On Being Creative* (Boston: Houghton Mifflin, 1932). Babbitt deplored the absence among intellectuals of "a general critical intelligence" and argued that what was needed to counter the tide of spreading propaganda was "the inner control" of the genuine puritan. "Without that inner control," he

insisted, "one remains a mere modernist and not a thoroughgoing and complete modern, for the modern spirit and the critical spirit are in their essence one."

11. Quoted in Aaron, *Writers on the Left*, 234.

12. Granville Hicks, *The Great Tradition* (Chicago: Quadrangle Books, 1969), 272.

13. T. S. Eliot, "The Humanism of Irving Babbitt," in Eliot, *Selected Essays of T. S. Eliot* (New York: Harcourt, Brace & Co., 1950), 422.

14. Joseph Wood Krutch, *The Modern Temper: A Study and a Confession* (New York: Harcourt, Brace & Co., 1929), 46.

15. Michael Gold, the novelist, who became editor of *The New Masses* in 1928, is thus quoted in Aaron, *Writers on the Left*, 241.

16. Edmund Wilson, *Letters on Literature and Politics, 1912–1972*, ed. Elena Wilson (New York: Farrar, Straus & Giroux, 1972), 204.

17. Ibid., 207.

18. Ibid., 211.

19. Ibid., 211.

20. Ibid., p. 222. The manifesto Wilson helped to draft emphasized that the present "crisis of the world" was more than "a mere crisis of politics or economics"—it was, rather, "a crisis of human culture" that called for "new social forms, new values, a new human order." It proposed "a temporary dictatorship of the class-conscious workers, as the necessary instrument for abolishing all classes based on material possession which shall release the energies of man to spiritual and intellectual endeavor."

21. The headlines about "the starving Armenians," refer, of course, to an earlier time—the period between 1915 and 1925 when following two separate attempts by the Turkish government to destroy the Armenians living on their ancestral lands (in 1915 nearly 2 million Armenians were massacred), the Armenians were rendered homeless and destitute. It was the impassioned report of the American ambassador, Henry Morgenthau, to the U.S. State Department about "the destruction of the Armenian race in Turkey" that awakened Americans to the desperate plight of these uprooted people. In 1916, with the staunch cooperation of the press (in particular the editorials of John F. Finley of *The New York Times*), a campaign was launched to raised $100,000 for the general relief of 200,000 Armenian survivors. The full story is told in Henry Morgenthau's magnificent book *Ambassador Morgenthau's Story* (New York: Doubleday, Page & Co., 1918*).

22. William Saroyan, "Homage to Emerson," in *Learning* (March 1978). In explaining his relationship to Emerson, Saroyan writes,

> It was at Emerson School [the Fresno grammar school and high school Saroyan attended until age twelve] that I became, in a very real sense but in total ignorance, Emerson himself, Ralph Waldo, or enough like him to be able to say almost sixty years later that I became a preaching writer, and an American one, certainly more American than Armenian, although also deeply Armenian.

23. Walt Whitman, "A Backward Glance," in *Walt Whitman: Poetry and Prose*, ed. Justin Kaplan (New York: Library of America, 1983), 657.

24. Despite Saroyan's continuous publication of autobiographical works in the last two decades of his life, he never ceased writing plays as well. I saw and read many of them in manuscript. They were never made available to production, because, as he put in in 1969, "the situation in that area is so bad . . . that for almost 30 years I haven't even offered my plays to the bankers, business-men,

public-relations specialists, real-estate experts and tax-avoidance geniuses who run Broadway." *Kenyon Review* 1 (1969): 60.

Saroyan also wrote a long novel in 1974 which he was unable to get published. According to one publisher's reader, it had "genius" material but lacked "the linguistic dimension of Joyce." (Quoted with permission of Harold Matson, from the file at Columbia University, Rare Books & Mss.)

It is also a fact that one of Saroyan's earliest stories, "Yea and Amen," was printed despite the misgivings of the *Hairenik* editor who found it anachronistic and inappropriate for their readers. As Mr. Tashjian reported to me in a private conversation, young Saroyan (or "Goryan") had gone over the heads of the paper's readers, because, while he was telling a simple enough tale about two innocent children's discovery of the miracle of birth as they watched a chick being hatched, the story's impressionistic prose was deemed highly unconventional.

25. An extract from *transition* (1937), 126. The work itself was presented as "The Slot-Machine" (Extracts).

26. In a letter by William Saroyan, 15 August 1935. (Quoted with permission of Kenneth A. Lohf, Librarian, Rare Books & Mss. Columbia University.)

27. *transition* (1929).

28. William Saroyan, "Some Thoughts About Gertrude Stein," *The Reporter*, 13 October 1953.

29. *The Flowers of Friendship*, ed. Donald Gallup (New York: Alfred A. Knopf, 1953), 291.

30. Edmund Wilson, *Axel's Castle: A Study in the Imaginative Literature of 1870–1930* (New York: Scribner's Sons, 1947), 239.

31. William Saroyan, letter to Harrison Smith (editor of *The Saturday Review of Literature*), 21 April 1934: "Harry Block returned my October novel of 1933, "Trapeze Over the Universe," (alternate title "Smiling Universe")." Its ending would be about "the weary swinging on the trapeze across geometric spaces, weary of wakefulness and sleep." *The Daring Young Man on the Flying Trapeze and Other Stories* was published that same year.

CHAPTER 2. THE THEORY AND PRACTICE OF BEING WILLIAM SAROYAN: EARLY STORIES

1. Howard Floan, *William Saroyan* (New York: Twayne, 1966), 20.
2. Lionel Trilling, *The Liberal Imagination* (New York: Viking, 1950), 12.
3. William Saroyan, "Self-Interview," KPFA Radio, Berkeley, California, 17 February 1976.
4. What is suggested in Saroyan's own story radically contradicts Aram Saroyan's pseudo-psychological evaluation, made in his two books about his father, *Last Rites, The Death of William Saroyan* (New York: William Morrow, 1982); and *William Saroyan* (Harcourt, Brace Jovanovich, 1983). Aram Saroyan claims that his father's early orphanhood left a scarring trauma on the writer that never healed. Far from inducing a severe emotional impact that developed into a lifelong "interior freeze," (Aram Saroyan's phrase), the early loss of his father appears to have awakened in William Saroyan an intuitive sense of oneness with others, of continuity beyond death. Capitalizing on his "unknown" roots, the impressionable youth could enlarge on what his imagination seized as the "truth." None of the symptoms that one associates with alienation, moreover—withdrawal, indifference, repression, exclusion—were ever observed in Saroyan's essential make-up;

certainly there were no such symptoms threatening to pervert his original vision. The dark thoughts and verbal self-abuse that crept into his prose in later years can be found only in the autobiographical writings, brought on quite normally by extreme pressures of personal circumstances; scarcely ever did the animus over-flow into his fiction, where he had his real being.

5. Ernest Hemingway's denigrating article about Saroyan appeared in *Esquire,* January 1935.

6. Agathangelos was the private secretary of King Tiridates of Armenia, the same king who, according to this chronicle, was converted to Christianity when, after suffering a cruel transmutation into a wild boar, St. Gregory (the first Arem-naian convert) restored him to his human form. In his foreword to his translation of *Agathangelos: The History of the Armenians* (Albany: State University of New York, 1976), vii. R. W. Thomson writes, "The work is enigmatic not only because it is a curious mixture of remembered tradition and invented legend; it also exists in several languages and different recensions, not all of which derive from the text extant 'in Armenian.'"

7. Jacques de Morgan, in *The History of the Armenian People, From the Remotest Times to the Present,* trans. Ernest F. Barry (Boston: Hairenik Press, 1918), 62, writes that Moses of Khoren confesses that he himself made out the earliest dynasties of the Armenians "from what he had discovered as certain in the ancient Histories, and to the best of his ability." De Morgan goes on to say that "these last works set the seal of improbability on all his narrative of events with which that writer was not contemporary."

8. In an essay titled "Armenia: Its Epics, Folksongs, and Mediaeval Poetry," published in *Armenian Legends and Poems,* compiled and illustrated by Zabelle C. Boyajian (New York: E. P. Dutton, 1916), Aram Raffi writes, "What is most remarkable is that at the beginning of the intellectual movement when the alphabet had just been formed [actually invented by St. Mesrop], the literary language was so highly developed, so rich and subtle, that it is more like the language which is the product of centuries of culture. This very fact shows that culture was no novelty in Armenia. The new movement only introduced a fresh era in Armenian civilization" (p. 154).

9. To Reuben Darbinian, 9 November 1934, (*Saroyan Memorial Issue: 104 Unpublished Letters of William Saroyan),* in *The Armenian Review* 34 (1981), No. 3-1-35, 250. A subsequent letter from Saroyan to Darbinian, dated 24 April 1936, bears quoting:

Now you are a Great Editor and they say I am a great writer. Where do we get our talents? As for you, you write in the Great Tongue, and I write in English, but we are both Armenians, thank God, and we must spring from a great literary heritage. Without such a teaching, our pens would be dull. I often feel that some Great Force is guiding my hand. I can't say it is Johnson or Shakespeare, or even Galsworthy, although I admire them. I am inclined to feel that it is Moses [of Khoren] and Raffi, Goryun [Armenian writers] and you, who sit at my desk. I feel them with me. I can't read Armenian, to my disgrace; but they are Great Writers, greater than I ever will be" (p. 229).

10. This account is taken from James Tashjian, introduction to Tashjian, ed., *My Name is Saroyan* (New York: Coward-McCann, 1983), 17–18. It is based on a private conversation with Tashjian on 29 June 1975. Saroyan told Tashjian how his uncle Aram had urged the *Hairenik* editor to advise Bill against trying to become a writer and to go to work, get married, have children, buy land, study, become a lawyer, etc." "Bardizian," Saroyan recalled, "was a short and rather

wiry man, with deepset eyes, and I warmed to him when he started talking quietly to me. . . . He asked about my writing and I told him I was always writing, but no one seemed to want to read what I wrote. He said, 'Keep writing. A man is his own best critic.'"

11. Charles Caldwell Dobie, to whom Saroyan wrote from San Francisco on 11 July 1929, was a writer for *The Bulletin.* Saroyan wrote with youthful, un-abashed ardor of his efforts "to connect with a newspaper and by thus surrounding [myself] with typewriters, paper, and a more or less guaranteed salary . . . To write short stories and what not." He goes on to tell of his attempts to find a job on one of the San Francisco newspapers.

> It is needless to say that I failed, which at first seemed strange. In the meantime I labored in other fields, but quite listlessly since my heart was not in the work, and every now and then I quit my job and made a fresh effort to get into the newspaper game. . . . I contributed something to the *San Franciscan* once in 1928 for which I was never paid, and I have made three contributions to the *Overland Monthly.* I am also a regular short story writer for a sheet known as *The Boulevardier,* published in Detroit, for which I receive $10.00 for any amount of words I happen to put into a short story, which is often from four to five thousand. Thus far my literary efforts have netted me exactly $3.00. I might add I am the sort of writer who also sends scripts to *The American Mercury, Scribners, The New Yorker.* These, of course are returned with slips attached, and I once got a story back from the *Bookman* via air mail, which is probably the most amusing thing that ever occurred to me in my career." Saroyan ends the letter thus: "These are the facts of the matter, and so I am humbly, Yours, William Saroyan."

There is no record of an answer. (The above is quoted through the courtesy of The Bancroft Library at the University of California, Berkeley.)

12. Tashjian, ed. *My Name is Saroyan,* 357. The poem, signed "William Saro-yan," appeared in *Hairenik Daily,* 14 January 1933. It was never republished, but Saroyan wrote of his remembrance of the Armenian singer in his autobiographical work, *Here Comes, There Goes You Know Who.*

13. Ibid, 358. "A First Fight for Armenia" was the first of Saroyan's stories to be published under the byline of "Sir Goryan" in *Hairenik Daily,* 9 and 10 May 1933. According to Mr. Tashjian, Sirak was the name of several of Saroyan's cousins, and "Goryan" or "Goriun" was a fifteenth-century Armenian writer. The story has not been republished, and Mr. Tashjian interprets the story as Saroyan's version of David and Goliath, "but here," he adds, "the Armenian loses the battle but wins the war."

14. Robert Mirak, *Torn Between Two Worlds: Armenians in America, 1980 to World War I* (Harvard University Press, 1984). In a chapter on the Fresno commu-nity Mr. Mirak writes that in the early part of the century, Armenians in Fresno were prohibited from owning land in "better neighborhoods"; they were excluded from social groups and called "undesirables," along with Negroes, Chinese, Japa-nese, Hindu and Turkish ethnics. They were designated as "not of the white or Caucasian race," though Armenians are, in fact, Caucasian. Mirak attributes some of this prejudice toward Armenians to jealousy, since Armenians became unusu-ally and quickly successful in the community, and moreover did not seem to have the "servile attitude" of most immigrants.

15. Tashjian, ed. *My Name is Saroyan,* 358. "The Broken Wheel," was pub-lished in *Hairenik Daily,* 2, 4, and 6 June 1933 and republished in Saroyan's second book, *Inhale and Exhale.* Krikor, in the story, is identified as Saroyan's brother, Henry.

16. Ibid, 358. "The Barbar's Apprentice" was first published in *Hairenik Daily,*

5 and 6 October 1933 and republished in *Hairenik Weekly,* 1 March 1935. It received Honorable Mention in Edward H. O'Brien's *Best Short Stories of 1934.*

17. Ibid, 359. "The Moment of Life" was first published in *Hairenik Daily,* 26 and 28 November 1933. Never republished.

18. Ibid, 359. "Noneh" was published in the same issues of *Hairenik Daily,* above. The character of Lucy was actually Saroyan's maternal grandmother, née Garoghlanian, the name he would use for the "Aram" stories. This story was also not republished.

19. Ibid, 360. "Yea and Amen" was published originally in *Hairenik Weekly,* 22 and 29 March 1934. It was republished in *Inhale and Exhale.*

20. William Saroyan, "His Collaborators," an essay printed in Paul P. Appel, ed., *Homage to Sherwood Anderson, 1876–1941* (Memaroneck, N.Y.: Paul P. Appel, 1970), 119–120.

21. Ibid.

22. Trilling, *The Liberal Imagination,* 26.

23. The tone Saroyan seemed obviously to be imitating was that of Ring Lardner in his famous story, "Haircut," which begins: "I got another barber that comes over from Carterville and helps me out Saturdays, but the rest of the time I can get along alone." In Lardner that tone persists, and the story ends, "Comb it wet or dry?"

CHAPTER 3. THE STORY AS DISCURSIVE DIALOGUE: THE EMERGENCE OF "A NEW KIND OF ARTIST"

1. Though well written with insights stemming from intimate knowledge, Aram Saroyan's biography of his father, *William Saroyan* (Harcourt, Brace Jovanovich, 1983) is sketchy and opinionated and marred throughout by filial embitterment. Written a year later, *Saroyan: A Biography* by Lawrence Lee and Barry Gifford (Harper & Row), succumbs too easily to the legend of the man at the expense of the many-sided and complex person behind it, depending too much on hearsay and the opinions of those who knew Saroyan only superficially. Worthy of perusal is a special issue of *Ararat* Quarterly (1985) devoted to Saroyan in which there are a number of recollections and sketches of interest.

2. *Overland Monthly and Outwest Magazine,* August 1928, 283–84.

3. Archie Minasian, who died in 1985, was one of Saroyan's favorite cousins. A would-be poet who settled into the vocation of house painter (in Palo Alto), he never gave up his writing ambitions and was encouraged and promoted by Saroyan to the end of his life. In a subsequent letter, dated 5 April 1930, Saroyan had already begun urging Archie to write and even offering to type his poems for him. His encouragement often took the form of urging Archie to read, especially "books of good poetry for ideas," and among the poets he singled out were Robert Frost, Vachel Lindsey, Edna St. Vincent Millay, and Carl Sandburg. Among prose writers, he recommended Ambrose Bierce, de Maupassant and O. Henry ("he is more interesting than sincere and honest"). He emphasized that whatever he wrote should "originate in yourself . . . Not something you have not personally experienced . . . You must stick to yourself, your own town, the people about you, the things you see, feel and dream about. Then your stuff will be honest and sincere."

4. Of special interest in this regard is Martha Foley's memoir, *The Story of*

Story Magazine, with an introduction and afterword by Jay Neugenboren (W. W. Norton, 1980).

5. From a letter to Whit Burnett, quoted in *The Literary Life and the Hell with It,* by Whit Burnett (Harper & Brothers, 1939), 197–202.

6. In the above mentioned memoir by Martha Foley, Foley writes, "One reason Random House was interested [in *Story* magazine] which I didn't realize at the time . . . was because they saw us as a good scouting arrangement to bring authors to them. They got Saroyan that way. Until that point, they'd been a reprint house. Now they were planning to bring out trade books" (202 n.).

7. Fred Lewis Pattee, in his book, *The Development of the American Short Story: An Historical Survey* (Harper & Brothers, 1923), reports the novelist Frank Norris as saying in an article, "Salt and Sincerity" (1902), that American literature must be democratized literature: "A literature that cannot be vulgarized is no literature at all and will perish. . . . If the modern novelist does not understand the Plain People, if he does not address himself directly to them, intelligibly and simply, he will fail. But he can never understand them by shutting himself away from them" (337–38).

8. From an article, "To Be a Writer, or Art and Imbecility," by William Saroyan, published in *My First Publication,* ed. James Hart (Book Club of California, 1961).

9. Reprinted in *Writers in America: The Four Seasons of Success,* by Budd Schulberg (Stein & Day, 1983).

10. In Frank Kermode's introduction to *The Short Story,* ed. (Thomas Nelson, 1941).

11. Louis Kronenberger, review of *The Daring Young Man on the Flying Trapeze, The Nation,* 7 November 1934.

12. Hirshel Brickell, review of *Inhale and Exhale, The New York Post,* 26 February 1936.

13. Otis Ferguson, review of *The Daring Young Man on the Flying Trapeze, The New Republic,* 7 November 1934.

14. Harold Strauss, review of Saroyan's *Little Children, The New York Times Book Review,* 15 August 1937.

15. Ernest Hemingway, "Notes on Life and Letters," op. cit. The article had some other strident words for Saroyan. "We have something else to write about," wrote Hemingway, "beside ourselves . . . you've only got one trick and that is that you're an Armenian. . . Most of us have written very little of what we know because it is very hard to write and we have learned how to handle what we are going to write. So we write the part of what we know we can handle with our equipment as we go along" (21 and 159).

16. H. E. Bates, the English writer and critic, in *The Modern Short Story: A Critical Survey* (Thomas Nelson, 1941). Written mainly on the basis of *The Daring Young Man on the Flying Trapeze,* Bates thus characterizes Saroyan's style: "A young American-Armenian, living in San Francisco . . . proceeds to unfold a range of very dazzling carpets of tricky design. . . . Every story was a carpet that had to be sold, and talk would sell it." He ends his comments by conceding that "Saroyan has shown yet one more phase of the short story's limitless possibilities. . . . [He] has shown that the short story can be stripped of every shred of convention, turned inside out and upside down, and yet remain the short story" (pp. 188–193)

17. The letters quoted hereafter between William Saroyan and his editor/publishers, Bennett Cerf and Donald Klopfer are from the Correspondence of Bennett

Cerf in the Rare Books and Mss. Division of Columbia University's Butler Library. They are quotes by permission of the Librarian, Kenneth A. Lohf.

18. Letter to Martha Foley, 9 January 1934, *Story,* March 1934. From the Archives of the Princeton University Collection.

19. Harold Strauss, review of *Inhale and Exhale, The New York Times Book Review,* 23 February 1936.

20. To Bennett Cerf and Donald Klopfer, 15 August 1935.

21. To Donald Klopfer, 8 October 1935. Another segment of the letter bears quoting: "As my publishers," wrote Saroyan, "it is your job to bring out these things, rather than to hinder by fears of tradition and worrying about the possible reactions of critics. I would be the last to say that the book is perfect, but I would like to know of any recent book that is more nearly perfect."

22. To Bennett Cerf, 11 November 1935.

23. Clifton Fadiman, review of *Inhale and Exhale, The New Yorker,* 22 February 1936.

24. Letter to James Laughlin, *Essays: Recollections of a Publisher* (Mt. Kisco, N.Y.: M. Bell, 1989) quoted here by his permission. In the segment I have read, Laughlin writes of his "wonderful friendship with Saroyan," and describes how as a struggling young writer he had felt liberated after reading Saroyan's first book. "[Saroyan] showed me," he writes, "that you didn't need conventional plotting, the structure of the story could be imagination and what the words did by themselves and excitement about life, people 'inhaling and exhaling.' It got me going again, though I knew I had to be careful not to sound like Saroyan. The real thing will not submit to imitation."

CHAPTER 4. THE ART OF THE SAROYAN STORY

1. From Clifton Fadiman's review of *Inhale and Exhale,* in *The New Yorker,* 22 February 1936.

2. In a letter by William Saroyan to Bennett Cerf on 7 March 1938. Quoted with the permission of Kenneth A. Lohf, Librarian of the Rare Book and Manuscript Library, Columbia University.

Saroyan goes on to say in this letter that *Inhale and Exhale* is "full of experiments of all kinds, which I know are influencing other writers. It is bound to be a source book and a text book of the art of the short story. It is probably the reason it failed with the public: it is a little difficult for the general reader, no less than *Ulysses* was and still is."

3. From "Poem, Story, Novel," in *Inhale and Exhale.* This "story" is really as essay that gives full measure of the writer's aim, ingenuously expressed. It remained in essence one he maintained throughout his long career. The meaning of the phrase quoted from page 288 is enhanced by what precedes it and so bears recording here:

The important thing is to remember that you may if you try hard enough become a form of yourself which can endure a rather long time, and a form of yourself which was not inevitable when you began to be. In other words, the important thing to do is to remember that it is possible, and that you have only to perceive the possibility of your wildest dreams.

4. Saroyan in a letter to Cerf (from the file given above), on 29 November 1936.

5. Ibid.

6. Saroyan in Lewis Gannett's column in *The New York Herald-Tribune,* 26 December 1936.

7. *My Heart's in the Highlands,* Saroyan's first play, was also the first to be produced and it had its first performance at the Guild Theatre in New York City on 13 April 1939.

8. Saroyan would enlarge on this scene in which a telegram messenger boy is asked to deliver personally the news of a soldier's death to his mother. In a moving passage of his 1943 novel, *The Human Comedy,* the messenger boy becomes the leading character, Homer Macauley.

9. Saroyan to Cerf (from the above file), 17 September 1936. The writer goes on to say: "I am writing one book. Trapeze is no more than one part of it, as well as *Inhale & Exhale,* as well as his latest one, *Little Children.* I don't write books. I write."

10. Harold Strauss, in his review of *Little Children,* in *The New York Times Book Review,* 15 August 1937.

11. Ibid.

12. David S. Calonne, in *William Saroyan: My Real Work is Being* (1983), 41.

13. Saroyan's romantic attachment to a young writer, Sanora Babb has until now remained private and obscure in detail. In its bare outline it can be traced in a file entitled "34 Letters from William Saroyan to Sanora Babb, 1931–1941," in the Bancroft Library of the University of California at Berkeley. Permission to quote from the file has been granted both by the library and by Ms. Babb.

The letters begin on a purely platonic note: two writers eager to exchange their experiences in the struggle to get published. In April 1932, when the correspondence gets going, they have not yet met. She lives in Los Angeles, he is writing from 348 Carl Street in San Francisco. (There is a reference to a short story she has sent him.) By September of that year they are beginning to take a more personal interest in each other and there is an exchange of photos (not shown in the file, and, according to Ms. Babb, not preserved). The tone is still formal— about the writing they are doing, the magazines they are writing for, etc. Six months later, in March 1933, Saroyan is still restrained, if less formal: he confesses to Ms. Babb that while on a recent visit to Los Angeles, he looked up her phone and nearly called. He wishes he had heard from her sooner so he could have felt free to call her.

The letters begin to get longer—some are as many as seven, single-spaced pages, but they remain mainly literary. They include discussions (always on target) about Zukofsky and the Objectivists, Gertrude Stein and William Carlos Williams, new and old magazines, *The New Republic,* H. L. Mencken, Archibald McLeish, the Swiss writer Amiel, and Clifton Fadiman (critic of *The New Yorker*). Some personal material in interspersed with the literary talk but it comes through like "asides," as if he were writing about some one else. He confides, for instance, his impatience with "false and silly talk," which he encountered so often on his travels and his determination to avoid "evasions" and live "pretty much inside" himself. He cues in Ms. Babb to an important aspect of his character: "a tendency to become that which I wished to know." Though he sends her three samples of his poetry, he confesses—unabashedly—that he is not educated, has no diploma, and is "technically known as a failure." He sums up his work experiences as a series of clerical jobs, lists them with their locations and ends with the final abandon: "clerk: everywhere else." Besides always being impecunious, he tells her, he counts himself an "outsider," one who "resists all accepted notions."

About his writing, he tells her that he is at work on a book of 350,000 words—"all great prose." And he speaks with equal enthusiasm about his new hobby, line drawings, which he would like to show her.

Now and then, as if embarrassed that he has gone on too long about himself, he comments on something she has written about herself, and there is a lyric moment when he tries to imagine her as a schoolgirl in the Midwest, wishing he might have been there to bring her "a sack of green apples, a blossoming twig." Finally, he reverts to her writing, "in all that you've done, in all that you plan to do." In April 1933 there is still no sign of a "relationship"—no reference of time spent together, and though he addresses her as "Sanora," he still signs his letters "yours, William Saroyan."

By the end of 1933, after writing virtually an essay-story about rain and the Pacific, language and silence, he appears to break down and confess his feelings, but all that he admits to is that he has been thinking of her a lot; then, in a kind of poetic conceit, he goes on to say he is telling her this not to please her (indeed, she may be displeased) but because "I wish primarily to write a letter that will not be in a language we have used . . . The language of the intellect alone." The remainder of the letter, however, becomes abstract and literary, reverting to the formal inquiries about her her writing, etc. He now signs the letter "your old friend and comrade, Will Saroyan."

Not until 3 April 1934 do the letters finally because permeated with a tone of unspoken love but with an oblique reference to the fact that their love is not meant to be. He now confesses to feeling "lonely, remembering you, yourself, your presence, seen and unseen, but always felt deeply." He does not know how to write about this, "what to say, what to mean." He admits he was jealous and wanted her never again "to feel any pleasure (or pain) in living that would not be of my own pleasure and pain." He also confesses to having had "trivial affairs," mostly "in mockery of myself, as amusement, to kill time, or to keep me from too great a violence of loneliness." He can now say "I think I wanted you, wholly, for myself and yourself and *when I found I could not have you* [italics mine], there was mockery again." The wedge that stands between them, he suggests, is that "I do not know the truth of you. . . . And not knowing it, I cannot know the truth of myself." Then, as if turning away from her, he reminds her, "I know it is pretty important for me to go on writing." And, like an afterthought, he tells her simply that Random House will publish his book of stories sometime that year.

It is not until a month later, in a letter dated May 1934, that the words are openly said at last: "Sanora, this only: humbly, quietly, my love. . . . For you I feel only the deepest, the deepest, there is only one word, and it has been torn to pieces, only the deepest love."

Sanora Babb has published many stories, one novel, *The Lost Traveler* (1958, both in England and America), and an autobiographical book about her childhood and youth in Colorado, *An Owl on Every Post* (1970, also both in England and America). She appears to have been an autodidact, like Saroyan, who started school late but caught up fast, having a nimble brain and boundless ambition. She was at one time a reporter for the Associated Press in Los Angeles and worked in the fields with migrant workers during the Depression. Ms. Babb herself has supplied this information to this writer in letters and telephone conversations and has given permission to use her comments on Saroyan for this book.

Sanora Babb admits to an abiding friendship with Saroyan, as well as deep affection, but she says there was no real "relationship." Nor was there a sudden break in communication; the correspondence lapsed when she was on assignment in Europe in 1936, and there was a period when both were in Hollywood and had no need to write to each other. A forthright and openly communicative person, Ms. Babb is convincing when she says no letters between them were deliberately destroyed.

Saroyan's final letter of August 1941, is veiled in its declaration that this may be his last to her: "There won't be any old-time letter writing. I'll be plain and honest—I just won't do it. Because if I did, you couldn't help knowing it was wrong—or at least not right. The right to write that way is no longer mine—and I don't regret that it isn't." He is reminded of the "old-time letters" because Ms. Babb has loaned him the letters he sent her and kept. He asks her for a few samples in connection with a book he is writing, which is so far titled, *How to Be Human.* Looking over the old letters, he writes (again somewhat cryptically), "I have never stopped thinking of you as somebody rare and extraordinary and fine and wonderful and truly beautiful, *no matter what you thought I have thought*" [italics mine]. Whatever the circumstances of their "parting" (Ms. Babb has little to say on the matter), the letter ends amicably, "all best always. Yours truly, William."

Ms. Babb was married to the Chinese-American Hollywood photographer, James Wong Howe, in 1949; he died in 1976.

14. Sanora Babb to Nona Balakian, 16 February 1988.

15. Saroyan describes such an encounter, with great humor, in his autobiographical work, *Sons Come and Go, Mothers Hang in Forever* (1976), 111–112. The incident occurred soon after he was fired from his script-writing job in Hollywood.

16. Budd Schulberg, in his chapter on Saroyan in *Writers in America* (1983), 83.

17. Alfred Kazin, *Starting Out in the Thirties,* 57.

18. William Saroyan to Sanora Babb, 3 May 1934. (From the Saroyan-Babb file at the Bancroft Library referred to above. Again with permission to quote.) The letter continues:

I really would like to get to a plain shack somewhere and start over again: for numerous reasons, but primarily for this one; to breathe deeply, cleanly, to see clearly, to stand solidly and lithe upon the earth, to be quietly great by being quietly humble, Jesus Christ, to be alive. But maybe this is stupid, too, I don't know. I suppose I am looking in the direction of nowhere. Do not mind, ever, anything I say that is stupid or false or glib. Your story in Trend is big: I think of you, Sanora. William.

19. William Saroyan to Sanora Babb, 12 April 1934. This letter goes on:

Five days in a row now no writing. I should be ramming my head into the wall . . . I get insanely lonesome for you and start to swear at innocent bystanders, sometimes female . . . You are lovely, Jesus, you are, and what am I to do, remember you? Is that it?

20. Philip Rahv, in his review of *Love, Here Is My Hat,* in *The Nation,* 26 March 1938.

21. "Conversation with Milan Kundera," conducted in Rennes, France, by Normand Biron for Radio Canada, summer 1976, and translated by Andreas Mytze and Victoria Nelson. Reprinted by *Threepenny Review* (Winter 1986).

22. Howard Floan in *William Saroyan* (1966), 54.

23. Ibid.

24. In a letter to Nona Balakian, 7 December 1987, Philip Cronenwett, curator of Manuscripts at Dartmouth University Library, confirms that Saroyan's story,

"The Tiger," from *The Trouble With Tigers* —a work donated to the library by the author in manuscript—was indeed written in 1935.

25. Saroyan to Whit Burnett, 6 February 1939. From the Whit Burnett-Martha Foley file at the Princeton University Library. Quoted with permission. The story appears in *Dear Baby.*

26. Richard H. Pells, in *Radical Visions and American Dream: Culture and Social Thought in the Depression Years* (1973), has an interesting chapter, "Documents, Fiction and the Depression," which elucidates this point, showing how there was a ready audience for the kind of writing Saroyan was doing. One passage, in particular, bears reprinting here:

> Behind this rediscovery of rural virtue lay an assertion of faith in a simpler, innocent, uncomplicated America. It had become desperately important for writers to find something alive and good in the United States despite the breakdown of its modern, complex political and economic system. If they could locate a fundamental stability and resilience in the American people, they might again feel at home in their native land. This search for roots led them to praise not only the past but also the democratic instincts of the common man" (200).

27. Henry Seidel Canby, in his review of *My Name is Aram,* in *Saturday Review,* 28 December 1940.

28. Christopher Morley, in *The Book of the Month Newsletter,* December 1940.

29. William Floan, *William Saroyan,* 83.

30. William Saroyan, "The Impossible Saroyans of Fresno," in *Country Beautiful* 2 (Elmgrove, Wisconsin), 22–23.

CHAPTER 5. TOWARD AN AMERICAN THEATER: A RADICAL CONVERSION

1. Mary McCarthy, *Sights and Spectacles* (New York: Farrar, Straus and Cudahy, 1956). Quotes on Saroyan are from pp. 46–52.

2. Ibid., 47. McCarthy goes on to say,

> Both Odets and Steinbeck are offering the public counterfeit literature: Odets is giving an imitation of a lacerated Bronx boy named Odets who once wrote a play. Steinbeck is giving an imitation of a serious novelist. Saroyan as a public figure does an impersonation of Saroyan, but as a writer he plays straight.

3. Ibid., xiii.

4. Walter Pritchard Eaton, *The Theatre Guild, The First Ten Years* (New York: Brentano's, 1929), 43, 44. Eaton explains in his historical survey that "[The Theatre Guild] could not experiment with undeveloped native work, however promising, as an amateur group could do, because they were definitely pledged to subscribers to produce finished entertainment."

5. Harold Clurman explains in his book *The Fervent Years: the Story of the Group Theatre* (New York: Alfred A. Knopf, 1950) the nature of O'Neill's discomfort in the theater of the thirties:

> The Twenties took heart in O'Neill's gloom. It proved, despite all the clamor and shouting, that we were keeping our wits about us. In any case, O'Neill struggled with his soul, and the riddle of the universe; with the chaos of the helter-skelter torrent. His work writhed

in a kind of nocturnal anguish, woke and smiled a bit, proclaimed fresh faith, fell asleep again and dreamed fitfully anew. Since the early Thirties there has been silence. How the issue has been resolved still remains a mystery (p. 21).

6. Eaton, *The Theatre Guild,* 43.

7. Chiefly responsible for this was the president of the Guild, Lawrence Langner, who pleaded eloquently on its behalf:

[I]t is the next step forward in playwrighting, the poetry of the unconscious to offset the stark realism of the conscious; the science of the new psychology and the mysticism of God the Father. This play contains in it more deep knowledge of the dark corners of the human mind than anything that has ever been written before. It proclaims O'Neill the great dramatic genius of the age" (quoted in Eaton, p. 104).

8. Cf. Virginia Woolf's essay, "The Leaning Tower," delivered originally as a lecture to the Workers Educational Association in London, May 1940.

9. Clurman. Ibid. n.p.

10. Quoted in C. W. E. Bigsby, *A Critical Introduction to Twentieth-Century American Drama* (New York: Cambridge University Press, 1984), 16.

11. Robert Lewis, *Slings and Arrows: The Theatre in My Life* (Stein and Day, 1984). Lewis, one of the youngest of The Group and a founder of Actors' Studio, recalls how after hearing Clurman's words on "a celebratory theatre," "many of [the members] would repair to Child's Restaurant on Columbus Circle and sit throughout the night talking some more about how we had to save the American theatre, and incidentally change the world" (p. 37).

12. McCarthy, *Sights and Spectacles,* 10.

13. In his chapter on Odets, Bigsby illuminates the nature of the relationship that existed between Marxism and many of the playwrights of the thirties. "The Marxism they embraced," he writes,

was less ideological than spiritual—it was an image of human unity, a conviction that capitalism had run its course (by which, more often than not, they seem to have meant that money should no longer be a defining factor, that war was simply a product of capitalist imperialism). But in truth the model which Odets no less than Steinbeck, treasured was closer to that embodied in Jefferson. What they looked for was a sense of spiritual and moral renewal (p. 176).

14. In a speech titled "Toward a New Theatre," delivered to the Theatre Union in 1933, Odets had laid it on the line. "The bourgeois theatre is truthfully the only theatre we know and IT IS NOT REAL THEATRE, but instead a highly disjointed bastardized form of entertainment worthy of no name but Death and Corruption . . . a real theatre is always a social theatre, used to express a communal idea or necessity." Quoted in Margaret Brennan-Gibson, *Clifford Odets: American Playwright. The Years from 1906–1940* (New York: Atheneum, 1981), 652.

15. Clifford Odets, *The Time is Ripe: The 1940 Journal* (New York: Grove Press, 1988), 18.

16. Ibid., 18–19.

17. Quoted in Brennan-Gibson, *Clifford Odets,* 428.

18. Harold Clurman, *Lies Like Truth* (New York: Macmillan, 1958), 4.

19. Ibid., 6.

20. John Mason Brown, *Broadway in Review* (W. W. Norton, 1940), 18–19.

NOTES TO CHAPTER 5

21. Maxwell Anderson, *Off Broadway*. (New York: William Sloane Associates, 1947), 51.

22. Stark Young wrote that some of the bursts of Anderson's eloquence "sound like a Stephen Phillips version of an Arthur Symons translation of a decadent German versifying of a lax translation of Euripides." Quoted in Edmund Wilson *The Shores of Light: A Literary Chronicle of the Twenties and Thirties* (New York: Farrar, Straus and Young, 1952), 677.

23. Joseph Wood Krutch, *The American Drama Since 1918: An Informal History* (New York: George Braziller, 1957), 286–318.

24. Edmund Wilson, in his review of "Winterset," 23 June 1937. Quoted in *The Shores of Light*, 680.

25. Archibald MacLeish, in his essay, "The Hope for Poetry in the Theatre," quoted in *New Theatre and Film, 1934–1937: An Anthology*, ed. Herbert Kline (New York: Harcourt Brace Jovanovich, 1985), 34.

26. If Saroyan sounds brash and conceited, Harold Clurman in the preface introducing the play sounds insipid and unctuous in its praise. "It has a pure kind of stage viability," he writes, "it has an endearing homeliness, affability and good companionship." Having called it initially "the purest type of country tale," he goes on to say that it has "restored a sound theatricality to the stage—good sense gaiety and loveliness. Thus for all its modest proportions, it is, in my opinion, an important contribution to the art of the theatre in this country" (pp. 7–11).

27. Robert van Gelder, *The New York Times Book Review*, 24 March 1940, 12.

28. From the afterword to *The Time of Your Life*, 201.

29. Ibid., 205.

30. Ibid., 205–6.

31. In his memoir, *Slings and Arrows*, Robert (Bobby) Lewis refers to *My Heart's in the Highlands* as "my true firstborn," his favorite to this day, mainly for the reason that I could build the production from scratch with no serious outside interference." He had been trying to make a foray into the lyric theater and saw in Saroyan's vehicle (still in the process of transformation from story into play) "a perfect libretto on which to build a poetic production by adding music, sound, color and movement to the enchanting dialogue." But in the process of "theatricalization" some odd things were done (pp. 103–104).

32. Archibald MacLeish, in his article "The Poet as Playwright," *Atlantic Monthly*, February 1955. The commentary in full reads, "The illusion of the real is indeed the principal business of poetry. It is to know our own reality as living, feeling beings that poetry is written."

33. As Clurman put it in *The Fervent Years*, "[Saroyan] did not approve of Bobby Lewis's delicate stylization, though he did not fail to borrow it later for his production of *The Beautiful People* " (p. 250).

34. Erich Auerbach, *Mimesis: The Representation of Reality in Western Literature*, trans. from the German by William Trask (New York: Doubleday/Anchor, 1957). Auerbach's cogent analysis of Virginia Woolf's technique is relevant here. Referring to a specific scene in *To the Lighthouse*, he writes, "The exterior events have actually lost their hegemony: they serve to release and interpret inner events, whereas before her time (and still today in many instances) inner movements preponderantly function to prepare and motivate significant exterior happenings" (p. 475).

35. The result of such condescending characterizations (coming even from enthusiastic critics) was at best to dilute and minimize the praise heaped on Saroyan. At its worst, it carried a covert racial slur.

36. Edmund Gagey, *Revolution in American Drama* (New York: Books for Libraries Press, 1947), 113–119. Gagey's estimate of Saroyan is thoroughly ambivalent. Though he calls him "a fantasist pure and simple, he calls into account his "credo," or ideas, which he labels as "limpid . . . infantile, repetitious, and unduly naive, showing little contact with the real world." He nonetheless ends by saying "one must admit that by some obscure miracle, his plays show more real originality than those of O'Neill, Green and Anderson put together."

37. An example of the uncritical criticism Saroyan received was John Mason Brown's commentary: "It throws open some welcome windows, even if it opens them upon a fog. The air it admits may be cloudy, but it is still moving and fresh and a joy to inhale." Quoted in *Broadway in Review*, 187. But in retrospect, George Jean Nathan was to call *My Heart's in the Highlands* "the best play of its year" (*The Magic Mirror*, 225).

38. Brooks Atkinson, *The New York Times*, 11 April 1939.

39. The Ballet Theatre's production of *The Great American Goof* with Eugene Loring in the lead, music by Henry Brant and sets by Boris Aronson was performed in 1940, while *The Time of Your Life* was still running and *Love's Old Sweet Song* was newly launched.

40. The prologue for the broadcast made on 23 February 1941 was written by the CBS staff for Saroyan's approval, and was edited by him.

41. In a letter to George Jean Nathan quoted by permission of Cornell University Library Archives. In this letter Saroyan tells of other titles he had considered, such as *The Light Fantastic, The Time of Your Life, St. Joe and Sister Kitty, Sunset Sonata, The Brothers and Sisters, Brother Joe and Sister Kitty,* and *Pacific Sonata.*

42. Letter from San Francisco, 27 August 1939. Quoted with permission of Cornell University Library Archives.

CHAPTER 6. A NEW DRAMATIC VISION: THE TIME OF YOUR LIFE

1. Marcel Proust, *On Art and Literature: 1896–1919,* trans. Sylvia Townsend Warner (New York: Carroll & Graff, 1984), pp. 100–104.

2. William Saroyan, preface to *The Time of Your Life* (New York: Harcourt, Brace & Co., 1939), 11.

3. William Saroyan, introduction to the paperback edition of *The Time of Your Life* (New York: Bantam, 1967), 2.

4. Ibid., 6.

5. At the time of its revival on 10 March 1976 on PBS, Saroyan wrote in an article for *TV Guide* 6 March 1976 titled "How to Write a Great Play": "I wrote it in six days early in May of 1939 while stopping in New York on my way to Europe for a second look before the holocaust, which I knew was coming—and had known for at least 10 years, while Roosevelt and Churchill hadn't."

6. Ecclesiastes, chapter 1.

7. Ibid., chapter 2.

8. Ibid., chapter 11.

9. This and the following quotation are, from the credo or preface to printed version of *The Time of Your Life* (Harcourt, Brace & Co., 1939). It reads as follows in full:

In the time of your life, live—so that in that good time there shall be no ugliness or death for yourself or for any life your life touches. Seek goodness everywhere, and when it is found, bring it out of its hiding-place and let it be free and unashamed. Place in matter and in flesh the least of the values, for these are the things that hold death and must pass away. Discover in all things that which shines and is beyond corruption. Encourage virtue in whatever heart it may have been driven into secrecy and sorrow by the shame and terror of the world. Ignore the obvious, for it is unworthy of the clear eye and the kindly heart. Be an inferior of no one, nor of any man be the superior. Remember that every man is a variation of yourself. No man's guilt is not yours, nor is any man's innocence a thing apart. Despise evil and ungodliness, but not men of ungodliness or evil. These understand. Have no shame in being kindly and gentle, but if the time comes in the time of your life to kill, kill and have no regret. In the time of your life, live—so that in that wondrous time you shall not add to the misery and sorrow of the world, but shall smile to the infinite delight and mystery of it.

10. Walter Kerr, *God on the Gymnasium Floor and Other Theatrical Adventures* (Simon & Schuster, 1971). Writes Kerr, "Funny, how we remember it wrong. No, we don't even remember it wrong. We get it wrong in the first place." In his new interpretation he proceeds to throw a pall over the whole play, seeing it as "really all about the day the last sun went down. There isn't any tomorrow in it for anybody . . . it is . . . the matrix for all the doomsday plays that have followed" (pp. 163, 167). Clearly, the critic has acquired new lenses in the interim through his exposure to absurdist drama (Beckett, Ionesco). Perhaps John Hirsch's "too mellow" production, is partly at fault, but Kerr has obviously bypassed the inner spirit of the play which is one of affirmation.

11. The young idealist narrating his story in "The Living and the Dead," has a moment of illumination at the end; he realizes suddenly that reforms are only superficial, encouraging further those who have not yet learned to live: "What good will it do when everybody has cake, comrades, what good will it do when everybody has everything, comrades, everything isn't enough, comrades, and the living aren't alive, brothers, the living are dead."

12. McCarthy, *Sights and Spectacles,* 52. Writing about Kit Carson, she says, "This kind of character undoubtedly belongs to the tradition of American life and especially to the West. It is Paul Bunyan and it is also the barker. But the tradition is dead now; it died when the frontier closed on the West Coast at some point in Saroyan's childhood."

13. Kerr, *God,* 167.

14. In a chapter called "The Dance" in *Here Comes There Goes You Know Who,* Saroyan writes of a memorable moment in his orphanage years—the day his mother brought him a wind-up tin man "that jigged on a tin platform," that seemed to him like a bribe. But "all the same I watched and listened." Watching the tin dancer, he had stopped crying. "I decided to wait and see and make do. I decided to figure it out, not for my mother, not for my family, not for my name, but for myself" (p. 38).

15. Perhaps the hardest character for us to accept today is Krupp—a police officer who appears totally "unconditioned" by his long confrontation with the life of crime. The loss of a sense of goodness would seem the natural thing, not the extraordinary. But in an era when the World's crime was so glaringly emphasized, Krupp's labor violence beat seemed comparatively mild.

CHAPTER 7. THE BROADWAY YEARS

1. Brooks Atkinson, *New York Times,* 3 May 1940.

2. See Brooks Atkinson/William Saroyan discussion of his "mindlessness" in "Preface" to *Love's Old Sweet Song* in *Three Plays,* Harcourt Brace & Co., 1940.

3. Saroyan, *Razzle Dazzle*, 1942, 179.

4. W. David Sievers, *Freud on Broadway*, New York: Hermitage House, 1955, 245.

5. Ibid., 247.

6. George Jean Nathan's assessment of Saroyan, his originality compared to "ten dozen other playwrights," and the regrettable shoddiness resulting from too-rapid writing is contained in his article "Saroyan" in *The Magic Mirror*, edited by Thomas Quinn Curtis (New York: Knopf, 1960).

7. Stark Young, *The New Republic*, 12 May 1941, 664.

8. Ibid.

9. This and all subsequent quotations concerning this play, in answer to Brooks Atkinson, come from a rebuttal essay printed as "Preface" to the published version of *Love's Old Sweet Song* in *Three Plays*, 7.

10. *Love's Old Sweet Song*, 51 (Elsa speaking).

CHAPTER 8. AND BEYOND: SAROYAN'S LATER WRITINGS

1. Howard R. Floan, *William Saroyan*, Twayne, 1966, 124.

2. Saroyan, *The Adventures of Wesley Jackson*, 154.

3. Saroyan, *Jim Dandy or Fat Man in a Famine*, 1947, 123.

4. *Kenyon Review*, Issue 1, 1969, 60.

5. Northrop Frye, "The Art of Literature and Common Sense," from *Lectures on Literature*, Harvard University Press, 1980, n.p.

6. "After Thirty Years," preface to a new edition of *Daring Young Man on a Flying Trapeze*, 1962, 112.

7. *Chance Meetings*, 1978, 3.

8. *Obituaries*, 1979, 153.

9. Vladimir Nabokov, "The Art of Literature and Common Sense," from *Lectures on Literature*, Harvard University Press, 1980, n.p.

Bibliography

PRIMARY SOURCES

The works of Saroyan discussed in this study are here listed in chronological order, since that is principally the approach to them in this work. Unless otherwise specified, Saroyan's publisher is Harcourt, Brace in New York.

The earliest of Saroyan's works referred to is "Preface to a Book Not Yet Written," which appeared in *Overland Monthly and Out West Magazine, 1928.* A series of early pieces appeared under the pseudonym of Sirak Goryan in the Armenian daily and weekly *Hairenik*: "The Broken Wheel." In three installments, 2, 4 and 6 June "A First Fight for Armenian." 9–10 May 1933, "The Barber's Apprentice," 15–16 October 1933; *Hairenik Weekly,* 1 March 1935; "The Moment of Life," *Hairenik Daily,* 26 and 28 November 1933; "Nonch" Ibid.; "Yea and Amen," *Hairenik Weekly,* 22 and 29 March 1934 (Reprinted in *Inhale and Exhale.*)

The Daring Young Man on the Flying Trapeze and Other Stories. New York: Random House, 1934.

Inhale and Exhale. New York: Random House, 1936.

Three Times Three. Los Angeles: The Conference Press, 1936.

Little Children. 1937.

The Trouble with Tigers. 1938.

Love, Here Is My Hat. New York: Modern Age Books, 1938.

My Heart's in the Highlands. 1939; also in *Three Plays,* 1940.

The Time of Your Life. In *Three Plays.* Reference made to Introduction in paperback edition. New York: Bantam Books, 1967.

Peace, It's Wonderful. New York: Starling Press, New York: 1939.

My Name is Aram. 1940.

A Special Announcement (radio play). New York: House of Books, 1940.

Three Plays. 1939, 1940.

Love's Old Sweet Song in *Three Plays*; also New York: Samuel French, 1941.

The Beautiful People. 1941.

Razzle-Dazzle. 1942.

The Human Comedy. 1943.

The Adventures of Wesley Jackson. 1946.

Jim Dandy or Fat Man in a Famine. 1947.

Don't Go Away Mad. 1949.

The Assyrian, and Other Stories. 1950.

Rock Wagram. New York: Doubleday, 1951.

The Bicycle Rider in Beverly Hills. New York: C. Scribner, 1952.

The Laughing Matter. New York: Doubleday, 1953.

The Whole Voyald and Other Stories. Boston: Little, Brown, 1956.

The Cave Dwellers. New York: Putnam, 1958.

Here Comes There Goes You Know Who. New York: Simon and Schuster, 1961.

Not Dying. 1963.

After Thirty Years: The Daring Young Man on the Flying Trapeze. 1964.

The Hungerers. New York: Samuel French, 1967.

Letters from 74 rue Taitbout. New York: World Publishing Co., 1969.

"His Collaborators" in *Homage to Sherwood Anderson 1876–1941.* Mameroneck, New York, 1970.

Places Where I've Done Time. New York: Dell, 1972.

Sons Come and Go, Mothers Hang in Forever. New York: McGraw Hill, 1976.

Chance Meetings. New York: Norton, 1978.

Obituaries. Berkeley: Creative Notebook Co., 1979.

Saroyan Memorial Issue: 104 Unpublished Letters of William Saroyan in *The American Review,* September 1981.

SECONDARY SOURCES

Aaron, Daniel. *Writers of the Left.* New York: Oxford University Press, 1977.

Agathangelos. *History of the Armenian People: From the Remotest Times to the Present.* Boston, *Hairenik Press,* 1918. New edition: State University of New York at Albany, 1976.

Agee, James and Walter Evans. *Let Us Now Praise Famous Men.* 1941.

Babbitt, Irving. *On Being Creative.* Boston: Houghton Mifflin, 1932.

Balakian, Nona. "So Many Saroyans," *The New Republic,* cxxiii, August 1950; "The Armenian-American Writer," AGBU, 1958.

Bates, H. E. *The Modern Short Story: A Critical Survey.* New York: Thomas Nelson, 1941.

Bigsby, C. W. E. *A Critical Introduction to Twentieth-Century American Drama.* New York: Cambridge University Press, 1984.

Blackmur, R. P. *American Short Novels.* New York: Crowell, 1960.

Burnett, Whit. *The Literary Life and the Hell with It.* New York: Harper Brothers 1939.

Calonne, David S. *William Saroyan: My Real Work is Being,* Chapel Hill: University of North Carolina Press, 1983.

Clark, Barrett H., *European Theories of the Drama.* New York and London: D. Appleton & Co., 1929.

Clurman, Harold. *The Fervent Years: The Story of the Group Theatre and the Thirties,* New York: Hill and Wang, 1957.

————. *Lies Like Truth.* New York: Macmillan & Co, 1958.

Cowley, Malcolm. *Exile's Return: A Literary Odyssey of the 1920's.* New York: Viking Press, 1951.

———. *The Dream of the Golden Mountain.* New York: Viking Press, 1950.

Dewey, John. *Art as Experience.* New York: Capricon, 1953.

———. *A Common Faith.* New Haven: Yale University Press, 1934.

———. *A Quest for Certainty: A Study of the Relation of Knowledge and Action.* New York: Minton, Balch & Co., 1929.

Eaton, Walter Pritchard. *The Theatre Guild: The First Ten Years.* New York: Brentano, 1929.

Floan, Howard. *William Saroyan.* New York: Twayne, 1966.

Gagey, Edmund. *Revolution in American Drama.* New York: Books for Libraries, 1947.

Gassner, John. *Form and Idea in the Modern Theatre.* New York: Dryden Press, 1956.

Gilson, Etienne. *The Christian Philosophy of St. Augustine.* New York: Random House, 1960.

Hicks, Granville. *The Great Tradition.* Chicago: Quadrangle Books, 1969.

Hiler, Hilaire. *Why Abstract? Henry Miller and William Saroyan.* New York: G. Wittemborn, 1946, 1962.

Kherdian, David. *A Bibliography of William Saroyan, 1934–64.* San Francisco: R. Beacham, 1965.

Kazin, Alfred. *Starting Out in the Thirties.* Boston: Little, Brown, 1965.

———. *On Native Grounds.* New York: Reynal & Hitchcock, 1942.

Kerr, Walter. *God on the Gymnasium Floor and Other Theatrical Adventures.* New York: Simon and Schuster, 1971.

Krutch, Joseph Wood. *The Modern Temper: A Study and A Confession.* New York: Harcourt, Brace & Co., 1929.

———. *The American Drama Since 1918: An Informal History.* New York: George Braziller, 1957.

Lee, Lawrence & Barry Gifford. *Saroyan: A Biography.* New York: Harper & Row, 1984.

Lewis, Robert. *Slings and Arrows: The Theatre in My Life.* New York: Stein and Day, 1984.

Lewis, R.W.B. *The American Adam, Innocence, Tragedy, and Tradition in the Nineteenth Century.* Chicago: University of Chicago Press, 1955.

Martin, Jay. *Nathanael West, the Art of His Life.* New York: Farrar, Straus & Giroux, 1970.

McCarthy, Mary. *Sights and Spectacles.* New York: Farrar, Straus & Cudahy, 1956.

Mirak, Robert. *Torn Between Two Worlds: Armenians in America 1890–World War I.* Cambridge: Harvard University Press, 1984.

Morgan, Jacques de. *The History of the Armenian People: From the Remotest Times to the Present.* Translated by Ernst P. Barry. Boston: Hairenik Press, 1918.

Moses of Khoren. *History of the Armenian.* Cambridge: Harvard University Press, 1978.

Nadel, Norman. *A Pictorial History of the Theatre Guild.* New York: Crown Publishers, 1969.

Pattee, Fred Lewis. *The Development of the American Short Story, A Historical Survey.* New York: Harper & Brothers, 1923.

Pells, Richard H. *Radical Visions and American Dreams: Culture and Social Thought in the Depression Years.* New York: Harper & Row, 1973.

Pritchard, John Paul. *Criticism in America.* Norman: University of Oklahoma Press, 1956.

Proust, Marcel. *On Art and Literature: 1896–1919.* Translated by Townsend Warner. New York: Carroll & Graff, 1984.

Saroyan, Aram. *William Saroyan.* New York: Harcourt Brace Jovanovich, 1983.

———. *Last Rites: The Death of William Saroyan.* New York: William Morrow, 1982.

Schulberg, Budd. *Writers in America: The Four Seasons of Success.* New York: Stein and Day, 1983.

Sievers, W. David. *Freud on Broadway: A History of Psychoanalysis and the American Drama.* New York: Hermitage House, 1955.

Sokel, Walter Herbert. *Anthology of German Expressionist Drama, a Prelude to the Absurd.* Garden City, N.Y.: Doubleday, 1963.

Tashjian, James. *My Name is Saroyan.* New York: Coward-McCann, 1983.

Trilling, Lionel. *The Liberal Imagination.* New York: Viking, 1950.

Toqueville, Alexis de. *Democracy in America.* New York: Washington Square Press (paperback), 1968.

Wilson, Edmund. *Letters on Literature and Politics, 1912–72.* New York: Farrar, Straus & Giroux, 1977.

Index